A World More Attractive

A WORL

A VIEW (

b

POLITICS AND THE NOVEL

MODERN LITERATURE AND POLITICS

Irving Howe

Essay Index Reprint Series

BOOKS FOR LIBRARIES PRESS
FREEPORT, NEW YORK

Copyright © 1963 by Irving Howe

Reprinted 1970 by arrangement with
Horizon Press, New York

INTERNATIONAL STANDARD BOOK NUMBER:
0-8369-1958-0

LIBRARY OF CONGRESS CATALOG CARD NUMBER:
70-134096

PRINTED IN THE UNITED STATES OF AMERICA

For Nina and Nicholas Howe
Connoisseurs in Affection

Contents

Introduction ix

THE HERO AND HISTORY

T. E. Lawrence: The Problem of Heroism 1

CONTOURS OF AMERICAN FICTION

Edith Wharton: Convention and the Demons of
    Modernism 41
The Quest for Moral Style 59
Mass Society and Post-Modern Fiction 77
Black Boys and Native Sons 98
A Quest for Peril: Norman Mailer 123

THREE AMERICAN POETS

Walt Whitman: "Garrulous to the Very Last" 131
Robert Frost: A Momentary Stay 144
Wallace Stevens: Another Way of Looking at the
    Blackbird 158

SOME EUROPEAN MODERNS

George Gissing: Poet of Fatigue	169
Céline: The Sod Beneath the Skin	192
Sholom Aleichem: Voice of Our Past	207
The Fiction of Anti-Utopia	216

POLITICS AND CULTURE

Images of Socialism	227
This Age of Conformity	251
A Mind's Turnings	283
God, Man and Stalin	291
Edmund Wilson and the Sea Slugs	300

INTRODUCTION

Composed in the years between 1950 and 1963, the essays in this book range in kind from literary criticism to political analysis, from intellectual portraiture to cultural polemic. They cover a wide spectrum of topics and figures, but if varied in subject, they are, I believe, unified in outlook. Behind almost all of them can be found a stable complex of values and convictions, a persistent concern with problems and ideas, having to do primarily with that style of experience and perception sometimes called the "modern." By the "modern" I have in mind neither the merely contemporary nor the momentarily fashionable, either in our culture or our politics. I have in mind the assumption that the twentieth century has been marked by a crisis of conduct and belief that is perhaps unprecedented in seriousness, depth and extent.

The "modern," as it refers to both history and literature, signifies extreme situations and radical solutions. It summons images of war and revolution, experiment and disaster, apocalypse and skepticism; images of rebellion, disenchantment and nothingness. To claim that all of these are visibly present in the essays that follow, would be absurd; but I would say that the sense of their presence has been a dominant pressure, setting both the terms and the limits, of what I have written here.

Whether it be strictly literary, or primarily political, or a crossing of the two—as in the study of T. E. Lawrence, which forms the centerpiece of the book because it brings together so many of its themes—the work presented in these pages takes its meaning and its shape as a response to the problem of the "modern."

A number of the essays are literary in character, written from the assumption that literary criticism, like literature itself, can be autonomous but hardly self-sufficient. There is strong reason to stress the integrity of the work of literature, as an object worth scrutiny in its own right and in accordance with its own nature; but I would also insist—and in the last two decades it has become quite necessary to insist—that the work of literature acquires its interest for us through a relationship, admittedly subtle, difficult and indirect, to the whole of human experience. The kind of detailed or close analysis of particular texts which has been favored in recent years and which I have occasionally undertaken in lengthier studies, will not be found here. What I have tried for has been to provide a description of the characteristic qualities, the defining mode of vision, by which a writer can be recognized and valued; I have hoped to isolate the terms through which he confronts the experience of our time.

The few strictly political pieces in this book are drawn from a larger body of writing in which I have tried to speak for, even while criticizing, the tradition of socialism. Being a socialist in the mid-twentieth century means, for anyone who aspires to seriousness, a capacity for living with crisis, doubt and reconsideration. The ideal of socialism has become a problematic one, but the problem of socialism remains an abiding ideal. Some traditional doctrines of socialism now seem to me outmoded or mistaken, but I remain convinced of the need for a democratic and radical renovation of society, through which to give a fresh embodiment to the values of freedom and fraternity. A good part of the effort to preserve the animating purpose of socialist criticism in the past decade can be observed by turning to the files of *Dissent,* the quarterly of which I have been an editor; but some of that effort, the more speculative and less topical side of it, can be found in these pages.

If one side of my political writing has required the kind of self-questioning and reorientation which must today go on among serious socialists, another side has been devoted, in the years since the war, to an attack upon the growing acquiescence and conservatism of the American intellectual community. The early 'fifties in particular struck me as a time in which too many intellectuals abandoned their traditional privilege and responsibility of criticism. In "This Age of Conformity"—a polemic in which certain references may be seem dated but the controlling ideas of which seem to me still valid —I joined in a counter-attack which a few intellectuals launched against the turn to political quietism and conformity, the acceptance of the social *status quo,* the dilution of liberalism into a kind of genteel conservatism. Now, only a few years later, I find myself especially eager that such writings speak to those younger people who have recently come to their intellectual maturity and seem not quite to recall what happened in this country only a decade ago.

I have brought together in this volume about half my periodical writing over the last twelve or thirteen years. Whatever struck me as merely journalistic or too closely interwoven with a transient polemic, has been omitted. Yet I have included a few pieces that are journalistic and polemical, first because I believe them to possess a certain value in commenting upon significant discussions of the past decade, and second because I wish to write, not for some dim posterity, but for living men and women caught up, as I am caught up, with the problems and interests of our time.

"In my eyes," Leon Trotsky once wrote, "authors, journalists and artists always stood for a world that was more attractive than any other. . . ." One need not accept Trotsky's political outlook in order to appreciate the force of his remark, both as it indicates respect for the intellectual life and a complex, perhaps, ironic sense of the difficulties faced by those who would preserve a relationship between politics and literature, action and reflection. A world more attractive—from sentiments of this kind I have tried to live and work, and what has made the effort possible is above all else the presence of friends serving as models, colleagues, and teachers.

To name them would be presumptuous. But let me say a word of gratitude to a number of editors who have been kind enough to encourage my work while honest enough to criticize it. I wish to record my gratitude to Margaret Marshall, some years ago the book editor of *The Nation;* William Phillips and Philip Rahv, editors of *Partisan Review;* Robert Evett and Gilbert Harrison at *The New Republic;* and closest of all, the devoted men who have shared with me the burdens and pleasures of putting out *Dissent.* I am especially grateful to my friend Lewis Coser for permitting me to publish the essay entitled "Images of Socialism," of which he is co-author.

Finally, I should like to record my gratitude to the Bollingen Foundation whose generosity gave me the time to complete the literary part of this book.

—I.H.

The hero and history

T. E. LAWRENCE: THE PROBLEM OF HEROISM

> I wanted only to try to live in obedience to the promptings which came from my true self. Why was that so very difficult?
> —Demian

Time has mercifully dulled the image he despised yet courted: T. E. Lawrence is no longer the idol of the 'twenties, no longer "Lawrence of Arabia." But for the minority of men to whom reflection upon human existence is both a need and a pleasure, Lawrence seems still to matter. He is not yet a name to be put away in history, a footnote in dust. He continues to arouse sympathy, outrage, excitement. If we come to him admiring whatever in his life was extraordinary, we remain with him out of a sense that precisely the special, even the exotic in Lawrence, may illuminate whatever in our life is ordinary.

During the early 'twenties, after his return from Arabia, Lawrence became a national hero, the adventurer through whom Englishmen could once more savor the sensations of war and rescue emotions of sentimental grandeur. What he had done in Arabia—more important, what he had experienced—was epic in its proportions, and even a glance at his life prompts one to speculate about the nature of heroism in our century. But transplanted from the desert to the lantern-slides of the Albert Hall, where Lowell Thomas was conjuring for the English their stainless version of "Lawrence of Arabia," the whole war-time experience shrank to farce. Partly to salvage it from vulgarities which he himself had condoned, Lawrence wrote *The Seven Pillars of Wisdom,* a bravura narrative packed with accounts of battle yet finally the record of his search for personal equilibrium and value. By then, however, his public image had acquired a being and momentum of its own. So the book too, though in some ways esoteric, became popular—and helped sustain the image it was meant to subvert.

This sad comedy was to continue to the end. In *The Seven Pillars of Wisdom* the ideal of a forthright manly heroism, which Lawrence had supposedly rescued for an unheroic age, was soon transformed into the burden of self-consciousness, a burden he was never to escape. The dynamiter of railroads and bridges turned out to be an intellectual harassed by ambition and guilt. The literary man who had read Malory between desert raids and later worried over the shape and rhythm of the sentences in his book, made himself into a pseudonymous recruit tending the "shit-cart" of his camp. And these were but a few of his transfigurations.

I

Thomas Edward Lawrence was born in 1888, the second of five sons in a comfortable Victorian family. The father, a reserved gentleman who is said never to have written a check or read a book, devoted himself to the domestic needs of his family and a number of mild sports. The mother, clearly of lower rank, was a strong-spirited Scotch woman, ambitious for her sons, eager to share in their growth, the true psychic center of the family. Mrs. Lawrence raised her boys to be straightforward Christians—and the unambiguous piety with which two of them later met their death in the trenches of France must command respect even from those who might prefer a touch of rebellion.

In his youth Lawrence shared the family devoutness, serving briefly as a Sunday school teacher; but whatever mark this religious training left upon him, he refused all formal belief during his adult years. Almost all his biographers have noted strong religious traits in Lawrence, strainings toward some absolute of value by which to brace his conduct. Fewer have remarked on the tacit assumption he shared with many serious persons of our century: that the religious sensibility could be nurtured only in a culture of radical skepticism. (His friend, Eric Kennington, has recorded a conversation in which the adult Lawrence, asked about religion, spoke of a "process without aim or end, creation followed by dissolution, rebirth, and then decay to wonder at and to love. But not a hint of a god and certainly none of the Christian God.")

"Lessons," wrote Mrs. Lawrence, "were never any trouble to Ned [Lawrence's boyhood name], he won prizes every year . . . In the senior locals in 1906, he was place first in English language and literature . . . and thirteenth in the first class of some 10,000 entrants." Like a good many of the achievements that would later be dredged up from Lawrence's boyhood, this is impressive, but hardly as remarkable as his admirers have wished to suggest. Ned Lawrence was a bright, lively, inquiring boy; not a prodigy.

One trait merits special notice. In a family where all the sons were encouraged to a modest independence of bearing, Ned Lawrence stood out for his nervous boldness, a readiness to risk himself. His escapades and feats of physical endurance, both as a boy and then as a student at Oxford, were in part the proofs of strength that a small-bodied person feels obliged to thrust at the world, in part symptoms of a vanity which took the form of needing always to seem original. But these escapades and feats can also be seen as anticipations of his adult view that life is a test through which the human will, to assert its mastery over contingency and pain, denies the flesh not only its desires but its needs.

At some point before entering Oxford in 1907 Lawrence discovered that he and his brothers, apparently the sons of a respectable Oxford gentleman, were actually of illegitimate birth. His father, an Anglo-Irish baronet named Sir Thomas Chapman, had left a wife and four daughters in Ireland to run off with a former nurse, the woman who now figured both in public and at home as his wife. In letters written many years later to Mrs. Bernard Shaw—letters that may be read but cannot be quoted—Lawrence would claim that he had known these facts since before the age of ten. Like other of his stories about his past, this claim seems implausible: a defensive mechanism is at work here.

How deep a shock the discovery of illegitimate birth caused Lawrence, we do not really know. To what extent it should be regarded as a source of his sense of "homelessness" during the later years and his need to keep asserting himself in a series of new identities—this question demands speculation but does not permit a firm conclusion. One may see in the boy's discovery a matrix for those predispositions to suffering which would mark the later Lawrence. One may see it as a blow to his pride and self-esteem. But it is surely a vast simplification to claim, as does Richard Aldington in his venomous biography, that Lawrence received a wound that would leave him crippled for life. The bare facts—his gift for leadership, his success in winning the loyalty of distinguished men, his ability to complete a major literary work—all show that Lawrence was not permanently disabled by the effects of this adolescent trauma, if trauma it was. I add this last qualification because we must allow for the possibility that whatever pain the revelation caused him, Ned Lawrence, as an English boy raised on romantic notions and romantic books, might have felt it *inter-*

esting to have a father capable of such unconventionality in behalf of love.

Large parts of the boy's experience were intellectually vital and traditionally wholesome. A fondness for history led him to take bicycle trips through the south of England and make rubbings of monumental brasses. On his bedroom walls were pasted life-size portraits of knights who had performed heroic deeds in the Crusades. He devoured the medieval romances of William Morris with a relish that—hard as it may be for us to grasp—he would retain throughout his life. He attended lectures by Flinders Petrie that helped spark his interest in antiquities. And he began spending time at the Ashmolean Museum in Oxford, where he met the archaeologist D. G. Hogarth, who would become his mentor, friend, protector—at critical moments, a kind of father.

During the summers of 1906, 1907, 1908, on bicycle trips through France, Ned Lawrence visited cathedrals and castles, made careful notes, and wrote letters to his mother which, if a trifle too "composed," are still notable for an exactness of observation and phrasing beyond the usual capacity of an eighteen or nineteen-year-old boy. In the summer of 1909 he undertook a more adventurous trip: a walking tour of Syria, the interior of which was almost inaccessible to Europeans. His purpose was to prepare an Oxford thesis on the Crusaders castles. When he inquired about Syria from C. M. Doughty, whose *Arabia Deserta* he knew and loved, the older man sent back a note advising that the journey would be too risky, especially if undertaken alone. "Long daily marches," warned Doughty, "a prudent man who knows the country would consider out of the question." But Lawrence went.

Suffering heat, fever and a beating at the hands of a thief, Lawrence tramped eleven hundred miles through Syria, an average of twenty a day when on the move. He lived with Arab village families, ate *leben*, the Syrian yoghurt, and bread "almost leathery when fresh." He photographed some fifty castles and established to his own satisfaction the main point of his thesis.

Perhaps for the first time we come upon qualities in Lawrence that may be considered remarkable: —an intense fascination with the past, a ruthless insistence upon seeing things for himself, a readiness to submit to the customs of a strange, often hostile people, an eagerness to pursue an idea or action to its extreme limits. And something else, still more important: In Syria Lawrence came to feel the hypnotic pull of an utterly alien style of life, one that was almost the antipode of Western civilization. Toward the Arabs he would now be drawn by ties both stronger and less tender—certainly more abstract—than love. As he wrote a few years later to a friend: "You guessed right that the Arab appealed to my imagination. It is the old, old civilization which has refined itself clear of household gods, and half the trappings which ours hasten to assume."

By his twenty-first year Lawrence was beginning to think seriously about a career in archaeology—though whether he thought seriously about the close work required by archaeological scholarship is another matter. Through the help of D. G. Hogarth, Lawrence became attached in 1910 to a British Museum expedition that was to dig at Carchemish on the banks of the Euphrates. For most of the next three years—the happiest of his life, he called them—Lawrence worked as an assistant, miscellaneous, nimble and erratic, to the head of the expedition, first Hogarth and then Leonard Woolley.

At Carchemish Lawrence formed a close—and as it seems in retrospect, significant—friendship with Sheik Hamoudi, the foreman of the dig; and when he took another hike through Syria in the summer of 1911 which ended in bouts of fever and dysentary, it was Hamoudi who nursed him back to life. "He is our brother," the Arab would later say about Lawrence, "our friend and leader. He is one of us." *One of us:* a tribute that would have pleased Lawrence, amused him in its distance from truth, and finally disturbed him. For in stumbling upon Conrad's phrase, which for us evokes the whole tangle of fraternity and aloneness in human relationships, Hamoudi touched unwittingly upon the problem of bad faith that would torment Lawrence throughout his time in Arabia.

One fact more about the early Lawrence: In January 1914, as the world hurried toward war, he and Woolley went off on a trip through the area that runs south of Gaza and Beersheba and east of Akaba, ostensibly to retrace the routes of Biblical journeys for the Palestine Expeditionary Fund, actually to provide the British army with maps of a zone under Turkish sovereignty. For once there is justice in a complaint by Richard Aldington: "None of the intellectuals writing on Lawrence has expressed the faintest regret or indignation at this official abuse of science and religion to screen politico-military activities. . . ." Had Lawrence been anything but a man of austere moral sensibilities, this "official abuse," not the worst deed of our century, would hardly be worth noticing. Had he justified it in the name of military need, criticism might be given pause. But what disturbs one is that there was a side of Lawrence—the eternal British undergraduate with his sneaking admiration for "public school" pranks—that would regard such an incident as a lark. If the essential Lawrence was a man whose ordeal in Arabia burned every bit of pomp out of him, there was another Lawrence, a Kiplingesque schoolboy susceptible to romantic vanities about the mission of England, who was never quite to disappear. During the war years this other Lawrence would break out in a giggling superciliousness toward those military men he found dense and an equally callow adulation of those, like Allenby, he found enlightened. And who knows? Perhaps without this lesser Lawrence we should not have had the man who would come to write *The Seven Pillars of Wisdom*.

II

In the spring of 1916 Sherif Hussein of the Hejaz, descendent of the Prophet and protector of the faith, launched a revolt against the Turks. For some time the British had been tempting him with promises of post-war independence; but this shrewd fanatic had played a cautious game, rightly enough from his point of view, since he neither trusted the infidel British nor cared to risk the vengeance of the Turks.

At first the Arabs gained a few local victories, hardly decisive and, in their very success, exposing a poverty of purpose and leadership. But having lost the advantage of surprise and unable, with their irregular bands, to do more than harass entrenched Turkish posts, they now faced the danger of being wiped out by counterattack. The Arabs were ignorant of modern warfare; they had no master plan and barely an idea of why one might be needed; their main advantage lay not in any capacities of their own but in the sluggishness of the Turks. To provide help and soothe Hussein, British headquarters in Cairo sent an experienced official, Ronald Storrs, as envoy to the Hejaz. With him went T. E. Lawrence, who until then had spent the war months as an impudent and quite undistinguished staff captain in Military Intelligence.

In *The Seven Pillars of Wisdom* Lawrence has left a brilliant description of his first exploratory visit from one Arab camp to another, studying Hussein's three elder sons, each of whom led a body of troops. Ali, Abdullah, Feisal: which of these princes could become the focal point of rebellion, the embodiment of Arab desire? The picture of Lawrence plunging into the chaos of the Arab world, measuring the worth of its leaders and quickly bringing order to its ranks—this picture is surely overdrawn if one judges by the limited powers Lawrence actually enjoyed at the moment. Not until after his return to Cairo and his assignment as British Liason officer to the Arab troops in the winter of 1917 did he even begin to command such authority. Yet the picture is essentially faithful if one grants Lawrence the right—he won it in the desert and then through his book—to treat his own experience as a fable of heroism: the right, that is, to assign a scheme of purpose to hesitant improvisations which in the end did come to bear such a purpose.

It was Hussein's third son, Feisal, decided Lawrence, who could serve as the "armed prophet" of revolt: Feisal, "very tall and pillar-like," who displayed a posture of assurance and a patience for mediating tribal feuds. And it had better be added: Feisal responsive to the cues of this darting little Englishman with his "kitchen Arabic," his love for flamboyant dress, his curious pleasure in bending himself to the ritual and guile of Arab politics.

The speed with which Lawrence now became a leader of the revolt is astonishing, yet not difficult to explain. Between the xenophobic suspicions of the Arabs, who saw infidels descending upon them, and the routine military outlook of the British, who saw inefficiency all about them—which is to say, between two kinds of narrow-mindedness, each reflecting a different century—there arose in the Hejaz a vacuum of leadership. For the revolt to survive, the vacuum had to be filled. And it could be filled only by a man able to endow it with a coherent idea such as would appeal both to the predatory caution and reckless fanaticism of the Arabs.

The idea Lawrence first brought to the Arab revolt was not primarily a military one; nor did it yet have in his private reflections those metaphysical bearings that would later absorb him. Lawrence began by approaching the revolt not as a partisan but as a strategist. He approached it as a problem in dynamics: what was needed to move these people into action and, given their notorious inconstancy, to keep them in action? what kind of an enterprise could they reasonably be expected to assume and complete? To ask such questions was to enter the realm of politics, not as a system of ideas but as a makeshift theory of national psychology.

The tribal Arabs with whom Lawrence had now to deal, unlike the city intelligentsia and middle class of Syria, had almost no tradition of nationalism; they knew at best glimmers and anticipations of national feeling. The Arabs were not a nation at all; they were remnants and shards of what might once have been a nation; they contained perhaps the elements from which a nation might be forged. But Lawrence could not wait (nor could the Arabs) until they became one; he could only think of a course of action which, if they were enabled to pursue it with some freedom, would stir the Arabs into behaving *as if* they were a nation.

What might bring this about? Primarily the belief that they could or should be a nation; a burgeoning sense of their possibilities, such as they themselves could barely express; and a strategy of conflict that pressed them into momentary coherence without risking the full-scale warfare for which they were not prepared, since they were as quick to drop into discouragement as to flare into passion. Lawrence had to improvise a strategy of national politics for a cluster of tribes that neither was a nation nor had a politics. He had to find symbols and tactics for transforming their primitive antagonism to the Turks into a facsimile of a modern purpose: but a modern purpose that could retain its thrust only by drawing upon the sources of the primitive resentment.

Such considerations were obviously beyond the reach of most British officers, who saw only the noisy surface of Arab chaos and felt therefore that the best policy would be to bring in a sizable body of disciplined European troops. The French mission in the Hejaz, understanding Lawrence better, feared him more. It knew that any mobilization of Arab consciousness, no matter how useful at the moment, would threaten the structure of Allied power in the mid-East. No wonder that Lawrence complained in *The Seven Pillars of Wisdom* about the "blindness of European advisors, who would not see that rebellion was not war: indeed, was more of the nature of peace—a national strike perhaps." The moment Lawrence understood this, he was ready for his task.

In so reconstructing his situation, I do not mean to imply that Lawrence fully understood the workings of Arab society and religion, or the role of colonial rivalries among the great powers, or the general problem of nationalism in our century. Far from it. But what he grasped with absolute mastery was that the revolt could succeed only if it wore the face of freedom, only if it used the language of autonomy, only if it became a cause. To become a cause, it would have to be fought mainly by the Arabs themselves and appear to be led mainly by the Arabs themselves. If they could not be trained to positional warfare in the style of the period, they would have to be directed to other varieties of combat in which the more experienced Turkish army could not decimate them. British troops, except for a few technical advisors, would have to be kept away from the desert, at least until the Arabs gained some sense of their own powers. Good light weapons and a steady flow of gold were indispensable. Upon the tribal rivalries, the greed, the religious particularism of the Arabs there would have to be grafted a façade of unity: from which, if skillful enough, there might yet come the reality of national existence.

Lawrence was not deluded. He understood that the nationalism of the colonial countries was often devious and venal; that today's oppressed might be tomorrow's oppressors; that once freedom was won there might follow a moral relapse which would make the whole effort seem a waste. But he also sensed that meanwhile there lay imbedded in this nationalism an unformed yearning for dignity. If, for a time, the Arabs could be brought to act by this yearning, the revolt might succeed. If not, it would fail.

Lawrence saw the revolt in its political wholeness and

moral dynamism: not merely as it was, fouled by intrigue, cupidity and narrowness of spirit, but as it might become, an ideal possibility. He possessed the vision which, historically, was the Arabs' privilege: that was a cause for elation. He knew they could not sustain his vision: that was a cause for despair. Balancing elation and despair Lawrence, while still below thirty, reached full knowledge of the burdens of leadership.

Am I here endowing Lawrence with a coherence he would later claim but never really possess? Or assigning to him perceptions he would reach, if at all, only after the event? The record of his work and writings must stand as answer, but consider at least this sequence of passages, written before, during and immediately after the revolt:

1915
I want to pull them all [the "little powers" of Arabia] together, & to roll up Syria by way of the Hejaz in the name of the Sherif. You know how big his repute is in Syria . . . we can rush right up to Damascus, & biff the French out of all hope of Syria. It's a big game. . . . (From a letter to D. G. Hogarth)

1916
A difference in character between the Turkish and Arab armies is that the more you distribute the former the weaker they become, and the more you distribute the latter the stronger they become. (From *The Arab Bulletin*)

1917
The Arab movement is a curious thing. It is really very small and weak in its beginning, and anybody who had command of the sea could put an end to it in three or four days. It has capacity for expansion however—in the same degree—over a very wide area. It is as though you imagine a nation or agitation that may be very wide, but never very deep, since all the Arab countries are agricultural or pastoral, and all poor today. . . .

On the other hand the Arab movement is shallow, not because the Arabs do not care, but because they are few—and in their smallness of numbers (which is imposed by their poverty of country) lies a good deal of their strength, for they are perhaps the most elusive enemy an army ever had. . . . It is indiscreet only to ask what Arabia is. It has an East and a West and a South Border—but where or what it is on the top no man knoweth. I fancy it is up to the Arabs to find out! (From a letter to his parents)

1920
. . . but suppose we were an influence (as we might be), an idea, a thing invulnerable, intangible, without front or back, drifting about like a gas? Armies were like plants, immobile as a whole, firm-rooted, nourished through long stems to the head. We might be a vapour, blowing where we listed. Our kingdoms lay in each man's mind, and as we wanted nothing material to live on, so perhaps we offered nothing material to the killing.

. . . The Turk . . . would believe that rebellion was absolute, like war, and deal with it on the analogy of absolute warfare. Analogy is fudge, anyway, and to make war upon rebellion is slow and messy, like eating soup with a knife.

. . . We had seldom to concern ourselves with what our men did, but much with what they thought. . . . We had won a province when we had taught the civilians in it to die for our ideal of freedom; the presence or absence of the enemy was a secondary matter. (From "The Evolution of a Revolt")

These passages chart Lawrence's growing mastery of statement, but far more important, a development of thought and value almost to the point of establishing him as a new person. First, the simple-minded scheme for "biffing" the French. In 1917 the notation of a newly-seen complexity: a notation somewhat distant, neutral, but not unsympathetic. And finally the last statement, which Lawrence would work into *The Seven Pillars of Wisdom*, rising to an earned and measured eloquence: the revolt as idea, as undefiled conception. Yet this pattern is surely too neat, for Lawrence did not shed his earlier views, he buried them beneath his later ones. And the further qualification must be added that if the last passage gives us the essence of what the revolt could still mean to

Lawrence,—for by 1920 it often turned to ashes in his mouth, —the earlier passages provide evidence as to its less exalted realities.

In regard to so complex and elusive a mind as Lawrence's, no simple distinction can be enforced between action and response, what "really" happened and what he made of it in memory. Lawrence neither was nor could be a detached observer; he was leader, follower, victim all in one. He tells us that his first commanding view of the revolt came to him in March 1917 when for ten days he lay sick in the camp of Abdullah. Perhaps, in writing *The Seven Pillars of Wisdom*, Lawrence gave dramatic form to his memories by condensing a long experience of discovery into a moment of sudden realization. But this possibility should not be allowed to blur the fact that there was discovery. Even in Arabia history is not all muddle or chance; there *is* intelligence, plan, purpose. And to the extent that these were present in the revolt, they were significantly Lawrence's: not his alone, but his most forcefully.

It is possible that the innovations in military tactics claimed for Lawrence were neither so revolutionary nor calculated as has been supposed—though by now only specialists and old friends will have strong opinions about Lawrence as commander. It is possible that a good many of his glamorous desert raids were of uncertain value—though in guerrilla warfare bold acts can have consequences beyond their immediate military effects. It is possible that without British gold Lawrence could not have held together the Arab chieftains—though the crucial question is whether anyone else could have done it with twice as much gold. But one thing seems certain: it was Lawrence who grasped the inner logic of the revolt as a moral-political act and it was Lawrence who breathed into it a vibrancy of intention it had not previously known.

What his plunge into the desert meant to Lawrence he never fully said, perhaps because the main concern in his

writings was to present his relations to the Arabs as a problem
—a problem that could not be reduced to his private needs or
desires.* From fragments of evidence left by Lawrence and
those who were close to him, one may cautiously reconstruct
some of his responses.

Lawrence, the cocky young officer who had been disliked
so fiercely by the military regulars in Cairo, saw the Arabian
campaign as an adventure in the simplest, most *English* sense
of the word. This Lawrence took eagerly to the whole ritual-
pageant of the Arab camps and Arab ceremonies and Arab
pow-wows, though he knew that half the time they were mere
displays veiling weakness. This Lawrence suddenly found
himself cast in a role such as might satisfy the wildest fantasies of a middle class English youth raised on romantic
literature. With a sharp eye for stylized effects, he continued
in his own way the tradition of those English visitors to the
mid-East who have managed to penetrate native life without
ceasing to be immaculately English.

He loved to ride with Feisal at the head of a racing camel
army. He loved to dress in spotless white robes, sometimes
scarlet and white. He loved to sit in Feisal's tent, gravely
listening and dropping an occasional word during negotiations
with tribal chiefs who were edging toward the Arab cause.
He loved to compete with Auda Abu Tayi, leading sheik of
the Howeitat, a warrior out of the barbaric past. And he took
a special delight in acquiring for himself a bodyguard of dark-
skinned Ageyl fighters who formed a legion obedient to his

---

* Some private desires there surely were. *The Seven Pillars of Wisdom*
bears a fervid dedication in verse to "S.A.," who is generally taken to be
an Arabian Lawrence knew before the war. It has also been surmised,
from teasing hints dropped by Lawrence to his biographers, that one
motive for wishing to undertake the campaign in the desert was to reach
"S.A." But whether this person was, as Robert Graves insists, a woman
Lawrence had met in Syria or whether it was the Arab boy Sheik
Ahmoud whom he had befriended at Carchemish, we do not know. There
are other possibilities, but they are little more than guesses.

command. An English officer, meeting Lawrence at Akaba in 1918, found him

> . . . a small man dressed in extremely good and expensive Bedouin clothes, a richly braided and decorated goat's hair cloak over all, and on his head a wonderful silk kufaiyeh held in position by a gold agal. His feet were bare, and he had a gold Hejazi dagger in his belt. . . .

But even to act out this somewhat operatic role, Lawrence had to pay so terrible a price that one comes to disregard the flash and histrionics. From his return to the Hejaz until the day the British and Arabs entered Damascus, Lawrence accepted an appalling quantity of hardship. He learned to walk barefoot on hot sands with the aplomb of an Arab; to ride camels on lacerating marches; to go for days without food and then plunge his fingers into fatty stews; to show a contempt for pain which would win the respect of the most savage tribesman; to yield his body to exhaustion and then force it once again into war; to be on guard against those who might betray him for gold or wish him out of the way so they might pillage without check; to witness, often in necessary silence, repeated outbursts of cruelty (for the Arab's "sterile experience robbed him of compassion and perverted his human kindness to the image of the waste in which he hid.") And there were other, more intimate causes of suffering.

Lawrence never wished to persuade the Arabs that he had become one of them. Not only would that have been ludicrous, it would have threatened his mode of leadership. He did something more subtle and, in their eyes, impressive: he convinced the Arabs that in basic stoicism, outer bearing and daily practice he could become remarkably like them. The dream of "going back," of stripping to a more primitive self, which has so often fascinated Western man, was an authentic motive in his Arabian experience; but it was also consciously used by Lawrence to further his public role.

For a man who was so deeply drawn to the idea and the experience of *overcoming*—particularly a self-overcoming in the sense foreshadowed by Nietzsche—the war in Arabia came to be a test through radical humiliation and pain.

As he immersed himself in the life of the desert, repeating again and again the cycle of exertion—a moment of high excitement, a plunge into activity, then sickness, self-scrutiny, the wild desire to escape and finally a clenched return—Lawrence saw his experience as more than a romantic escapade or fearful discipline. Since in the bareness of the desert he had to remold his existence in order to meet an historical demand, he also found there the possibility of an action through which to carve out a chosen meaning for his life. From the trivia, the ugliness, the absurdity, the assured betrayal of events he would snatch a trophy of freedom.

In themselves courage and pain meant very little; men were being killed in France who also knew pain and showed courage. But they were mere dumb bodies led to slaughter. Lawrence, however, found himself in a situation where he might determine the character of his experience—or so it seemed to him in occasional moments of lucidity. To help make the Arabs into a free people was a task worthy of an ambitious man. To help steer the revolt past an enemy that would destroy it and allies that would disarm it, was a challenge worthy of a serious man. The fighting, to be sure, brought moments when such visions seemed utterly fatuous. There were wretched little raids where he had to use all his strength just to keep his forces from disintegrating, since the Arabs, indifferent to consequences, took pillage as the natural fruit of victory. There was the despair that followed a discovery that Zeid, Feisal's younger brother, had stupidly squandered a large sum of money and imperilled the revolt. There was the shock of learning that Auda, disgruntled in his greed, had entered secret negotiations with the Turks. But through it all Lawrence kept hoping that he might do something fine in the desert, perhaps something extraordinary.

He seized upon the Arabian campaign as an occasion for heroism not merely or primarily as it meant courage and recklessness, but as it meant the possibility for stamping intelligence and value upon a segment of history. To leave behind the settled life of middle class England which seemed to offer little but comfort and destruction; to abandon the clutter of routine by which a man can fill his days, never knowing his capacity for sacrifice or courage; to break with the assumption that life consists merely of waiting for things to happen; to carve out an experience which, in the words of Georg Simmel would "determine its beginning and end according to its own formative power"—these were the yearnings that Lawrence discovered in the revolt. And these are the motifs of his conduct that have made him so attractive to an age in which the capacities for heroism seem constantly to diminish.

Put aside the posturing and play-acting, put aside the embroidered robes and gold daggers, and there still remains the possibility of that rare action by which a man, rising above the limitations of moment and place, reaches the heart of excellence—a possibility, as Lawrence knew, that comes but rarely and must be seized with total desire, if seized at all. In the words of the hero of Malraux's *The Royal Way*, he wished to "put a scar on the map."

It is also in this sense, so utterly unlike the one I noticed a page or two back, that Lawrence undertook the Arabian campaign as an adventure: the sense, in Simmel's words, that an adventure is like a work of art, "for the essence of the work of art is . . . that it cuts out a piece of endlessly continuous sequence of perceived experience, giving it a self-sufficient form as though defined and held together by an inner core. . . . Indeed, it is an attribute of this form to make us feel that in both the work of art and the adventure the whole of life is somehow comprehended and consummated." Exactly what Lawrence came to hope for in the desert: that somehow, through an unimaginable exertion, the whole of his life would be comprehended and consummated.

At one decisive point, however, Lawrence's career turns sharply from the pattern suggested by Simmel. "The adventurer of genius," writes Simmel, "lives, as if by mystic instinct, at the point where the course of the world and the individual fate have, so to speak, not yet been differentiated from one another." About Lawrence this was not true, and everything that led him to think of his experience in Arabia as an imposture shows it could not be true. Consider the qualities implied by Simmel when he evokes the hero or, as he prefers to call him, "the adventurer of genius." The hero is a man with a belief in his inner powers, a confidence that he moves in rhythm with natural and historic forces, a conviction that he has been chosen for his part and thereby lifted above personal circumstances. At moments Lawrence felt one or another of these, but surely not with classic fulfillment or ease. Though his "individual fate" was indeed yoked to "the course of the world," in the end the two moved in profound opposotion to one another.

Lawrence found it hard to believe in the very deeds he drove himself to perform. His apparent fulfillment of the hero's traditional tasks was undercut at every point by a distrust and mockery of the idea of heroism. He could not yield himself to his own *charisma;* he was never certain of those secret gifts which for the hero ought to be an assured possession; he lived on the nerve's edge of consciousness, forever tyrannized by questions. At the end he abandoned his adventure with a feeling that inaction might be the most enviable of states and a desire to transform heroism into a discipline for the purging of self.

Is it fanciful to think that we have here a distinctly "modern" mode of heroism? So it seemed to Herbert Read when he reviewed *The Seven Pillars of Wisdom* in 1928. "About the hero," wrote Read, "there is an essential undoubting directness . . . essentially he is self-possessed, self-reliant, arrogant, unintelligent. Colonel Lawrence was none of these. . . . He was a lame duck in an age of lame ducks; a soldier spoilt by introspection and self-analysis; a man with a load on his mind. . . . [Lawrence's mind was] not great with thought, but tortured with some restless spirit that drives it out into the desert, to physical folly and self-immolation, a spirit that never triumphs over the body and never attains peace." Except for the ungenerous phrase about "physical folly," Read was here both accurate and perceptive. Read meant his remarks as a partial depreciation, but they point, I think, to the very ground for our continued interest in Lawrence. By now it is almost impossible to accept as a model of the heroic the sort of divine ox that Read claimed to admire. For better or worse, the hero as he appears in the tangle of modern life is a man struggling with a vision he can neither realize nor abandon, "a man with a load on his mind."

As Lawrence assumed greater burdens of responsibility in the desert campaign, his feeling that he had become a creature apart, isolated from both the Arabs and English, kept steadily growing. So too did his need to subject himself to the cruelest accusations. Some of Lawrence's difficulties were of a personal character and would have troubled him, though perhaps less violently, even if he had never come to Arabia; others followed from the very nature of warfare. All of them converging, they forced him into a mode of life that has come to be described as the experience of extreme situations.

In the fall of 1917, during a scouting expedition into enemy territory, Lawrence was captured by the Turks at Deraa. Fortunately not recognized, he was taken to be a deserter and brought before the local commandant, "a bulky man [who] sat on the bed in a night gown, trembling and sweating as though with fever. . . ." There followed a scene in which physical torture and sexual violation merged in a blur of pain. Later, in *The Seven Pillars of Wisdom*, Lawrence would describe it with a cold, almost clinical hysteria:

> I remembered the corporal kicking with his nailed boot to get me up . . . I remembered smiling at him, for a delicious warmth, probably sexual, was swelling through me: and then that he flung up his arm and hacked the full length of his whip into my groin. This doubled me half-over, screaming, or rather, trying impotently to scream, only shuddering through my open mouth. One giggled with amusement. A voice cried, 'Shame, you killed him.' Another slash followed. A roaring, and my eyes went black: while within me the core of life seemed to heave slowly up through the rending nerves. . . .

The two or three pages which recapture Lawrence's ordeal at Deraa anticipate a library of recollections by the victims of twentieth century totalitarianism. Few are more terrible than Lawrence's, though even in this extreme self-exposure, so honest about that side of himself which sought for masochistic pain, he could not quite succeed in being candid about the extent of his violation. From it he never fully recovered; for years he would impress people as a man battling his nerves to maintain the appearance of control.

The incident at Deraa would have been enough to break stronger and more secure men, but one reason it so tortured Lawrence in memory has to do with his sexual life. That Lawrence did not have what today we call a normal relationship with a woman, seems an incontrovertible fact. He shied away from women unless they were notably maternal, and his repeated expressions of disgust concerning the sexual act go far beyond the bounds of timidity or fastidiousness. Whether Lawrence was a practicing homosexual it is not possible to say here with any authority: the evidence of his friends ranges from genuine bewilderment to special pleading. There are passages in *The Seven Pillars of Wisdom* which show that

Lawrence was drawn to the idea or image of homosexuality as it occurred with apparent simplicity and purity among his young Arab warriors. But if, as one suspects, his sexual impulses were usually passive and suppressed, that would have been all the more reason for suffering a poignant sense of isolation in the desert, where he was thrown into an exclusively male society and the habits of the Bedouins were accepted without fuss or judgment.

There were other, more public reasons for his despair. By the summer of 1917 he knew about the Sykes-Picot treaty, a secret arrangement among Britain, France and Russia for perpetuating imperialism in the mid-East. This agreement made a farce of the promises of independence that had been given by Lawrence—though not by him alone—to the Arabs. Lawrence smarted under the knowledge that no matter what he would now say or do, he had no choice but to further this deceit. He had hoped, as he flamboyantly wrote in the suppressed preface for *The Seven Pillars of Wisdom*, "to restore a lost influence, to give 20 millions of Semites the foundations on which to build an inspired dream-palace of their national thoughts." The reality, which made him all the sicker as he became a legendary figure among the Arabs, was "a homesickness [which] came over me stressing vividly my outcast life among the Arabs, while I exploited their highest ideals, and made their love of freedom one more tool to make England win." And when, at a moment of climax in the Arabian campaign, Lawrence delivered a "halting, half-coherent speech" to the Serahin tribe—

> There could be no rest-houses for revolt, no dividend of joy paid out. Its style was accretive, to endure as far as the senses would endure, and to use each such advance as base for further adventure, deeper privation, sharper pain. . . . To be of the desert was, as they knew, to wage unending battle with an enemy who was not of the world, nor life, nor anything but hope itself;

and failure seemed God's freedom to mankind. . . . Death would seem best of all our works, the last free loyalty within our grasp, our final leisure. . . .

—he was speaking from the center of his new beliefs, assaulting his listeners at the point where he could make "their worldliness fade," but also, as he felt, enticing them into a net of deception.

Lawrence knew the Arabs had been selfish, narrow, treacherous all through the campaign—but wondered whether in the light of self-interest they had not been justified. He knew Doughty had been right in saying the Arabs had "a presumptuous opinion of themselves, yet [also] a high indolent fantasy distempered with melancholy. . . ." Victory, wrote Lawrence, "always undid an Arab force." And in a fine sentence in *The Seven Pillars of Wisdom* he brought together his complex feelings about the Arabs: "The Arab respected force a little: he respected craft more, and often had it in an enviable degree: but most of all he respected blunt sincerity of utterance, nearly the sole weapon God had excluded from his armament."

Had Lawrence been a principled anti-imperialist for whom sentiments of national pride were irrelevant, his problem might have been easier to bear. But he was not a principled anti-imperialist and he did retain sentiments of national pride. In fact, his shame and guilt derived precisely from a lingering belief in the British claim to fairness. Despite superb intuitions, he never reached a coherent view of the world political struggle in which finally he too was another pawn. There were moments when he saw, but he could not long bear the vision, that his whole adventure had been absorbed by a mere struggle for power. Lawrence was a man—hopeless, old-fashioned romantic!—who believed in excellence and honor; he came at the wrong time, in the wrong place.

On his thirtieth birthday, during a peaceful day shortly

before the entry into Damascus, Lawrence tried to examine himself honestly, without delusion:

> Four years ago I had meant to be a general and knighted when thirty. Such temporal dignities (if I survived the next four weeks) were now in my grasp. . . . There was a craving to be famous; and a horror of being known to like being known. . . . The hearing other people praised made me despair jealously of myself. . . . I began to wonder if all established reputations were founded, like mine, on fraud. . . . I must have had some tendency, some aptitude, for deceit. Without that I should not have deceived men so well, and persisted two years in bringing to success a deceit which others had framed and set afoot. . . .

As it now seemed to him, almost everything he had done was negligible in scale and value, a triviality of success. This judgment he would later express most forcibly in the preface he wrote for *The Seven Pillars of Wisdom,* and the summary of this preface that André Malraux has provided might almost have been written by Lawrence himself:

> . . . he was carried away at first by the appeal of liberty and was so completely committed to its service that he ceased to exist; he lived under the constant threat of torture; his life was ceaselessly crossed by *strange longings fanned by privations and dangers;* he was incapable of subscribing to the doctrines he preached for the good of his country at war . . . he ceased to believe in his civilization or in any other, until he was aware of nothing but an intense solitude on the borderline of madness; and what he chiefly recalled were *the agony, the terrors and the mistakes.*

When the British and Arabs marched into Damascus, the war came to an end for Lawrence. "In the black light of victory, we could scarcely identify ourselves."

III

Lawrence returned to England in November 1918, hoping, as he had written to his friend Vyvyan Richards, for "a long quiet like a purge and then a contemplation and decision of future roads." Nothing of the sort proved to be possible. The Versailles peace conference was a few months away; Feisal would be coming, ill-prepared and vulnerable; the Arab cause required pleading. Time and again Lawrence found himself wishing to shake off his responsibilities to the Arabs, who seemed far less admirable in peace than in war. It was not hard to surmise by now the order of civilization they would be bringing to the mid-East: a mixture of the worst of several possible worlds. But having yielded himself to an historical action, Lawrence felt that as a matter of honor he had to see it through.

He remained, to all appearances, a figure coiled with energy and purpose. His mind was never more supple than during these months in which he prepared to sabotage French and then British ambitions. But in his writings of the period—the impression is strengthened by memoires of his friends—one gains a sense of teeth clenched, hands tightened, a weariness beyond measure: as if he were trying to complete a necessary task and then lapse into silence.

In England Lawrence sent a memorandum to the cabinet proposing the creation of several independent Arab states, with Hussein's sons as limited monarchs and with moderate guidance and help to come from the West. That the Arabs were not ready for independence Lawrence knew quite well; no long-suppressed people ever is, except as it breaks past the limits of its suppression. Lawrence reached the core of the problem in an article he published in 1920: "We have to be prepared to see [the Arabs] doing things by methods quite unlike our own, and less well; but on principle it is better that they half-do it than that we do it perfectly for them."

Lawrence realized that his proposal would be bitterly fought by the French, if only because it allowed independence to the Syrian coastal area which the Sykes-Picot treaty had reserved for France. He understood that the British, to gain any peace at all, would have to compromise with their main ally. What he did not foresee—and here one may charge him with political naïveté—was that strong voices in England would be eager to work out an arrangement giving Syria to the French and allowing Britain to dominate Iraq.

At the peace conference his status was ambiguous. Formally he acted as advisor to the British delegation; actually, in the words of the Swedish writer Erik Lönnroth, he "functioned as representative of several Arab states which did not yet exist, and whose still vague contours he himself had greatly helped to form." The French, by now well briefed on his opinions and temper, treated him with frigid correctness. "If he comes as a British colonel, in an English uniform," read the instructions of the French foreign minister, "we will welcome him. But we will not accept him as an Arab. . . ." Yet it was precisely "as an Arab" that Lawrence did come, to badger and court Lloyd George, Balfour, Colonel House and even Clemenceau.

As negotiations dragged into the summer of 1919, it became clear that the British had decided to let France take Syria; in the labyrinth of cynicism and interest that would comprise the Versailles treaty, this was a small part of the bargain. The Arabs, sensing defeat, began to put up a show of truculence, notably in a popular congress held in Syria which proclaimed Feisal its head and independence its goal. The French, determined on a stern policy, were itching to drive Feisal's troops out of Damascus. And Lawrence, alone and powerless, grew increasingly estranged from his countrymen.

In the spring he had taken an airplane flight to Cairo with the intention of collecting his notes for *The Seven Pillars of Wisdom,* and when the plane crashed near Rome, had suffered a broken collarbone and rib fractures. The painful accident, together with the recent death of his father and the crumbling of his hopes at Versailles, brought him to a state approaching nervous exhaustion. It was now his predicament that as his reputation grew, his capacities declined. When the

French heard of the flight to Cairo, they set up a panicky cry that he was returning to the mid-East to lead an Arab resistance; in reality, Lawrence was in no condition to lead anything. As he returned to Paris, all he could do was persist in a quixotic loyalty to the Arabs, a loyalty resting more on principle than affection. And this stubborness—let us call it by its true name: this absolute unwillingness to sell out—began to strike his British colleagues as *unreasonable*, an embarrassment to their diplomacy.

On July 17 Lord Curzon telegraphed Balfour that Lawrence should not be allowed to work with Feisal any longer, since this would "cause us serious embarrassment with the French." An official of the British Foreign Office attached to the Paris delegation wrote in confidence: "While fully appreciating the value of Lawrence as a technical advisor on Arab affairs, we regard the prospect of his return to Paris in any capacity with grave misgivings. We and the War Office feel strongly that he is to a large extent responsible for our troubles with the French. . . ." At a peace conference, a man of principle can be decidedly irksome.

Lawrence kept searching for possibilities to maneuver. He appealed to the Americans in the name of self-determination; wrote pleading notes to the English leaders; sent a letter to the London *Times* arguing the Arab case and declaring—though this the editor did not print—that he regretted his war-time actions since the British government clearly had no intention of living up to the promises it had authorized him to make the Arabs. But it was hopeless, a lost cause. "By the mandate swindle," as Lawrence later said, "England and France got the lot." What Lawrence now felt came to far more than personal disappointment; it was a rupture of those bonds of faith that had made him a good and, in some respects, characteristic Englishman of his day. Now he "looked at the West and its conventions with new eyes: they destroyed it all for me."

By the end of 1919 the strain had become too great. Lawrence told himself that he had failed, perhaps betrayed, the Arabs. He harassed himself mercilessly in the writing of *The Seven Pillars of Wisdom.* And then, at the very moment of failure, he was thrust into public notoriety through Lowell Thomas' illustrated lecture, "With Allenby in Palestine and Lawrence in Arabia," a spectacle that in London alone drew over a million adoring spectators. Lawrence became a popular legend—cheap and vulgar—through the devices of a skillful journalist.

But also, one must add, through his own connivance: a connivance in which vanity and masochism joined to betray him. "I'm a sublimated Aladdin, the thousand and second Knight, a Strand-Magazine strummer," moaned Lawrence in early 1920, for he was far too intelligent not to see what Thomas was doing to him. Yet he failed to correct the numerous distortions, even after Hubert Young, his war-time companion, protested Thomas' statement that the British officers in Arabia had not accompanied Lawrence to the front. And he went to hear Thomas' lecture at least five times, apparently relishing his transformation into "a Strand-Magazine strummer." When "spotted," reports Thomas, "he would turn crimson, laugh in confusion, and hurry away with a stammered word of apology."

How was this possible? Why did Lawrence permit and even encourage Thomas to continue? There is no single answer, only a complex of possible reasons. The vaudeville in which Lawrence was cast as prince of the desert, served as a balm to feelings that had been hurt at Versailles: there was pleasure of a kind in being recognized at the Albert Hall and stared at in the streets. His new public role appealed to his sense of the sardonic, his sense of the distance between hidden truth and outer parody. It stimulated a kind of self-mortification, a twisting of the knife of public shame into the wounds of his ego. But at best these are explanations, and neither justify nor excuse. The truth is that it is hard to understand this episode, and harder still to accept it, unless of course we are prepared to show a little kindness toward a stricken man.

Yet not a hopelessly stricken man, for on one side of him Lawrence continued to behave like a tough and bouncy Irishman. Precisely during this period of failure, heart-sickness and notoriety Lawrence kept working away with an insatiable ambition, often for whole days and nights, at *The Seven Pillars of Wisdom*. Largely written in 1919, the manuscript was lost, completely and painfully redone, and in 1922 set up in proof at the Oxford *Times*. How ambitious he was Lawrence revealed in a letter to Edward Garnett:

> Do you remember my telling you once that I collected a shelf of 'Titanic' books (those distinguished by greatness of spirit, 'sublimity,' as Longinus would call it): and that they were *The Karamazovs, Zarathustra* and *Moby Dick*. Well, my ambition was to make an English fourth. You will observe that modesty comes out more in the performance than the aim.

"An English fourth" Lawrence did not quite make. Still, the book is one of the few original works of English prose in our century, and if Lawrence's name lives past the next half century it may well be for the book rather than the experience behind it. The book is subtitled "a triumph," and in regard to the Arabian campaign, formally its central action, this must surely be read as an irony. In another sense, however, it *is* a triumph: a vindication of consciousness through form.

As autobiography *The Seven Pillars of Wisdom* is veiled, ambiguous, misleading; less a direct revelation than a performance from which the truth can be wrenched. Nor can it be taken as formal history, since it focuses too subjectively, too obsessively, perhaps too passionately on its theme: which is the felt burden of history rather than history itself. Yet the book *as an act* has become part of the history of our politics, and is as necessary for comprehending the twentieth century as Brecht's poems or Kafka's novels or Pirandello's plays.

Primarily the book is a work of art, the model for a genre that would become all too characteristic of the age: a personal narrative through which a terrible experience is relived, burned out, perhaps transcended. This genre, to be perfected by the victims of totalitarianism, is a perilous one, succumbing too easily to verbal mannerism and tending to wash away the distinction between history and fable.

The Seven Pillars of Wisdom is a work of purgation and disgorgement. It is also, in order to resist the pressures of memory, a work of the most artful self-consciousness in which Lawrence is constantly "arranging words, so that the one I care for most is either repeated, or syllable-echoed, or put in a startling position." Robert Graves has said that "the nervous strain of its ideal of faultlessness is oppressive," and Lawrence himself found that the book is "written too hard. There are no flat places where a man can stand still for a moment. All ups and downs, engine full on or brakes hard on." The feverish state in which Lawrence composed the book, especially the early drafts—

> I tie myself into knots trying to reenact everything, as I write it out. It's like writing in front of a looking-glass, and never looking at the paper, but always at the imaginary scene.

—may help to explain why the book is "written too hard."

Its power depends upon a doubleness of perspective. It can be read as a narrative of high excitements and descriptive flourish. The scene is rendered with fierce, exotic particularity, as if to force the reader into a sensuous participation in Lawrence's experience. Details are thrust out with brutal, even shocking intent; for in this kind of narrative the reader must not be allowed to settle into any comfort of expectation. The bleakness of the desert, the sudden killing of an Arab soldier, the horror of an assault upon helpless Turkish prisoners, the nomadic grandeur of a man like Auda, the nightmare detachment of the Deraa incident and then, at increasingly frequent intervals, the turnings toward aloneness, the merciless guerrilla raids Lawrence conducted against his self—these and a thousand other bits comprise the agitated surface of the book.

Yet at every crucial point the writing, through wrenchings of metaphor and perspective, pulls attention away from the surface. It turns toward something else, at first a mere scattering of sentiments and then the growing and molding "I" of the book: an "I" that is not at all the conventional first-person narrator but an approximation of a figure who comes into being, like Melville's Ishmael, through the writer's struggle to write his book. It is the emergence of this self which keeps *The Seven Pillars of Wisdom* from being a mere recital of excitements and horrors.

Because he tries to maintain an almost intolerable pitch of intensity, Lawrence seems repeatedly to fall into a state of exhaustion, and the book to crumble into a series of set-pieces, sections detailing a more or less complete incident. By the nature of the set-piece, these sections are detachable and can be read as self-contained accounts of human exhaustion. Being detachable, they are so packed with nervous bravado and ambitious phrasing as to call attention to their life *as a form*, a series of compositional feats matching the feats of Lawrence's adventure. Yet through this accumulation of set-pieces there recurs the struggle of a self in formation; and therein the book gains a kind of unity.

To an age that usually takes its prose plain, Lawrence's style is likely to seem mannered. Unquestionably there are passages that fail through a surplus of effort; passages that betray the hot breath of hysteria; passages that contain more sensibility than Lawrence could handle or justify. But it is dangerous to dismiss such writing simply because we have been trained to suspect the grand. Lawrence was deliberately trying to achieve large-scale effects, a rhetoric of action and passion that may almost be called baroque: the style pursuing the thought. And while the reader has every reason to discriminate among these effects, it would be dull to condemn Lawrence merely for their presence.

Lawrence strives for a style of thrust and shock, and then, by way of balance, for passages of extreme sensibility. He often uses words with a deliberate obliqueness or off-meaning, so as to charge them with strangeness and potential life. The common meaning of these key words is neither fully respected nor wholly violated; but twisted, sometimes into freshness, sometimes into mere oddity. All of this followed from conscious planning: "I find that my fifth writing . . . of a sentence makes it more shapely, pithier, stranger than it was. Without that twist of strangeness no one would feel an individuality, a differentness, behind the phrase."

It is a coercive prose, as it is a coercive book, meant to shake the reader into a recognition of what is possible on this earth. No one can end it with emotions of repose or resolution; there is no pretense at conciliatory sublimation. The result, throughout, is a tensing of nerves and sensibility, a series of broken reflections upon human incompleteness. It is a modern book.

For Lawrence there was now to be one more significant entry into public life. Within a few months after the signing of the Versailles treaty, it became clear that he had been entirely right about the mid-East, and the massed heads of the French and British governments entirely wrong. By 1920 the British were pouring millions of pounds into Iraq in order to suppress Arab insurgents; the French were bombarding Damascus and spreading hatred with each discharge of their cannon. Soon the British decided they would have to modify their policy, which had been neither effective nor economical, and when Winston Churchill took over the Colonial Office in 1921 he offered Lawrence a post as advisor on mid-East affairs.

Lawrence now joined in political conferences in Cairo and for a brief time returned to the desert, where he helped work out a *modus vivendi* between the British and Arabs. A greater measure of autonomy was granted the Arabs in Iraq; the British army but not the RAF withdrawn; Feisal allowed to assume the throne; and peace momentarily restored. Lawrence said that justice had finally been done but the Arabs, wishing complete independence, took a less sanguine view.

His labor in composing *The Seven Pillars of Wisdom* and then the interval of service under Churchill had distracted Lawrence from himself. Now that both were done and nothing appeared to absorb or consume him, there could be no evading the central fact of his post-war years: *that, in his freedom, he no longer knew how or why to live.* It was the problem faced by many sensitive men of his generation, and Lawrence, who more than most had earned the right to speak of it, could find no solution, no way out.

He was physically wearied, morally depleted, a man without the strength of true conviction. He had run through life too fast, and now had to face the cruel question of how to continue living though his life was done. The ordinary ways of middle-class England he could not settle into; the literary world, which he admired to excess, made him wildly uncomfortable; and politics seemed dirty, mean, a mug's game. Religion as dogma or institution left him as cold as in the past, yet there burned in him a desire for some enlarging selfless purpose he could neither find nor name. Lord Halifax was surely right when he said that "some deep religious impulse moved him . . . some craving for the perfect synthesis of thought and action which alone could satisfy his test of ultimate truth and his conception of life's purpose." If this craving be a delusion, it is one from which the world is fast recovering.

Perhaps Lawrence's trouble was simply that of a man who, at the end of a great adventure, returns home and finds it impossible to slide into quiet and routine. (Some years later he would choose to translate the *Odyssey,* a book about a hero whose return is endlessly delayed.) Whatever the reason, his life was painfully distraught. He would walk the streets of London for nights on end, lost in moodiness and self-examination. He ate poorly, carelessly. His home in Oxford, palled by the death of two brothers in the war, was unbearable. A mist of affection separated him from his mother. After his return from Paris, she has remembered, he would sit motionless as stone for entire mornings. In London he found new friends, many of them famous men, to whom he could occasionally burst out in oblique confession; but goodwill and understanding were not enough. "The worst thing about the war generation of introspects," he wrote several years later to the novelist Henry Williamson, "is that they can't keep off their blooming selves." Caught up as he was with his "blooming self," Lawrence would lapse into bouts of self-pity and puerile shows of vanity. It is easy enough to dislike and judge the Lawrence of these days. But there were times when he expressed with a rare clarity and poignance, the sense of drift he shared with so many of his contemporaries.

"What more?" he wrote to Eric Kennington in 1922. "Nothing. I'm bored stiff: and very tired, and a little ill, and sorry to see how mean some people I wanted to respect have grown." A year later, after he had joined the RAF, he wrote to Lionel Curtis: "It's terrible to hold myself voluntarily here: and yet I want to stay here till it no longer hurts me. . . . Do you think there have been many lay monks of my persuasion? One used to think that such frames of mind would have perished with the age of religion: and yet here they rise up, purely secular."

Somewhat later Lawrence wrote in a letter to Robert Graves: "You see, I know how false the praise is: how little the reality compared with the legend: how much luck: how little merit. Praise makes a man sick, if it is ignorant praise." And when Graves remarked that there were two selves in Lawrence, a Bedouin self "longing for the bareness, simplicity, harshness of the desert—that state of mind of which the desert is a symbol—and the over-civilized European self," Lawrence answered: "The two selves, you see, are mutually destructive. So I fall between them into the nihilism which cannot find, in being, even a false god in which to believe." Later still, in a note to an unknown correspondent, probably in 1929, Lawrence wrote:

> I have done with politics, I have done with the Orient, and I have done with intellectuality. O, Lord, I am so tired! I want so much to lie down and sleep and die. Die is best because there is no reveille. I want to forget my sins and the world's weariness.

And in the early thirties Lawrence told a friend that he felt himself to be "an extinct volcano, a closed oyster, and I must discourage treasure-hunters from the use of tin-openers. . . ."

Taken from over a decade of Lawrence's life and grouped together in isolation, such passages unavoidably form a melodramatic picture. They omit the plateaus of ordinariness which fill the bulk of any life. They omit the moments of commonplace satisfaction. But that they are faithful to what Lawrence felt most deeply, that they show the most important side of his post-war life, seems beyond doubt. Through these years Lawrence suffered from a loss of *élan*, a sense of the void, the terror of purposelessness. He suffered from a nihilism which revealed itself as a draining of those tacit impulses, those root desires and values which make men continue to live.

This condition was by no means unique to Lawrence. When Hemingway wrote his stories, with their variations on the theme of *nada;* when Pirandello drove skepticism to intolerable extremes in his plays; when so somber a figure as Max Weber could speak of the "disenchantment of the world" and the likelihood that "not summer's bloom lies ahead of us, but rather a polar night of icy darkness and hardness"—they too were confronting the sense of the void, the sense that human life had entered a phase of prolonged crisis in which all of its sustaining norms had lost their authority. Lawrence reached these feelings in a unique way, through the desert of Arabia rather than the trenches of France. But once this strain of the exotic is put aside, there remains a common lot, a shared dilemma.

I would suggest that it is this Lawrence—the hero who turns into a bewildered man suffering the aftermath of heroism—who now seems closest to us. Had Lawrence simply returned to the wholesome life of an English gentleman, writing neither *The Seven Pillars of Wisdom* nor the remarkable letters to Lionel Curtis, he would still have been noteworthy. Such a man, however, could hardly have captured the imagination of reflective people as the actual Lawrence did. His war-time record was remarkable, the basis for all that was to come; without it he might have been just another young man afflicted with post-war malaise. But what finally draws one to Lawrence, making him seem not merely an exceptional figure but a representative man of our century, is his courage and vulnerability in bearing the burden of consciousness. "One used to think that such frames of mind would have perished with the age of religion: and yet here they rise up, purely secular."

Tensions of the kind Lawrence suffered during the years after the war cannot be borne indefinitely. In August 1922, as if to wipe out all he had once been, Lawrence joined the Royal Air Force as an ordinary recruit under the name of John Hume Ross. Six months later, when his identity became known, he was forced to leave but allowed to join the regular army. There he remained until 1925, when his pleas and the intervention of powerful friends persuaded Air Marshall Trenchard to accept him again, this time under the name of T. E. Shaw. Until his death in 1935 Lawrence served the RAF as clerk and mechanic, in England and India.

For a man to whom power, fame and money were within reach, Lawrence's decision to bury himself in the ranks was an extraordinary one; for a man who had fought all his life against the force of his own ambition, it was a climax of self-mortification, an act of symbolic suicide. No single explanation can account for thirteen years spent in a military whose spirit was at war with his passion for freedom, whose discipline chafed and humiliated him. All the explanations together are also unsatisfactory, except perhaps as they come to an absolute need to break from his old self, the heroic Lawrence and the helpless Lawrence both.

"Honestly," he wrote to Robert Graves,

> it was a necessary step, forced on me by an inclination toward ground-level: by a despairing hope that I'd find myself on common ground with men . . . by an itch to make myself ordinary in a mob of likes: also I'm broke. . . . It's going to be a brain-sleep, and I'll come out of it less odd than I went in: or at least less odd in other men's eyes.

And in a preface that he wrote for the catalogue to Eric Kennington's exhibit of Arab portraits, there is a brief but perhaps deeper statement of motive: "Sometimes we wish for chains as a variety."

There were other, slightly different explanations. "Partly, I came here to eat dirt till its taste is normal to me. . . ." Less candidly, he told some people he had joined the RAF to insure himself a regular income. To Lionel Curtis, who brought out his metaphysical side, he wrote:

> Free-will I've tried, and rejected: authority I've rejected (not obedience, for that is my present effort, to find equality only in subordination. It is domination whose taste I have been cloyed with): action I've rejected: and the intellectual life: and the receptive senses: and the battle of wits. . . .

Somehow he managed to live through the torments of basic training, for which he was ten years and one war too old. He learned to claw his way past the obscenities that filled the barracks where he slept. He found odd sensations of pleasure and pain in breaking himself to obey men he knew to be unworthy of his obedience. And at times there was a rough companionship, a peace of sorts. Today we would call it an "adjustment."

But again: why did he do it? To stamp forever upon his conscience the need for refusing power; to put himself beyond the possibility of taking power; to find some version of the monasticism he craved; to make up for the guilts that lingered from the war; to return to the commonest of common life; to punish himself and test again his capacity for accepting pain; to distinguish himself in suffering—truth lies in all these but in none alone. We should not sentimentalize. Except for the months of basic training, Lawrence did not feel himself to be suffering acutely. He was happy, or if not happy, then peaceful for long stretches of time. Whether he was stationed in England or Karachi did not seem to matter much: he was the same in one place as another. Still, it would also be sentimental to forget that he had surrendered, had accepted his dispossession:

> I was an Irish nobody. I did something. It was a failure. And I became an Irish nobody.

Throughout the years in service there were small pleasures, bits of compensation. Like a character in Conrad, he achieved a severe responsibility in his daily work, the "job-sense" that sees one through. ("One had but to watch him scrubbing a barrack-room table," recalled a corporal from the tank corps, "to realize that no table had been scrubbed just in that way before.") He found physical pleasure and a sense of freedom in racing his motorcycle across the narrow English roads. He made lasting friends in both the army and RAF, with whom he lived on terms of intermittent ease. He made friends, as well, with some of the greatest writers of the day: Bernard Shaw, E. M. Forster, Thomas Hardy. (Hardy he venerated with a filial emotion which is one of the most simply "human" of his qualities.) He tried his hand at critical essays, which are neither quite first-rate nor merely commonplace: a fine one on Landor, a respectable one on H. G. Wells. He turned the *Odyssey* into firm, often pungent English prose—some classicists have balked, but it is a living book. He finished *The Mint*, a severely chiselled picture of barrack life: Joycean in style, sometimes brilliant in evocation, structured as a series of set-pieces, showing a decided advance in control over *The Seven Pillars of Wisdom*, but too markedly an exercise, a self-conscious effort to *write*. And he conducted a wide, often pleasing correspondence with an army of friends.

His letters, though hardly a substitute for the definitive biography which some Englishman has still to write, give a more faithful picture of the shifts and turns in Lawrence's life than do either his own books or the books written about him. They are not letters written systematically out of one impulse or idea, a rigid notion of what a letter should be. Some, like the early ones, are interesting because they show us a typically intelligent English youth of a time we find increasingly hard to remember or imagine. Some, like the few from the war years, are valuable simply as a glass, transparencies upon action. Some, like those to Lionel Curtis, form a grave impersonal confession, not an unburdening of secrets, but the statement of a man in agony and quest. Others hold one by sudden bolts of power in expression, sudden breakthroughs to candor of speech. Whether they are "great letters," in the sense Keats' are, need not trouble us for a moment. They are the letters of a man who deserves to live in the imagination of his time.

In May, 1935, to avoid two errand boys coming toward him on a road, Lawrence crashed his motorcycle and died a few days later, never having recovered consciousness. Like much of his life, his death was no completion; it failed to round off his drama or his problem. He left his name entangled with a cluster of unanswered questions, this prince of our disorder.

Contours of American fiction

EDITH WHARTON: CONVENTION AND THE DEMONS OF MODERNISM

"Justice to Edith Wharton"—this was the title, and the motivating plea, of an essay Edmund Wilson wrote soon after Mrs. Wharton's death in 1937. Years have passed; a modest quantity of critical writing about her work has appeared; she still commands the respect of a certain number of readers, just as some, though not enough, of her books are still in print. But if one judges by the treatment she receives in our standard literary histories, the attention given her in the universities, the influence she exerts upon present-day writers, the feelings serious literary people are likely to have about their faded memories of her novels—then justice has not yet come to Edith Wharton. And this seems particularly true if one believes her to be a writer of wit, force and maturity—not the peer of Hawthorne, Melville and James, but several strides ahead of many twentieth century novelists who have received far more praise than she has.

I

It is difficult to imagine a study of Mrs. Wharton's apprentice fiction in which sooner or later the word "clever" failed to appear. I quote a few characteristic sentences from her early stories:

> The most fascinating female is apt to be encumbered with luggage and scruples.
>
> Her body had been privileged to outstrip her mind, and the two . . . were destined to travel through an eternity of girlishness.
>
> His marriage had been a failure, but he had preserved toward his wife the exact fidelity of act that is sometimes supposed to excuse any divagation of feeling; so that, for years, the tie between them had consisted mainly in his abstaining from making love to other women.

Such writing yields pleasure of a kind, but in context it often seems willful and strained. One senses too quickly the effort behind the cleverness, the claw inside the glove. Dealing with personal relationships among the leisured classes, these stories are usually brittle and contrived, reflections of the conflict in Mrs. Wharton between a worldliness that had not yet been raised to a style and a moralism that had not yet broken past the rationalistic and conventional.

The early stories hardly prepare one for the work to come. For with *The House of Mirth* (1905), a full-scale portrait of a lovely young woman trapped between her crass ambitions and her disabling refinements of sensibility, Mrs. Wharton composed one of the few American novels that approaches the finality of the tragic. The book is close in philosophic temper to European naturalism, though constructed with an eye toward "well-made" effects that are quite distant from the passion for accumulating evidence that we associate with the naturalistic novel. At its best Mrs. Wharton's style is terse, caustic, and epigrammatic—a prose of aggressive commentary and severe control. At points of emotional stress, however, she succumbs to a fault that is to mar all her novels except *The Age of Innocence:* she employs an overcharged rhetoric to impose upon her story complexities of meaning it cannot support and intensities of feeling it does not need. If not her most finished work, *The House of Mirth* is Mrs. Wharton's most powerful one, the novel in which she dramatizes her sense of the pervasiveness of waste in human affairs and the tyranny that circumstance can exert over human desire.

Technically, Mrs. Wharton was not an audacious writer. She felt little sympathy with the experiments that were being undertaken during her lifetime by the great European and American novelists. In reading her books one is always aware that for Mrs. Wharton the novel is essentially a fixed form, a closely designed if somewhat heavy container of narrative, the presence of which we are never invited to forget. Unlike such impressionist writers as Conrad and Faulkner, she does not seek for that illusion of transparency which might tempt a reader to suppose he is "in" the world of the novel. She wishes her audience always to be aware of her firm guiding hand, to regard it as a force of assurance and control. In the several senses of the term, she is a *formal* writer.

Mrs. Wharton composed the kind of novel in which the plot stands out in its own right, like a clear and visible line of intention; in which the characters are taken to be rationally apprehensible, coherent figures to be portrayed through their actions rather than dissolved into a stream of psychology; and in which the narrative point of view is quickly established and limited, even if most of the time it comes through the austere tones of Mrs. Wharton's own voice. Her locale and subject-matter are usually American, but her view of the possibilities and limitations of the novel as a form makes her seem closer to such Europeans as Flaubert than to Americans like Melville and Twain.

She is a writer of limited scope. The historic span of her novels is narrow, usually confined to those late nineteenth century realignments of power and status that comprise a high moment in the biography of the American bourgeoisie.

The social range is also narrow, dealing with clashes among segments of the rich or with personal relationships as these have been defined, or distorted, by the conventions of a fixed society. Mrs. Wharton had no gift for the large and "open" narrative forms, those sprawling prose epics which in modern fiction have been employed to depict large areas of national experience. Nor, despite an intense awareness of the pressure of impulse in human life, does she care to encounter the murk and puzzle of the unconscious. She respects it, she fears it, she would as soon keep it at a distance. The arena of her imagination is the forefront of social life, where manners reveal moral stress, and accepted forms of conduct may break under the weight of personal desire. "Civilization and its discontents"—the phrase from Freud could stand as an epigraph for her books. She writes as a convinced rationalist, but in her best work as a rationalist who knows how desperately besieged and vulnerable human reason is.

Within these traditional limits, and despite her coolness to modernist innovations, Mrs. Wharton was a restless writer, forever seeking new variations of tone and theme, and in her several important novels after *The House of Mirth* rarely troubling to repeat a success. In *The Reef* (1912) she composed a subtle though tenuous drama of personal relations, Jamesian in manner and diction, which deals largely with the price and advantage of moral scruple. In *The Custom of the Country* (1913) she turned to—I think it fair to say, she was largely the innovator of—a tough-spirited, fierce, and abrasive satire of the barbaric philistinism she felt to be settling upon American society and the source of which she was inclined to locate, not with complete accuracy, in the new raw towns of the Midwest. Endless numbers of American novels would later be written on this theme, and Sinclair Lewis would commonly be mentioned as a writer particularly indebted to *The Custom of the Country;* but the truth is that no American novelist of our time—with the exception of Nathanael West—

has been so ruthless, so bitingly cold as Mrs. Wharton in assaulting the vulgarities and failures of our society. Her considerable gifts for caricature reached their fruition in *The Custom of the Country*, a novel that is hard to endure because it provides no consoling reconciliations and has therefore never been properly valued or even widely read. And finally in the list of her superior novels there is *The Age of Innocence* (1920), a suavely ironic evocation of New York in the 1870's, blending Mrs. Wharton's nostalgia for the world from which she came with her criticism of its genteel timidities and evasions.

On occasion Mrs. Wharton was also a master of the shorter forms of prose fiction. A fine selection could be made from her short stories, and there are three short novels or novelettes —*Ethan Frome* (1911), *Summer* (1917) and *The Bunner Sisters* (1916)—which are of permanent interest. *Ethan Frome*, a severe depiction of gratuitous human suffering in a New England village, is a work meant to shock and depress; it has often been criticized, wrongly, for being so successfully the *tour de force* Mrs. Wharton meant it to be—that is, for leaving us with a sense of admiration for the visible rigor of its mechanics and a sense of pain because of its total assault upon our emotions. *Summer*, a more complex and thoughtful piece of writing, is also set in rural New England, displaying a close knowledge of locale and character which would surprise those who suppose Mrs. Wharton merely to be the chronicler of the New York rich. *The Bunner Sisters*, an account of the sufferings of two poor women in New York, is not only a masterpiece of compressed realism but a notable example of Mrs. Wharton's ability to release through her fiction a disciplined compassion that is far more impressive than the rhetoric of protest cultivated by many liberal and radical writers. One or two other novelettes by Mrs. Wharton, such as the melodramatic *The Old Maid*, also have a certain interest, for the short novel was a form in which her fondness for economy of effects—a sweeping narrative line, a brisk prose, a rapid disposition of theme and figures—served her well.

The remaining novels? A few are dull and earnest failures, like *The Fruit of the Tree,* and too many others, like *The Glimpses of the Moon,* are barely superior to ladies' magazine fiction. In the novels written during the last fifteen years of her life, Mrs. Wharton's intellectual conservatism hardened into an embittered and querulous disdain for modern life; she no longer really knew what was happening in America; and she lost what had once been her main gift: the accurate location of the target she wished to destroy.

II

One reason justice has not yet come to Edith Wharton is the widespread assumption that she is primarily a disciple of Henry James—a gifted disciple, to be sure, but not nearly so gifted as the master. Now it is true that if you come to Mrs. Wharton's work with the expectation of finding replicas of the Jamesian novel, you will probably be disappointed; but then the expectation is itself a mistake. The claim that Henry James exerted a major influence upon Mrs. Wharton's fiction, repeated with maddening regularity by literary historians, reveals the reluctance of scholars to suppose that anything can spring directly from the art of a writer without also having some clearly specifiable source in an earlier writer.

I would contend that Mrs. Wharton is not primarily the disciple of James; that James's influence upon her work has either been overstated or misunderstood; and that, within certain obvious limits, she is an original writer.

In one large and pleasant way Mrs. Wharton did regard herself as permanently indebted to Henry James. For her, as for so many later writers, he loomed as a model of artistic conscience; his example made their calling seem a sacred one, his devotion to craft made everything else seem trivial. James persuaded her that the composition of a novel should not be a mere outpouring, but a craft to be studied and mastered; he was, as she said, "about the only novelist who had formulated his ideas about his art." In this respect, then, James was her "inspiration"—which is something rather different from an influence.

There is *some* evidence of a direct literary influence. A number of James's early novels left their mark upon that side of Mrs. Wharton's work which is concerned with the comedy of social manners. To say this, however, is to indicate a serious qualification: for if James began as a novelist of manners he soon became something else as well, and although Mrs. Wharton was skillful at observing manners and in most of her books more dependent than James upon the use of such observation, it is finally for the strength of her personal vision and the incisiveness of her mind that we should value her work. Perhaps one could say that it was the lesser James that influenced the lesser Mrs. Wharton.

The point seems to be enforced by E. K. Brown when he writes that "The picture of the Faubourg Saint Germain in *Madame de Treymes* [a story by Mrs. Wharton] owes as much to [James's] *The American* and *Madame de Mauves* as it does to direct observation." This is largely correct, but it affects only some minor instances of Mrs. Wharton's work and is not sufficient ground for the usual claim of a pervasive Jamesian influence. Brown is also correct in noting that "from the beginning to the end *The Reef* is Jamesian." Yet here too qualifications are needed: the refined agonies of conscience which Anna Leath experiences in this novel are of a kind that depend on Mrs. Wharton's "feminine" side and thereby are mostly beyond the reach of James, while the ending of the novel, so painfully tendentious and damaging to all that has preceded it, is also dependent on Mrs. Wharton's "feminine" side, as this time it takes upon itself the privilege of moral retaliation. Still, the presence of differences between two writers does not remove the possibility of influence, and in regard to *The Reef* that influence is clear.

Can we go any further? In a valuable essay Q. D. Leavis cites Mrs. Wharton's remark that James "belonged irrevocably to the old America out of which I also came," and that he was "essentially a novelist of manners, and the manners he was qualified by nature and situation to observe were those of the little vanishing group of people among whom he had grown up." Such statements form part of Mrs. Leavis's ground for calling Edith Wharton "the heiress of Henry James," but in taking those statements at face value she is, I think, being led somewhat astray.

Mrs. Wharton's description of James's novels is clearly inadequate, for it transforms him into a writer excessively like herself. His dependence on the manners of "the little vanishing group of people among whom he had grown up" was never very great and, as his art matured, was left almost entirely behind. And though a figure of "the old America," James came from a milieu quite different from the one in which Mrs. Wharton was raised and upon which she drew so heavily in her fiction. Though a New Yorker by birth and occasional residence, James had his closest ties of intellect and temperament with the New England of philosophical idealism, both as it came down to him in its own right and as it was recast in the speculations of his father Henry James, Sr. Now it is precisely this element of American thought to which the mind of Mrs. Wharton was closed: both to her literary profit, since she escaped its vapidity, and her literary loss, since a major lack in her writing is any trace of that urge to transcendence, that glow of the vision of the possible, which lights up even the darkest of James's novels. The intellectual backgrounds of the two writers are quite different, and that is one reason Mrs. Wharton could not respond favorably to James's later novels. The whole Emersonian tradition, so important a formative element in James sensibility and so pervasive in his later books, was alien to her.

The truth is that in Mrs. Wharton's most important novels it is hard to detect any *specific* Jamesian influence. Perhaps it can be found in her conception of the novel as a form, her wish to write with plan and economy; perhaps in the style of *The Custom of the Country,* which may owe something to the cold brilliance of James's prose in *The Bostonians.* But Mrs. Wharton's novelettes are in setting, theme, and characterization quite alien to James, while each of her three best novels —*The House of Mirth, The Custom of the Country* and *The Age of Innocence*—is a work notably different from either the early or late James. The somewhat naturalistic method of *The House of Mirth* and Mrs. Wharton's preoccupation with Lily Bart as victim of her social milieu, the caustic satire of *The Custom of the Country* and Mrs. Wharton's impatience with its feeble hero as an agent of traditional values, the modulated style of *The Age of Innocence* and Mrs. Wharton's involvement with the world of her birth—all this seems her own. Her characteristic style is sharper, clearer, more aggressive, and less metaphorical than James's in all but a few of his novels. Her narrative line is usually more direct than his. And her sense of life is more despondent, less open to the idea or even the possibility of redemption.

III

Mrs. Wharton's best novels portray the life of New York during the latter third of the nineteenth century. Economically and socially, this world was dominated by an established wealthy class consisting of the sons and grandsons of energetic provincial merchants. In the 1870's and 1880's this class did not yet feel seriously threatened by the competition and clamor of the *nouveaux riches;* it had gained enough wealth to care about leisure, and enough leisure to think of setting itself up as a modest aristocracy. The phrase *modest aristocracy* may seem a contradiction in terms, but it should serve to suggest the difficulty of building an enclave of social precedence in the fluid bourgeois society America was then becoming.

Quite free from any disturbing intensities of belief or aspirations toward grandeur of style, this class was strict in its decorum and narrow in its conventions. With tepid steadfastness it devoted itself to good manners, good English, good form. And it cared about culture too—culture as a static and finished quantity, something one had to possess but did not have to live by. Its one great passion was to be left alone, unchallenged and untroubled by the motions of history; and this of course was the one privilege history could not bestow. The nation was becoming industrialized; waves of immigrants were descending upon New York; financial empires were being established in the alien cities of the Midwest as well as in Wall Street itself. Such developments made it inevitable that the provincial ruling class of "old New York" should suffer both assault and assimilation by newer, more vigorous, and less cultivated segments of the American bourgeoisie.

In "old New York" no one soared and no one was supposed, visibly, to sink. Leisure ruled. Husbands rarely went to their offices "downtown," and there were long midday lunches and solemn entertainments in the evening. Good conversation, though of a not too taxing kind, was felt to be desirable. Taste and form were the reigning gods, not the less tyrannical for their apparent mildness of administration. As Mrs. Wharton remarked with gentle sarcasm in *The Age of Innocence*, it was a world composed of people "who dreaded scandal more than disease, who placed decency above courage, and who considered that nothing was more ill-bred than 'scenes,' except the behavior of those who gave rise to them." In the same novel she wrote: "What was or was not 'the thing' played a part as important in Newland Archer's New York as the inscrutable totem terrors that had ruled the destinies of his forefathers thousands of years ago." And above all, "old New York" was a world that had entered its decline. What was happening in the years of Mrs. Wharton's youth, as Louis Auchincloss remarks, was "the assault upon an old and conservative group by the multitudes enriched, and fabulously enriched, by the business expansion of the preceding decades." Mrs. Wharton kept returning to this theme, half in the cool spirit of the anthropologist studying the death of a tribe, half with the nostalgia of a survivor mourning the loss of vanished graces.

Toward the world in which she grew up Mrs. Wharton retained a mixture of feelings that anticipates those of later American writers toward their immigrant childhood and youth in a new New York. It was too fatally *her* world, beyond choice or escape, and it would serve her as lifelong memory, lifelong subject, perhaps lifelong trauma. She loved "old New York" with that mixture of grieving affection and protective impatience Faulkner would later feel toward Mississippi and Saul Bellow toward the Jewish neighborhoods of Chicago. Yet it also left her dissatisfied, on edge, unfulfilled. Her work, as Edmund Wilson has remarked, "was . . . the desperate product of a pressure of [personal] maladjustments. . . . At her strongest and most characteristic, she is a brilliant example of the writer who relieves an emotional strain by denouncing his generation." She yearned for a way of life that might bring greater intellectual risks and yield greater emotional rewards than her family and friends could imagine, and only after a time did she find it in her dedication to writing. Just as Faulkner's attitudes toward his home country have kept shifting from one ambiguity to another, so Mrs. Wharton combined toward her home city feelings both of harsh rejection and haughty defense. There are moments, especially in *The House of Mirth*, when she is utterly without mercy toward "old New York": she sees it as a place of betrayal, failure, and impotence. In her old age, when she came to write her autobiography, she was mellower—though perhaps the word should really be, harder—in spirit. "It used to seem to me," she wrote, "that the group in which I grew up was like an empty vessel into which no new wine would ever again be poured. Now I see that one of its uses lay in preserving a few drops of an old vintage too rare to be savored by a youthful palate. . . ."

For a novelist to be so profoundly involved with a known and measured society offers many advantages. Mrs. Wharton wrote about her segment of America with an authority few novelists could surpass, for she was one of the two or three among them who knew, fully and from the inside, what the life of the rich in this country was really like. Henry James had used that life as an occasion for fables of freedom and circumstance in his later books; F. Scott Fitzgerald, an interloper in the world of wealth, was to collect brilliant guesses and fragments of envious insight; John O'Hara has felt his way along the provincial outposts of the America that made its money late and fast. But no American writer has known quite so deeply as Mrs. Wharton what it means, both as privilege and burden, to grow up in a family of the established rich: a family where there was enough money and had been money long enough for talk about it to seem vulgar, and where conspicuous effort to make more of it seemed still more vulgar. One reason for continuing to read *The House of Mirth, The Custom of the Country,* and *The Age of Innocence* is the shrewdness with which Mrs. Wharton, through an expert scrutiny of manners, is able to discriminate among the gradations of power and status in the world of the rich. To read these books is to discover how the novel of manners can register both the surface of social life and the inner vibrations of spirit that surface reveals, suppresses, and distorts.

There were other advantages in being so close to her materials. As with Faulkner, the subject seems to have chosen the writer, not the writer the subject; everything came to her with the pressure and inexorability of a felt memory; each return to the locale of her youth raised the possibility of a new essay at self-discovery. And in books like *The House of Mirth* and *The Age of Innocence* she could work on the assumption, so valuable to a writer who prizes economy of structure, that moral values can be tested in a novel by dramatizing the relationships between fixed social groups and mobile characters.

As she herself knew quite well, there was little in Mrs. Wharton's world that could provide her with a subject large in social scope and visibly tragic in its implications. Had "old New York" gone down in blind and bitter resistance to the *nouveaux riches,* that might have been a subject appropriate to moral or social tragedy; but since there was far less conflict than fusion between the old money and the new, she had little alternative to the varieties of comedy that dominate her books. Only once in her novels did she achieve a tragic resonance, and that was in *The House of Mirth* where Lily Bart is shown as the victim of a world that had made possible her loveliness and inevitable her limitations. Even here we must reduce the traditional notion of the tragic to the pathetic on one side and bleak on the other, if the term is to be used with approximate relevance. In discussing this novel Mrs. Wharton showed a complete awareness of her problem. How, she asked herself, "could a society of irresponsible pleasure-seekers be said to have, on the 'old woes of the world,' any deeper bearing than the people composing such a society could guess?" And she answered: "A frivolous society can acquire dramatic significance only through what its frivolity destroys. Its tragic implication lies in its power of debasing people and ideas."

Toward the end of her career Mrs. Wharton found it more and more difficult to employ her material with the success that marks her work between 1905 and 1920. Her later novels are shoddy and sometimes mean-spirited in the hauteur with which she dismisses younger generations beyond the reach of her understanding or sympathy. These novels bristle with her impatience before the mysteries of a world she could not enter, the world of twentieth century America, and are notable for a truculence of temper, a hardening of the moral arteries. I would offer the speculation that Mrs. Wharton, whose intelligence should never be underestimated, was aware that the ground on which she took her moral stand was dissolving beneath her. At best the world of her youth had been an aristocracy of surface ("In that simple society," she recalled, "there was an almost pagan worship of physical beauty"), but she had always wanted it to be something better, something beautiful and truly distinguished. She had wanted to look upon it as potentially an aristocracy of value, and throughout most of her life she struggled with this desire and her recognition that it was an impossible, even unreasonable desire. But even when she recognized this, she still wondered to what extent the style and decorum of "old New York" had at least made possible some of the aspirations she had cherished since childhood. Having a thoroughly earthbound mind, she sought for tangible embodiments, in social groups or communities, of the values to which she clung—for she could not be content with the fabulous imaginings Henry James spun in his later novels. She turned, at times with open savagery and at other times with a feeling as close to wistfulness as she could tolerate, to the world of her birth, hoping to find there some token of security by which to satisfy the needs of her imagination. In the inevitable disappointment that followed, Mrs. Wharton, though extremely conservative in her opinions, proved to be the American novelist least merciful in her treatment of the rich. She kept harassing them, nagging at them in a language they could not, with the best will in the world, understand; and then she became glacial in her contempt, almost too willing to slash away at their mediocrity because she did not know anyone else to turn toward or against.

At the end she was alone. If the incongruity between desire and realization is a recurrent motif in her writing about personal relationships, it is an incongruity she also observed in her dealings with the public world. There were always available to her, once she settled in France, a number of personal friends, men and women of high if somewhat forbidding culture. But what emerges from a scrutiny of her work as a whole is that Mrs. Wharton, like so many of those younger deracinated novelists who both interested and disturbed her, was a solitary, clinging to values for which she could find no place, and holding fast, with tight-lipped stoicism, to the nerve of her pride. She was a writer haunted by what she disliked, haunted by the demons of modernism as they encircled her both in life and literature. She would have nothing to do with them, yet in her most important books they kept reappearing, both as agents of moral dissolution and as possibilities of fresh life that needed to be kept sternly in check.

IV

The texture of Mrs. Wharton's novels is dark. Like so many writers whose education occurred during the latter decades of the nineteenth century, she felt that the universe—which for her is virtually to say, organized society—was profoundly inhospitable to human need and desire. The malaise which troubled so many intelligent people during her lifetime—the feeling that they were living in an age when energies had run down, meanings collapsed, and the flow of organic life been replaced by the sterile and mechanical—is quite as acute in her novels as in those of Hardy and Gissing. Like them, she felt that somehow the world had hardened and turned cold, and she could find no vantage point at which to establish a protective distance from it. This condition is somewhat different from the strain of melancholy that runs through American literature, surely different from the metaphysical desperation that overcame Melville in his later years or the misanthropy that beset Twain. What Mrs. Wharton felt was more distinctly

"European" in quality, more related to that rationalist conservatism which is a perennial motif in French intellectual life and manifests itself as a confirmed skepticism about the possibilities of human relationships.

In Mrs. Wharton's vision of things—and we can only speculate on the extent to which her personal unhappiness contributed to it—human beings seem always to prove inadequate, always to fail each other, always to be the victims of an innate disharmony between love and response, need and capacity. Men especially have a hard time of it in Mrs. Wharton's novels. In their notorious vanity and faithlessness, they seldom "come through"; they fail Mrs. Wharton's heroines less from bad faith than from weak imagination, a laziness of spirit that keeps them from a true grasp of suffering; and in a number of her novels one finds a suppressed feminine bitterness, a profound impatience with the claims of the ruling sex. This feminist resentment seems, in turn, only an instance of what Mrs. Wharton felt to be a more radical and galling inequity at the heart of the human scheme. The inability of human beings to achieve self-sufficiency drives them to seek relationships with other people, and these relationships necessarily compromise their freedom by subjecting them to the pain of a desire either too great or too small. Things, in Mrs. Wharton's world, do not work out. In one of her books she speaks of "the sense of mortality," and of "its loneliness, the way it must be borne without help." I am convinced she meant by this more than the prospect of death. What "must be borne without help" is the inexorable disarrangement of everything we seek through intelligence and will to arrange.

Mrs. Wharton's general hostility toward "modern" ideas must have predisposed her against Freudian psychology, yet one is repeatedly struck by the fact that, at least in regard to the *possibilities* of the human enterprise, there is an underlying closeness of skepticism between her assumptions and Freud's theories. Mrs. Wharton had a highly developed, perhaps overdeveloped, sense of the power of everything in organized social existence which checks our desires. Like Freud, she believed that we must endure an irremediable conflict between nature and culture, and while she had at least as healthy a respect as he did for the uses of sublimation, she also knew that the human capacity for putting up with substitute gratifications is limited. From this impasse she could seldom find any way out.

A good many of Mrs. Wharton's critics have assumed that she was simply a defender of harsh social conventions against all those who, from romantic energy or mere hunger for meaning in life, rebel against the fixed patterns of their world. But this is not quite true for many of her books, and in regard to some of them not true at all. What is true is that most of her plots focus upon a clash between a stable society and a sensitive person who half belongs to and half rebels against it. At the end he must surrender to the social taboos he had momentarily challenged or wished to challenge, for he either has not been able to summon the resources of courage through which to act out his rebellion, or he has discovered that the punitive power of society is greater than he had supposed, or he has learned that the conventions he had assumed to be lifeless still retain a certain wisdom. Yet much of Mrs. Wharton's work contains a somewhat chill and detached sympathy for those very rebels in whose crushing she seems to connive. Her sense of the world is hardly such as to persuade her of its goodness; it is merely such as to persuade her of its force.

Mrs. Wharton understands how large is the price, how endless the nagging pain, that must be paid for a personal assertion against the familiar ways of the world, and she believes, simply, that most of us lack the strength to pay. Yet she has no respect for blind acceptance, and time after time expresses her distaste for "sterile pain" and "the vanity of self-sacrifice." It is hard to imagine another American writer for whom society, despite its attractions of surface and order, figures so thoroughly as a prison of the human soul. And there, she seems to say, there it is: the doors locked, the bars firm. "Life," she wrote in *The Fruit of the Tree*, "is not a matter of abstract principles, but a succession of pitiful compromises with fate, of concessions to old traditions, old beliefs, old tragedies, old failures." This sense of fatality has, in her best work, a certain minor magnificence, what might be called the magnificence of the bleak.

In a final reckoning, of course, Mrs. Wharton's vision of life has its severe limitations. She knew only too well how experience can grind men into hopelessness, how it can leave them persuaded that the need for choice contains within itself the seeds of tragedy and the impossibility of choice the sources of pain. Everything that reveals the power of the conditioned, everything that shreds our aspirations, she brought to full novelistic life. Where she failed was in giving imaginative embodiment to the human will seeking to resist defeat or move beyond it. She lacked James's ultimate serenity. She lacked his gift for summoning through images of conduct the purity of children and the selflessness of girls. She lacked the vocabulary of happiness.

But whatever Mrs. Wharton could see, she looked at with absolute courage. She believed that what the heart desires brings with it a price, and often an exorbitant price. Americans are not trained to accept this view of the human situation, and there is nothing to recommend it except the fact that it contains at least a fraction of the truth. How well, with what sardonic pleasure, Mrs. Wharton would have responded to the lines of W. H. Auden:

> Every farthing of the cost
> All the bitter stars foretell
> Shall be paid.

THE QUEST FOR MORAL STYLE

"I went to the woods," wrote Henry David Thoreau, "because I wished to live deliberately, to front only the essential facts of life, and see if I could not learn what it had to teach and not, when I came to die, discover that I had not lived." It is no mere fancy to suggest that in this one sentence Thoreau released the dominant concern of nineteenth century American writing, especially that segment of it composed in New England under the influence of the transcendental philosophers. Not many American writers have cared, literally, to go to the woods: Hawthorne would have preferred a warm study. But in the mid-nineteenth century most of them believed that, by discovering a new freedom in the openness of the natural world, man could reach out toward both God and his inmost self—the two were not always kept distinct in Emerson's New England—without having first to be greatly concerned about the intervening barriers of society. The first major outburst of American writing, as it comes to us in the work of Emerson, Hawthorne, Melville and Whitman, is at once intimate, dealing with problems of personal being, and metaphysical, seeking to establish a fresh sense of man's relation to the universe. But of social forms, conventions, institutions, ambitions and burdens there is very little.

Only during the last decades of the nineteenth century does the idea of society as an overwhelming and inescapable force appear in American literature. The important writers of this period differ radically in their responses to society: Mark Twain looks upon it as insidiously enclosing and asphyxiating, Henry James regards it as both the solvent of innocence and the necessary theatre for high drama, William Dean Howells treats it simply as the neutral and sometimes benign medium of daily existence, and for Frank Norris it becomes a mysterious agency dispensing pleasure and destruction with promiscuous brutishness. But all of these writers, both those who announce their contempt and those who relax in acceptance, confront society with a vigilance that is new to American literature.

In two later novelists, Theodore Dreiser and Edith Wharton, the *idea* of society becomes a central preoccupation. Though utterly different in literary method and social opinion, Dreiser in *Sister Carrie* and Mrs. Wharton in *The House of Mirth* assume that society exists, intractably, and that it can be examined in terms of relationships of power, economic interest and social status. For such novelists society becomes a force, an actor apart from the central characters and not to be reduced to a mere "background." It breaks the will of the characters or bends to their desires; and it takes on a "thickness," a hovering and often menacing presence, that cannot be found in the earlier American novelists.

In their eagerness to observe social detail and their commitment to the view that the power of circumstance is a power over the human soul, Dreiser and Mrs. Wharton are closer to the central tradition of the nineteenth century novel both in England and continental Europe than they are to the American writers preceding or following them. Unlike the Melville of *Moby Dick* or the Hemingway of *The Sun Also Rises,* they believe that the web of society is the true locale of man's destiny and that his salvation can be found, if found at all, within society. But Dreiser and Mrs. Wharton are not mere passive recorders, mere photographers of the world as it is. Like every other sensitive writer of the past hundred years, they also need to question—even if, in some of Mrs. Wharton's novels, strongly to reaffirm—traditional views governing our moral existence. They too are involved in that peculiarly anxious and persistent search for values which forms so prominent an aspect of the moral history of our time—the search for secure assumptions, unbroken justifications, which can give direction and coherence to human conduct.

II

That search is by now not only a familiar but an expected component of the serious novel; a tradition has been established in which it figures conspicuously and often omniverously, so that readers have come, with a certain loss of historical perspective, to regard it as a necessary part of literary experience.

For the generation of American writers, however, that began publishing shortly after the First World War, the crisis of traditional values was no longer a problem in quite the way it had been for writers in the late nineteenth century. By now the crisis of values was an accepted fact, and therefore not so much a painful conclusion toward which their novels and poems might reach as a necessary assumption from which their novels and poems had to begin.

This attitude found an important anticipation in the stories of Sherwood Anderson, a writer who began to publish only a few years before Hemingway and Fitzgerald but who was clearly a man of an older generation, his mind and temper having been formed in the rural mid-west. The younger writers would soon be brushing Anderson aside as a sentimentalist, which in part he was; but at his best, in the haunting tales and sketches he wrote about American loneliness, he helped prepare the way for the modernist writing of the 'twenties.

Anderson did this through the example of his life, particularly that moment of climax, soon to become a legend in our culture, when at the age of thirty-six he abandoned his paint factory, wife and children to strike out for the bohemia of Chicago, devote himself to the cult of art and thereby, as he might have said, "front only the essential facts of life." His work, too, set a significant example. *Winesburg, Ohio* is a classic American portrait of human bewilderment, conveying a vision of the native landscape cluttered with dead stumps, twisted oddities, grotesque and pitiful remnants of human creatures. Confronted with this world of back-street grotesques, for whom nothing can happen because everything is too late, one hardly feels it enough to speak of a crisis of values. Things have gone beyond that, and what *Winesburg* reveals is the debris of crisis, the cost of collapse. As it abandons the naturalist impulse of a Dreiser to represent society in overwhelming detail and moves toward an expressionist tableau of human deformity, *Winesburg* helps to confirm the younger writers in their sense of American life and their desire to find a way of imaginatively transcending it.

Perhaps the most vivid account of this new generation of writers, a generation that begins to publish after the First World War and reaches its finest achievement during the mid-'twenties, has come from the poet and critic John Peale Bishop. In his essay "The Missing All"—the title is taken from an Emily Dickinson poem that begins "The missing All prevented me from missing minor things"—Bishop described how the young literary men returning from the war felt they had been cheated not merely of health and time but more important, of truth and honor. They formed "really the first literary generation in America. There had been groups before, but they were not united by a communion of youth, a sense of experience shared and enemies encountered. . . ." They felt themselves to be cut off from the world of all who had come immediately before them, all who held power and spoke with authority. They were not in rebellion against the political order of Western capitalism, but in revulsion from its moral disorder. As Bishop wrote:

> The most tragic thing about the war was not that it made so many dead men, but that it destroyed the tragedy of death. Not only did the young suffer in the war, but every abstraction that would have sustained and given dignity to their suffering. The war made the traditional morality inacceptable; it did not annihilate it; it revealed its immediate inadequacy. So that at its end the survivors were left to face, as they could, a world without values.

This sense of having been betrayed and left adrift was powerful among young people in all the Western countries, where it formed the psychic foundation for that "communion of youth" Bishop so keenly observed. It is one of the strongest feelings behind the writing of the 'twenties, and nowhere has it been expressed so poignantly as in the introduction T. E. Lawrence would write for *The Seven Pillars of Wisdom:*

> We were wrought up with ideas inexpressible and vaporous, but to be fought for. We lived many lives in those whirling campaigns, never sparing ourselves any good or evil: yet when we achieved and the new world dawned, the old men came out again and took from us our victory and remade it in the likeness of the former world they knew. Youth could win, but had not learned to keep, and was pitiably weak against age. We stammered that we had worked for a new heaven and a new earth, and they thanked us kindly and made their peace.

When Emily Dickinson spoke of "the Missing All," she meant the God of her fathers, the God of Christianity; when Bishop borrowed her phrase, he had in mind not merely the image of God but a whole way of life that had been the heritage of classical Christianity, even if hardened and distorted in America by Puritanism, and that was now clearly in the process of crumbling. This perception—it is more a perception than a belief or idea—is seldom the dominant subject in the work of Hemingway and his contemporaries, but it is the dominant fact that needs to be known about their work. It is the premise from which they start, a premise that strikes them as so entirely obvious they feel no need to demonstrate or dramatize it. They do not even discuss it—only their critics do. The hopelessness of the familiar social world, the pointlessness of trying to change it, and the necessity for some credo of private disaffiliation (Hemingway's "separate peace") are assumption in their work quite as the need to grapple with inherited but fading Christian pieties form an assumption in the work of Hawthorne and Melville.

For writers like Hemingway, Fitzgerald, Cummings and the early Dos Passos there could no longer be any question of clinging to traditional values. But more important, there could not even be a question of trying to find a new set of values; they were beyond such ambitions or delusions, they knew it was their lot to spend their lives in uncertainty, and the problem that troubled them most was how to do this without violating their feelings about courage and dignity. To be sure, the very desire to find an honorable style of survival in a time of moral confusion indicates a certain strength of moral intent; and the hope of preserving courage and dignity while experiencing a crack-up of values implies the continued hold of certain values. Even these, however, become extremely problematic when they are raised to the level of a troubled self-consciousness.

The writers we are here discussing went through just this kind of crisis. Almost by instinct they backed away from large-scale beliefs or ideals: they had had enough of rhetoric, enough of "idealism," and lived in a magnified fear of platitudes. They had given up, if they had ever had it, the hope of achieving a coherent and ordered moral perspective; they were concerned with something more desperate, more fragmentary, more immediate. They were struggling to survive, as men of sensibility who had lost their way and knew it. They saw their task as a defensive one: the preservation of residual decencies even when they could not quite provide sufficient reasons for wishing to preserve them. And if that seemed too ambitious, they were ready to settle for a severe insistence upon keeping honest among, and with, themselves. Though often bohemian and sometimes dissolute, these writers nourished a sense of their calling as austere and finally as monastic as Flaubert's. It was if they had taken upon themselves the obligation to keep alive an undefiled word, not because they grasped its full meaning but because they felt that to keep it alive would allow others, later on, to grasp it.

The best of these writers were in search of what I propose to call a *moral style*. I mean by this improvised phrase: a series of tentative embodiments in conduct of a moral outlook they could not bring to full statement; or a series of gestures and rituals made to serve as a substitute for a moral outlook that could no longer be summoned; or a fragmentary code of behavior by which to survive decently, as if there were—the drama consisting in the fact that there is not—a secure morality behind it. The search for a moral style, which I take to be fundamental to the best American writing between the First World War and the depression years, is a search undertaken by men who have learned that a life constricted to the standard of *faute de mieux* can still be a rigorous, even an exalting obligation. Or to put it in more homely terms, the idea of moral style is a twentieth century equivalent—only far more urgent and desperate—of the New England notion of "making do." How one "makes do," whether with grace or falsity, courage or evasion, is the great problem.

III

The great problem, above all, in the work of the most influential American novelist of our time, Ernest Hemingway. Of all the writers who began to print after the First World War, Hemingway seems best to have captured the tone of human malaise in an era of war and revolution; yet it is noteworthy that, while doing so, he rarely attempted a frontal or sustained representation of life in the United States, for he seems always to have understood that common experience was not within his reach. By evoking the "essence" of the modern experience through fables of violence that had their settings in Africa and Europe, Hemingway touched the imagination of American readers whose lives, for all their apparent ordinariness, were also marked by the desperation which would become his literary signature and which is, indeed, central to all "modernist" writing. These readers, in turn, often tried to endow their lives with meaning and value by copying the gestures of defiance, the devotion to clenched styles of survival, which they found in Hemingway's work. Because he had penetrated so deeply to the true dilemmas of the age, Hemingway soon began to influence its experience—not for the first time, life came to imitate art.

Who, by now, is not familiar with the shape and colors of Hemingway's world? His recurrent figures are literary expatriates in the wastes of *nada*, bullfighters who have lost their nerve and skill, rich young men without purpose, wounded soldiers who would sign "a separate peace" in order to withdraw from the world's battles, distraught young women grasping at physical sensations as if they were a mode of salvation, tired gangsters, homeless café-sitters, stricken Spaniards: men and women always on the margin, barely able to get by from day to day. There emerges from this gallery the characteristic hero of the Hemingway world: the hero who is wounded but bears his wound in silence, who is sensitive but scorns to devalue his feelings into words, who is defeated but finds a remnant of dignity in an honest confrontation of defeat. In almost all of Hemingway's books there is a tacit assumption that the deracination of our life is so extreme, everyone must find a psychic shelter of his own, a place in which to make a last stand.

But note: to make a last stand—for if defeat is accepted in Hemingway's world, humiliation and rout are not. His fictions present moments of violence, crisis and death, yet these become occasions for a stubborn, quixotic resistance through which the human capacity for satisfying its self-defined obligations is both asserted and tested. "Grace under pressure": this becomes the ideal stance, the hoped-for moral style, of Hemingway's characters. Or as he puts it in describing Romero's bullfighting in *The Sun Also Rises:* "the holding of his purity of line through the maximum of exposure." All of Hemingway's novels and stories can be read as variants upon this theme, efforts to find improvised gestures and surrogate codes for the good, the true, even the heroic.

The Hemingway hero is a man who has surrendered the world in order to remake a tiny part of it, the part in which he can share honor and manner with a few chosen comrades. Jake Barnes, Frederick Henry, most of Hemingway's heroes, are men who have seen too much, who want no more of this world and now seek to act out the choregraphy of heroism as a kind of private charade. The bull-ring becomes, for some of them, a substitute for the social world; the combat with the bull, a version of the manly testing which this world does not allow; the circle of *aficionados,* a monastic order of crippled heroes.

It may be true, as Edmund Wilson claims, that Hemingway shows a taste for scenes of killing, but at his best he wishes to squeeze from them some precarious assertion—or perhaps more accurately, some credible facsimile—of value. The Hemingway hero turns to his code, a mixture of stylized repression and inarticulate decencies, so that manners become the outer sign of an inexpressible heroism and gestures the substance of a surviving impulse to moral good. And what is this code? The determination to be faithful to one's own experience, not to fake emotions or pretend to sentiments that are not there; the belief that loyalty to one's few friends matters more than the claims and dogmas of the world; the insistence upon avoiding self-pity and public displays; the assumption that the most precious feelings cannot be articulated and that if the attempt is made they turn "rotten"; the desire to salvage from the collapse of social life a version of stoicism that can make suffering bearable; the hope that in direct physical sensation, the cold water of the creek in which one fishes or the purity of the wine made by Spanish peasants, there will be found an experience that can resist corruption (which is one reason Hemingway approaches these sensations with a kind of propitiatory awe, seldom venturing epithets more precise than "fine" and "nice," as if he feared to risk a death through naming). Life now consists in keeping an equilibrium with one's nerves, and that requires a tight control over one's desires, so that finally one learns what one cannot have and then even not to want it, and above all, not to make a fuss while learning. As Jake Barnes says in *The Sun Also Rises:* "I did not care what it was all about. All I wanted was how to live in it."

Hemingway was always a young writer, and always a writer for the young. He published his best novel *The Sun Also Rises* in his mid-twenties and completed most of his great stories by the age of forty. He started a campaign of terror against the fixed vocabulary of literature, a purge of style and pomp, and in the name of naturalness he modelled a new artifice for tension. He struck past the barriers of culture and seemed to disregard the reticence of civilized relationships. He wrote for the nerves.

In his very first stories Hemingway struck to the heart of our nihilism, writing with that marvellous courage he then had, which allowed him to brush past received ideas and show Nick Adams alone, bewildered, afraid and bored, Nick Adams finding his bit of peace through fishing with an exact salvaging ritual in the big two-hearted river. Hemingway struck to the heart of our nihilism through stories about people who have come to the end of the line, who no longer know what to do or where to turn: nihilism not as an idea or a sentiment, but as an encompassing condition of moral disarray in which one has lost those tacit impulsions which permit life to continue. There is a truth which makes our faith in human existence seem absurd, and no one need contemplate it for very long: Hemingway, in his early writing, did. Nick Adams, Jake Barnes, Lady Brett, Frederick Henry, and then the prize-fighters, matadors, rich Americans and failed writers: all are at the edge, almost ready to surrender and be done with it, yet holding on to whatever fragment of morale, whatever scrap of honor, they can.

Hemingway was not so foolish as to suppose that fear can finally be overcome: all his best stories, from "Fifty Grand" to "The Short Happy Life of Francis Macomber" are concerned to improvise a momentary truce in the hopeless encounter with fear. But Hemingway touched upon something deeper, something that broke forth in his fiction as the most personal and lonely kind of experience but was formed by the pressures of 20th Century history. His great subject was panic, the panic that follows upon the dissolution of nihilism into the blood-stream of consciousness, the panic that finds unbearable the thought of the next minute and its succession by the minute after that. We all know this experience, even if, unlike Jake Barnes, we can sleep at night: we know it because it is part of modern life, perhaps of any life, but also because Hemingway drove it into our awareness.

Hemingway's early fiction made his readers turn in upon themselves with the pain of measurement and consider the question of their sufficiency as men. He touched the quick of our anxieties, and for the moment of his excellence he stood ready to face whatever he saw. The compulsive stylization of his prose was a way of letting the language tense and retense, group and regroup, while beneath it the panic that had taken hold of the characters and then of the reader kept spreading inexorably. The prose served both as barrier and principle of contrast to that shapelessness which is panic by definition, and through its very tautness allowed the reader finally to establish some distance and then perhaps compassion.

The poet John Berryman once said that we live in a culture where a man can go through his entire life without having once to discover whether he is a coward. Hemingway forced his readers to consider such possibilities, and through the clenched shape of his stories he kept insisting that no one can escape, moments of truth come to all of us. Fatalistic as they often seem, immersed in images of violence and death, his stories are actually incitements to personal resistance and renewal.

A code pressing so painfully on the nervous system and so constricted to symbolic gratifications is almost certain to break down—indeed, in his best work Hemingway often shows that it does. After a time, however, his devotion to this code yields him fewer and fewer psychic returns, since it is in the nature of the quest for a moral style that the very act of approaching or even finding it sets off a series of discoveries as to its radical limitations. As a result the later Hemingway, in his apparent satisfaction with the moral style he has improvised, begins to imitate and caricature himself: the manner becomes that of the tight-lipped tough guy, and the once taut and frugal prose turns corpulent.

IV

At first glance F. Scott Fitzgerald's novels seem closer to the social portraiture of Edith Wharton than to the moral fables of Hemingway. Few American writers have commanded so fine a sense of social gradations, not merely in terms of class relationships but even more in the subtle nuances of status which in our country often replace or disguise class relationships. Fitzgerald is a writer very much of the historical moment, the laureate of the twenties, the *wunderkind* of the jazz age, and his talent, profligacy and tragic personal fate seem symbolic tokens of that historical moment. But in addition to the Fitzgerald who made of his "extreme environmental sense" a foundation of his gift for rendering social manners, there was the Fitzgerald who had been seized and driven by a vision of earthly beatitude which, all through his life, allowed him neither rest nor fulfillment.

Fitzgerald was an eternal adolescent infatuated with the surfaces of material existence. He worshipped money, he worshipped glamour, he worshipped youth, but above all, he worshipped the three together in a totality of false values. Like Keats before the candy shop, he stared with a deep yearning at the blessings of the rich, the ease and security with which they moved through the years, apparently free from the tyranny of work and the burden of circumstance, and thereby enabled to cultivate their own sense of what life might be. He thought that in the American dream of money there lay imbedded a possibility of human realization, because money means power and when you have power you can do anything—you can even, as Jay Gatsby supposes, obliterate the past. He felt that youth was the greatest of human possessions, indeed a kind of *accomplishment* for which the young should be praised. His work was a glittering celebration of immaturity, the American fear of aloneness and limitation.

The preceding paragraph condenses the kind of critical attacks to which Fitzgerald was subject during his career: it is true, all of it true, but not the whole truth about his writing.

For the man who composed *The Great Gatsby* and *The Last Tycoon* was a writer who had gone to war against the unexamined convictions of his youth, and at a terrible price in suffering and blood, had triumphed. This was the writer who noted that "all the stories that came into my head had a touch of disaster in them—the lovely young creatures in my novels went to ruin, the diamond mountains of my short stories blew up, my millionaires were as beautiful and damned as Thomas Hardy's peasants." Fitzgerald knew—it was to anchor this knowledge that he put Nick Carraway into *The Great Gatsby* as narrator—that the vitality and ambition of Jay Gatsby were lavished on a "vast, vulgar and meretricious beauty." He knew—it was to release this knowledge that he created the looming figure of Monroe Stahr in *The Last Tycoon* —that "life is essentially a cheat and its conditions are those of defeat, and that the redeeming things are not 'happiness and pleasure' but the deeper satisfactions that come out of struggle." As one of Fitzgerald's critics, Andrews Wanning, has remarked: "his style keeps reminding you . . . of his sense of the enormous beauty of which life, suitably ornamented, is capable; and at the same time of his judgment as to the worthlessness of the ornament and the corruptibility of the beauty."

The preceding paragraph condenses the kind of critical praise with which Fitzgerald was honored in the years after his death; it is true, all of it true, but only if one also remembers how accurate were the attacks against him.

Yet there is more to Fitzgerald than this counterposition of early illusion and later self-discovery. In his best writing— which consists not merely of one or two novels and several stories but also of a succession of extraordinary passages appearing almost anywhere in his books, like sudden flares of beauty and wisdom—Fitzgerald confronted both early illusion and later self-discovery from a certain ironic distance. ("The test of a first-rate intelligence," he once wrote, "is the ability to hold two opposed ideas in his mind at the same time, and still retain the ability to function.") Supremely American that he was, Fitzgerald tried to preserve something of the sense of human potentiality which had first led him to be enticed by the vulgarity of money and the shallowness of youth. He knew how impotent, and finally irrelevant, was that depreciation of material values in the name of some moralistic ideal which had become a set attitude in American thought and writing. He sensed that, endlessly rehearsed, this depreciation had actually come to reinforce the power of material values, partly because it could not come to grips with the society that drove men to concern themselves with money and partly because any claim of indifference to such a concern was in America likely to be a mere Sunday pose. As Fitzgerald had worshipped wealth, youth and glamour, they were surely false; as he later turned upon them, his turning was true; but even in his turning he kept some essential part of his earlier worship, and—one is inclined to say—he was right to do so.

Where Hemingway had tried to salvage a code for men at the margin of society, Fitzgerald tried to construct a vision of human possibility at its center. He enjoyed neither doctrinal support in religion nor a buoying social goal nor even a firm awareness of traditional culture that might have helped him sustain and enlarge this vision. Necessarily, it was sporadic, marred and precarious, more a series of flickering intuitions than assured values. Fitzgerald was struggling to achieve something of vast importance for our society, even though he could hardly have named it and we, in turn, can seldom enlarge upon it. He tried to create a moral style out of the urgencies of desire and talent, and finally it came to a search, at the very least, for a mode of gracefulness in outer life and, at the very best, for some token of grace in a world where grace could no longer be provided by anyone but man himself.

V

William Faulkner, last of the three major American novelists to begin writing in the decade after the First World War, enjoyed a more secure sense of social place and moral tradition than either Hemingway or Fitzgerald. The impact of the fundamentalist Protestantism of the South was still fresh to his imagination, even if more as a discipline than a dogma; the power of a commanding historical myth, the myth of heroic Southern reistance and defeat in the Civil War, was everywhere to be felt in the world of his youth; and the idea of kinship, a deep tacit awareness of the bonds of family and clan, was still a reality in his early experience, as it would later be in the series of novels set in Yoknapatawpha County.

In one major respect, however, Faulkner began as a thoroughly "modern" writer, caught up with the same emotion of uprootedness and uncertainties of value which afflicted Hemingway: his early novels *Soldier's Pay* and *Sartoris* reflect, though not nearly so well as those of Hemingway, the belief of a generation that it is adrift, "lost" in the aftermath of a terrible war. Provincial though the early Faulkner was, he had nevertheless been bruised by the troubles of the outer world, and for all his attachment to the Southern homeland he always retained a lively conviction as to the pervasiveness of malaise in modern life. But he had available, both as man and writer, resources which Hemingway and Fitzgerald lacked. Where Hemingway turned in his novels and stories to a marginal world he had partly observed and partly imagined, and Fitzgerald tried to impose his vision of human possibility upon such recalcitrant material as the lives of the very rich and very young, Faulkner could still turn back to a living segment of American society—back to the familiar places of the South, the homeland he knew with an intimacy beyond love or hate.

Each of Faulkner's novels written during his great creative outburst—from *The Sound and the Fury* in 1929 to *Go Down, Moses* in 1942—represents an increasingly severe and fundamental criticism of the homeland. Not merely of the South alone, to be sure; for when Faulkner composed his despairing estimate of social loss in *The Sound and the Fury* he was also portraying some of the central disabilities of modern civilization. But the foreground subject in the Yoknapatawpha novels is the immediate present and recent past of the South: the way in which its claims to grandeur prove to be aspects of delusion; its pretensions to gentility, elements of corruption; and its compulsive racialism, a poison coursing through its whole moral life. In the novels written during this period Faulkner ranged through almost every area of Southern life, beginning with a wish for nostalgia and ending with the bleakness of accepted truth.

At every point in these novels Faulkner had available— or wrote as if there were still available—persons, places and principles to which he could look for moral support and standards. He *turned back*, as neither Hemingway nor Fitzgerald could, to the hillsmen, the poor farmers, the Negroes and the children, all of whom seemed to him apart and pure, surviving in the interstices of a decadent society, unable significantly to change its course, yet vital enough to serve as figures of moral and dramatic contrast. The MacCallums, Dilsey, Cash Bundren, Lena Grove, Ike McCaslin, Lucas Beauchamp, Miss Habersham, Ratliff—these are some of the characters in Faulkner's world who embody in their conduct some portion of goodness and charity. Defeated as they may often be, they are nevertheless *there*, and because they are there Faulkner did not yet need to invent a moral style in the sense Hemingway and Fitzgerald did.

Now, in what is obviously a simplification, one can regard the whole development of Faulkner's Yoknapatawpha saga as a gradual discovery that these figures, for all their attractions and virtues, prove less and less competent as moral guides for the contemporary world. That Faulkner clearly sees as much is suggested by the history of Ratliff, the choric figure in the Snopes trilogy who is so marvellously self-assured in *The Hamlet* but so fumbling in *The Mansion* when he must approach the modern South. Slowly, Faulkner has been exhausting the psychic and moral resources he had supposed to be present for him in the world of Yoknapatawpha; slowly, he has been emerging to the same needs and bewilderments that other writers now feel. The idea of a return to primitive simplicity retains its strength in Faulkner's books insofar as it is kept by him at a certain distance from the present, or can be recognized as metaphor rather than prescription. In his later books Faulkner still turns for moral contrast and support to the kinds of characters he had admired in the earlier ones— the back-country saints, the earthy madonnas, the Negroes, the children, the good simple men. But now it is with very little of the old conviction: you need only contrast his use of Nancy in *Requiem for a Nun* with Dilsey in *The Sound and the Fury*. He turns to such figures because he has nowhere else to go, and he turns to them not with any firm conviction as to their moral power but simply in the hope of imposing on and through them his own hopes and standards. With the figures who had once been for him the bulwarks of life he must now try to "make do," late in his career; and not very skillfully, learn to improvise a moral style.

The search for moral style is recurrent in modern writing. It places a tremendous burden upon literature, almost the burden of demanding that literature provide us with norms of value we find impossible to locate in experience. It tends to demand from literature a kind of prophetic gratification which would have seemed decidedly strange to earlier generations of readers. Yet precisely this aspect of the work of such modern figures as Hemingway, Fitzgerald and Faulkner makes them seem close to us, writers whom we continue to regard as the spokesmen for our needs and our desires.

MASS SOCIETY AND POST-MODERN FICTION

Raskolnikov is lying on his bed: feverish, hungry, despondent. The servant Nastasya has told him that the landlady plans to have him evicted. He has received a letter from his mother in which she writes that for the sake of money his sister Dounia is to marry an elderly man she does not love. And he has already visited the old pawnbroker and measured the possibility of murdering her.

There seems no way out, no way but the liquidation of the miserly hunchback whose disappearance from the earth would cause no one any grief. Tempted by the notion that the strong, simply because they are strong, may impose their will upon the weak, Raskolnikov lies there, staring moodily at the ceiling. It must be done: so he tells himself and so he resolves.

Suddenly—but here I diverge a little from the text—the doorbell rings. A letter. Raskolnikov tears it open:

Dear Sir,
It is my pleasure to inform you, on behalf of the Guggenheim Foundation, that you have been awarded a fellowship for the study of color imagery in Pushkin's poetry and its relation to the myths of the ancient Muscovites. If you will be kind enough to visit our offices, at Nevsky Prospect and Q Street, arrangements can be made for commencing your stipend immediately.

(signed) Moevsky

Trembling with joy, Raskolnikov sinks to his knees and bows his head in gratitude. The terrible deed he had contemplated can now be forgotten; he need no longer put his theories to the test; the way ahead, he tells himself, is clear.

But Dostoevsky: is the way now clear for him? May not Raskolnikov's salvation prove to be Dostoevsky's undoing? For Dostoevsky must now ask himself: how, if the old pawnbroker need no longer be destroyed, can Raskolnikov's pride be brought to a visible dramatic climax? The theme remains, for we may imagine that Raskolnikov will still be drawn to notions about the rights of superior individuals; but a new way of realizing this theme will now have to be found.

It is a common assumption of modern criticism that Dostoevsky's ultimate concern was not with presenting a picture of society, nor merely with showing us the difficulties faced by an impoverished young intellectual in Czarist Russia. He was concerned with the question of what a human being, acting in the name of his freedom or disenchantment, may take upon himself. Yet we cannot help noticing that the social setting of his novel "happens" to fit quite exactly the requirements of his theme: it is the situation in which Raskolnikov finds himself that embodies the moral and metaphysical problems which, as we like to say, form Dostoevsky's deepest interest.

The sudden removal of Raskolnikov's poverty, as I have imagined it a moment ago, does not necessarily dissolve the temptation to test his will through killing another human being; but it does eliminate the immediate cause for committing the murder. Gliding from fellowship to fellowship, Raskolnikov may now end life as a sober Professor of Literature. Like the rest of us, he will occasionally notice in himself those dim urges and quavers that speak for hidden powers beyond the assuagement of reason. He may remember that once, unlikely as it has now come to seem, he was even tempted to murder an old woman. But again like the rest of us, he will dismiss these feelings as unworthy of a civilized man.

The case is not hopeless for Dostoevsky: it never is for a writer of his stature. He can now invent other ways of dramatizing the problem that had concerned him in the novel as it was to be, the novel before Moevsky's letter arrived; but it is questionable whether even he could imagine circumstances—imagine circumstances, as distinct from expressing sentiments—which would lead so persuasively, so inexorably to a revelation of Raskolnikov's moral heresy as do those in what I am tempted to call the unimproved version of *Crime and Punishment*.

From which it will not be concluded, I hope, that a drop in our standard of living is needed in order to provide novelists with extreme or vivid situations. I am merely trying to suggest that in reading contemporary fiction one sometimes feels that the writers find themselves in situations like the one I have here fancied for Dostoevsky.

II

Let us assume for a moment that we have reached the end of one of those recurrent periods of cultural unrest, innovation and excitement that we call "modern." Whether we really have no one can say with assurance, and there are strong arguments to be marshalled against such a claim. But if one wishes to reflect upon some—the interesting minority—of the novels written in America during the past 15 years, there is a decided advantage in regarding them as "post-modern," significantly different from the kind of writing we usually call modern. Doing this helps one to notice the distinctive qualities of recent novels: what makes them new. It tunes the ear to their distinctive failures. And it lures one into patience and charity.

That modern novelists—those, say, who began writing after

the early work of Henry James—have been committed to a peculiarly anxious and persistent search for values, everyone knows. By now this search for values has become not only a familiar but an expected element in modern fiction. It has been a major cause for that reaching, sometimes a straining toward moral surprise, for that inclination to transform the art of narrative into an act of cognitive discovery, which sets modern fiction apart from a large number of 18th and even 19th century novels.

Not so frequently noticed, however, is the fact that long after the modern novelist had come to suspect and even assault traditional values there was still available to him—I would say, until about the Second World War—a cluster of stable assumptions as to the nature of our society. If the question, "How shall we live?" agitated the novelists without rest, there was a remarkable consensus in their answers to the question, "How do we live?"—a consensus not so much in explicit opinion as in a widely shared feeling about Western society.

Indeed, the turn from the realistic social novel among many of the modern writers would have been most unlikely had there not been available such a similarity of response to the familiar social world. At least some of the novelists who abandoned realism seem to have felt that modern society had been exhaustively, perhaps even excessively portrayed (so D. H. Lawrence suggests in one of his letters) and that the task of the novelist was now to explore a chaotic multiplicity of meanings rather than to continue representing the surfaces of common experience.

No matter what their social bias, and regardless of whether they were aware of having any, the modern novelists tended to assume that the social relations of men in the world of capitalism were established, familiar, knowable. If Joyce could write of Stephen Dedalus that "his destiny was to be elusive of social or religious orders," that was partly because he knew and supposed his readers to know what these orders were. If

Lawrence in his later works could write a new kind of novel that paid as little attention to the external phenomena of the social world as to the fixed conventions of novelistic "character," that was partly because he had already registered both of these—the social world and the recognizable solid characters—in *Sons and Lovers*. The observations of class relationships in the earlier novels are not discarded by Lawrence in the later ones; they are tacitly absorbed to become a basis for a new mode of vision.

Values, as everyone now laments, were in flux; but society, it might be remembered, was still there: hard, tangible, ruled by a calculus of gain. One might not know what to make of this world, but at least one knew what was happening in it. Every criticism that novelists might direct against society had behind it enormous pressures of evidence, enormous accumulations of sentiment; and this, one might remark to those literary people who bemoan the absence of "tradition," this is the tradition that has been available to and has so enriched modern fiction. A novelist like F. Scott Fitzgerald, whose gifts for conceptual thought were rather meager, could draw to great advantage upon the social criticism that for over a century had preceded him, the whole lengthy and bitter assault upon bourgeois norms that had been launched by the spokesmen for culture. That Fitzgerald may have known little more than the names of these spokesmen, that he drew upon their work with only a minimum of intellectual awareness, serves merely to confirm my point. The rapidity with which such criticism was accumulated during the nineteenth century, whether by Marx or Carlyle, Nietzsche or Mill, enabled the modern novelists to feel they did not need to repeat the work of Flaubert and Dickens, Balzac and Zola: they could go beyond them.

Between radical and conservative writers, as between both of these and the bulk of non-political ones, there were many bonds of shared feeling—a kinship they themselves were often unable to notice but which hindsight permits us to see. The sense of the banality of middle class existence, of its sensuous and spiritual meanness, is quite the same among the conservative as the radical writers, and their ideas about the costs and possibilities of rising in the bourgeois world are not so very different either.

If one compares two American novelists so different in formal opinion, social background and literary method as Theodore Dreiser and Edith Wharton, it becomes clear that in such works as *Sister Carrie* and *The House of Mirth* both are relying upon the same crucial assumption: that values, whether traditional or modernist, desirable or false, can be tested in a novel by dramatizing the relationships between mobile characters and fixed social groups. Neither writer felt any need to question, neither would so much as think to question, the presence or impact of these social groups as they formed part of the examined structure of class society. In both novels "the heart of fools is in the house of mirth," the heartbreak house of the modern city; and as Carrie Meeber and Lily Bart make their way up and down the social hierarchy, their stories take on enormous weights of implication because we are ready to assume *some* relationship—surely not the one officially proclaimed by society, nor a mere inversion of it, but still some complex and significant relationship—between the observed scale of social place and the evolving measure of moral value. It is this assumption that has been a major resource of modern novelists; for without some such assumption there could not occur the symbolic compression of incident, the readiness to assume that X stands for Y, which is a prerequisite for the very existence of the novel.

Beset though they might be by moral uncertainties, the modern novelists could yet work through to a relative assurance in their treatment of the social world; and one reason for this assurance was that by the early years of our century the effort to grasp this world conceptually was very far advanced. The novelists may not have been aware of the various theories concerning capitalism, the city and modern industrial society; it does not matter. These ideas had so thoroughly penetrated the consciousness of thinking men, and even the folklore of the masses, that the novelists could count on them without necessarily being able to specify or elaborate them. In general, when critics "find" ideas in novels, they are transposing to a state of abstraction those assumptions which had become so familiar to novelists that they were able to seize them as sentiments.

Part of what I have been saying runs counter to the influential view that writers of prose fiction in America have written romances and not novels because, in words of Lionel Trilling that echo a more famous complaint of Henry James, there has been in this country "no sufficiency of means for the display of a variety of manners, no opportunity for the novelist to do his job of searching out reality, not enough complication of appearance to make the job interesting." I am not sure that this was ever true of American fiction—the encounter between Ishmael and Queequeg tells us as much about manners (American manners), and through manners about the moral condition of humanity, as we are likely to find in a novel by Jane Austen or Balzac. But even if it is granted that the absence of clearcut distinctions of class made it impossible in the nineteenth century to write novels about American society and encouraged, instead, a species of philosophical romance, this surely ceased to be true by about 1880. Since then, at least, there has been "enough complication of appearance to make the job interesting."

Nor am I saying—what seems to me much more dubious—that the presumed absence in recent years of a fixed, stratified society or of what one critic, with enviable naïveté, calls "an agreed picture of the universe" makes it impossible to study closely our social life, or to develop (outside of the South) human personalities rooted in a sense of tradition, or to write good novels dealing with social manners and relationships. That all of these things can be done we know, simply because they have been done. I wish merely to suggest that certain assumptions concerning modern society, which have long provided novelists with symbolic economies and dramatic conveniences, are no longer quite so available as they were a few decades ago. To say this is not to assert that we no longer have recognizable social classes in the United States, or that distinctions in manners have ceased to be significant. It is to suggest that the modern theories about society—theories which for novelists have usually been present as tacit assumptions—have partly broken down; and that this presents a great many new difficulties for the younger writers. New difficulties, which is also to say: new possibilities.

III

In the last two decades there has occurred a series of changes in American life, the extent, durability and significance of which no one has yet measured. No one can. We speak of the growth of a "mass society," a term I shall try to define in a moment; but at best this is merely a useful hypothesis, not an accredited description. It is a notion that lacks common consent, for it does not yet merit common consent. Still, one can say with some assurance that the more sensitive among the younger writers, those who feel that at whatever peril to their work and careers they must grapple with something new in contemporary experience, even if, like everyone else, they find it extremely hard to say what that "newness" consist of—such writers recognize that the once familiar social categories and place-marks have now become as uncertain and elusive as the moral imperatives of the nineteenth century seemed to novelists of fifty years ago. And the something new which they notice or stumble against is, I would suggest, the mass society.

By the mass society we mean a relatively comfortable, half welfare and half garrison society in which the population grows passive, indifferent and atomized; in which traditional loyalties, ties and associations become lax or dissolve entirely; in which coherent publics based on definite interests and opinions gradually fall apart; and in which man becomes a consumer, himself mass-produced like the products, diversions and values that he absorbs.

No social scientist has yet come up with a theory of mass society that is entirely satisfying; no novelist has quite captured its still amorphous symptoms—a peculiar blend of frenzy and sluggishness, amiability and meanness. I would venture the guess that a novelist unaware of the changes in our experience to which the theory of mass society points, is a novelist unable to deal successfully with recent American life; while one who focussed only upon those changes would be unable to give his work an adequate sense of historical depth.

This bare description of the mass society can be extended by noting a few traits or symptoms:

1) Social classes continue to exist, and the society cannot be understood without reference to them; yet the visible tokens of class are less obvious than in earlier decades and the correlations between class status and personal condition, assumed both by the older sociologists and the older novelists, become elusive and problematic—which is not, however, to say that such correlations no longer exist.
2) Traditional centers of authority, like the family, tend to lose some of their binding-power upon human beings; vast numbers of people now float through life with a burden of freedom they can neither sustain nor legitimately abandon to social or religious groups.
3) Traditional ceremonies that have previously marked moments of crisis and transition in human life, thereby helping men to accept such moments, are now either neglected or debased into mere occasions for public display.
4) Passivity becomes a widespread social attitude: the feeling that life is a drift over which one has little control and that even when men do have shared autonomous opinions they cannot act them out in common.

5) As perhaps never before, opinion is manufactured systematically and "scientifically."
6) Opinion tends to flow unilaterally, from the top down, in measured quantities: it becomes a market commodity.
7) Disagreement, controversy, polemic are felt to be in bad taste; issues are "ironed out" or "smoothed away"; reflection upon the nature of society is replaced by observation of its mechanics.
8) The era of "causes," good or bad, comes to an end; strong beliefs seem anachronistic; and as a result, agnostics have even been known to feel a certain nostalgia for the rigors of belief.
9) Direct and first-hand experience seems to evade human beings, though the quantity of busy-ness keeps increasing and the number of events multiplies with bewildering speed.
10) The pressure of material need visibly decreases, yet there follows neither a sense of social release nor a feeling of personal joy; instead, people become increasingly aware of their social dependence and powerlessness.

Now this is a social cartoon and not a description of American society; but it is a cartoon that isolates an aspect of our experience with a suggestiveness that no other mode of analysis is likely to match. Nor does it matter that no actual society may ever reach the extreme condition of a "pure" mass society; the value of the theory lies in bringing to our attention a major historical drift.

If there is any truth at all in these speculations, they should help illuminate the problems faced by the novelists whose work began to appear shortly after the Second World War. They had to confront not merely the chronic confusion of values which has gripped our civilization for decades. In a sense they were quite prepared for that—the whole of modern literature taught them to expect little else. But they had also to face a problem which, in actually composing a novel, must have been still more troublesome: our society no longer lent itself to assured definition, one could no longer assume as quickly as in the recent past that a spiritual or moral difficulty could find a precise embodiment in a social conflict. Raskolnikov, fellowship in hand, might still be troubled by the metaphysical question of what a human being can allow himself; but Raskolnikov as a graduate student with an anxious young wife and a two-year-old baby—what was the novelist to make of him? Something fresh and valuable, no doubt; but only if he were aware that this new Raskolnikov had to be seen in ways significantly different from those of the traditional modern novelists.

How to give shape to a world increasingly shapeless and an experience increasingly fluid; how to reclaim the central assumption of the novel that telling relationships can be discovered between a style of social behavior and a code of moral judgment, or if that proves impossible, to find ways of imaginatively projecting the code in its own right—these were the difficulties that faced the young novelists. It was as if the guidelines of both our social thought and literary conventions were being erased. Or as a young German writer has recently remarked:

> There's no longer a society to write about. In former years you knew where you stood: the peasants read the Bible; the maniacs read *Mein Kampf*. Now people no longer have any opinions; they have refrigerators. Instead of illusions we have television, instead of tradition, the Volkswagen. The only way to catch the spirit of the times is to write a handbook on home appliances.

Taken literally, this is close to absurd; taken as half-comic hyperbole, it reaches a genuine problem.

The problem, in part, is the relationship between the writer and his materials. Some years ago Van Wyck Brooks had spoken of the conflict between the life of the spirit and the life of commerce, and had called upon American writers to make their choice. Most of them did. Almost every important writer in twentieth century America, whether or not he read Brooks, implicitly accepted his statement as the truth and chose, with whatever lapses or qualifications, to speak for the life of the spirit.

But was the conflict between spirit and commerce, between culture and society still so acute during the postwar years? Was not a continued belief in this conflict a stale and profitless hangover from the ideologies of the thirties? Might there not be ground for feeling, among the visible signs of our careless postwar prosperity, that a new and more moderate vision of society should inform the work of our novelists? It hardly matters which answers individual writers gave to these questions; the mere fact that they were now being seriously raised had a profound impact upon their work.

Those few who favored a bluntly "positive" approach to American society found it hard to embody their sentiments in vibrant—or even credible—fictional situations. The values of accommodation were there for the asking, but they seemed, perversely, to resist creative use. For almost two decades now there has been an outpouring of "affirmative" novels about American businessmen—Executive Suites in various shades; but I do not know of a single serious critic who finds these books anything but dull and mediocre. At least in our time, the novel seems to lend itself irrevocably to the spirit of criticism; as Camus has remarked, it "is born simultaneously with the spirit of rebellion and expresses, on the esthetic plane, the same ambition."

But what has been so remarkable and disconcerting is that those writers who wished to preserve the spirit of rebellion also found it extremely hard to realize their sentiments in novels dealing with contemporary life. Most of them were unable, or perhaps too shrewd, to deal with the postwar experience directly; they preferred tangents of suggestion to frontal representation; they could express their passionate, though often amorphous, criticism of American life not through realistic portraiture but through fable, picaresque, prophecy and nostalgia.

Morally the young novelists were often more secure than their predecessors. Few of them were as susceptible to money and glitter as Fitzgerald; few had Hemingway's weakness for bravado and swagger; few succumbed to hallucinatory rhetoric in the manner of Faulkner. Yet, as novelists, they were less happily "placed" than the writers who began to publish in the twenties and early thirties. They lacked the pressure of inevitable subjects as these take shape in situations and locales. They lacked equivalents of Fitzgerald's absorption with social distinctions, Hemingway's identification with expatriates, Faulkner's mourning over the old South. Sentiments they had in abundance and often fine ones; but to twist a remark of Gertrude Stein's, literature is not made of sentiments.

Literature is not made of sentiments; yet a good portion of what is most fresh in recent American fiction derives from sentiments. Better than any other group of literate Americans, our novelists resisted the mood of facile self-congratulation which came upon us during the postwar years. To be novelists at all, they had to look upon our life without ideological delusions; and they saw—*often better than they could say*— the hovering sickness of soul, the despairing contentment, the prosperous malaise. They were not, be it said to their credit, taken in. Yet the problem remained: how can one represent malaise, which by its nature is vague and without shape? It can be done, we know. But to do it one needs to be Chekhov; and that is hard.

My point, let me hasten to add, is not that novelists need social theories or philosophical systems. They do, however, need to live in an environment about which they can make economical assumptions that, in some ultimate way, are related to the ideas of speculative thinkers. Let me borrow a useful distinction that C. Wright Mills made between troubles and issues. Troubles signify a strong but unfocussed sense of disturbances and pain, while issues refer to troubles that have been articulated as general statements. Novelists, as a rule, concern themselves with troubles, not issues. But to write with assurance and economy about troubles, they need to be working in a milieu where there is at least some awareness of issues. And in the troubled years after the Second World War it was precisely this awareness that was often lacking.

A few serious writers did try to fix in their novels the amorphous "troubledness" of postwar American experience. In *The Violated,* an enormous realistic narrative about some ordinary people who reach adulthood during the war, Vance Bourjailly seemed consciously to be dramatizing a view of American society quite similar to the one I have sketched here. He chose to write one of those full-scale narratives composed of parallel strands of plot—a technique which assumes that society is distinctly articulated, that its classes are both sharply visible and intrinsically interesting, and that a novelist can arrange a conflict between members of these classes which will be dramatic in its own right and emblematic of large issues. But for the material Bourjailly chose—the lives of bewildered yet not uncharacteristic drifters during the past two decades —these assumptions could not operate with sufficient force; and as his characters, in the sameness of their misery, melted into one another, so the strands of his narrative, also having no inevitable reason for separate existence, collapsed into one another.

Norman Mailer, trying in *The Deer Park* to compose a novel about the malaise of our years, avoided the cumbersomeness of the traditional social novel but could find no other structure that would give coherence to his perceptions. Mailer tried to embody his keen if unstable vision in a narrative about people whose extreme dislocation of experience and feeling would, by the very fact of their extreme dislocation, come to seem significant. But in its effort to portray our drifting and boredom full-face, in its fierce loyalty to the terms of its own conception, *The Deer Park* tended to become a claustrophobic work, driving attention inward, toward its own tonal peculiarities, rather than outward, as an extending parable. Throughout the novel Mailer had to fall back upon his protagonist, through whom he tried to say that which he found hard to show.

IV

A whole group of novelists, among the best of recent years, has found itself responding to immediate American experience by choosing subjects and locales that are apparently far removed from that experience yet, through their inner quality, very close to it. These writers are sensitive to the moods and tones of postwar American life; they know that something new, different and extremely hard to describe has been happening to us. Yet they do not usually write about postwar experience *per se:* they do not confront it as much as they try to ambush it. The film critic Stanley Kauffmann has noted a similar phenomenon:

> When Vittorio de Sica was asked why so many of his films deal with adultery, he is said to have replied, "But if you take adultery out of the lives of the bourgeoisie, what drama is left?" It is perhaps this belief that has impelled Tennessee Williams into the areas that his art inhabits. He has recognized that most of contemporary life offers limited dramatic opportunities . . . so he has left "normal" life to investigate the highly neurotic, the violent and the grimy. It is the continuing problem of the contemporary writer who looks for great emotional issues to move him greatly. The anguish of the advertising executive struggling to keep his job is anguish indeed, but its possibilities in art are not large-scale. The writer who wants to "let go" has figuratively to leave the urban and suburban and either go abroad, go into the past, or go into those few pockets of elemental emotional life left in this country.

Abroad, the past, or the few pockets of elemental emotional life—many of our best writers have pursued exactly these strategies in order to convey their attitudes toward contemporary experience. In *The Assistant* Bernard Malamud has written a somber story about a Jewish family during the Depression years, yet it soon becomes clear that one of his impelling motives is a wish to recapture intensities of feeling we have apparently lost but take to be characteristic of an earlier decade. Herbert Gold's *The Man Who Was Not With It* is an account of marginal figures in a circus as they teeter on the edge of *lumpen* life; but soon one realizes that he means his story to indicate possibilities for personal survival in a world increasingly compressed. The precocious and bewildered boy in J. D. Salinger's *Catcher in the Rye* expresses something of the moral condition of adolescents today—or so they tell us; but clearly his troubles are not meant to refer to his generation alone. In *A Walk on the Wild Side* Nelson Algren turns to down-and-outers characteristic of an earlier social moment, but if we look to the psychic pressures breaking through the novel we see that he is really searching for a perspective for estrangement that will be relevant to our day. In *The Field of Vision* Wright Morris moves not backward in time but sideways in space: he contrives to bring a dreary Nebraskan middle-class family to a Mexican bull-fight so that the excitement of the blood and ritual will stir it to self-awareness. And while, on the face of it, Saul Bellow's *The Adventures of Augie March* is a picaresque tale about a cocky Jewish boy moving almost magically past the barriers of American society, it is also a kind of paean to the idea of personal freedom in hostile circumstances. Bellow's most recent novel *Henderson the Rain King* seems an even wilder tale about an American millionaire venturing into deepest Africa, in part, the deepest Africa of boy's books; but when he writes that men need a shattering experience to "wake the spirit's sleep" we soon realize that his ultimate reference is to America, where many spirits sleep.

Though vastly different in quality, these novels have in

common a certain obliqueness of approach. They do not represent directly the postwar American experience, yet refer to it constantly. They tell us rather little about the surface tone, the manners, the social patterns of recent American life, yet are constantly projecting moral criticisms of its essential quality. They approach that experience on the sly, yet are colored and shaped by it throughout. And they gain from it their true subject: the recurrent search—in America, almost a national obsession—for personal identity and freedom. In their distance from fixed social categories and their concern with the metaphysical implications of that distance, these novels constitute what I would call "post-modern" fiction.

But the theme of personal identity, if it is to take on fictional substance, needs some kind of placement, a setting in the world of practical affairs. And it is here that the "post-modern" novelists run into serious troubles: the connection between subject and setting cannot always be made, and the "individual" of their novels, because he lacks social definition and is sometimes a creature of literary or even ideological fiat, tends to be not very individualized. Some of the best postwar novels, like *The Invisible Man* and *The Adventures of Augie March*, are deeply concerned with the fate of freedom in a mass society; but the assertiveness of idea and vanity of style which creep into such books are the result, I think, of willing a subject onto a novel rather than allowing it to grow out of a sure sense of a particular moment and place. These novels merit admiration for defending the uniqueness of man's life, but they suffer from having to improvise the terms of this uniqueness. It is a difficulty that seems, at the moment, unavoidable and I have no wish to disparage writers who face it courageously. Still, it had better be said that the proclamation of personal identity in recent American fiction tends, if I may use a fashionable phrase, to be more a product of the will than of the imagination.

It may help strengthen my point—critics ought not to

strengthen such points too much—if I turn for a moment to the two most-discussed literary groups of the last few years: the "angry young men" in England and the "beat generation" writers of San Francisco.

Partly because they write in and about England, Kingsley Amis, John Braine and John Wain are blessed with something precious to a writer: a subject urgently, relentlessly imposing itself upon their imaginations. They have earned the scorn of a good many American critics—notable, of course, for asceticism—who point out that it is not clear whether it is a better or just a bigger share of the material and cultural goods in contemporary England that these writers want. But while you can feel righteous or even hostile toward Amis and Braine, you can hardly deny that in their early novels one finds something of the focussed desire, the quick apprehension and notation of contemporary life which, for reasons I have tried to suggest, has become somewhat rare in serious American fiction. These English writers face a predicament of the welfare state: it rouses legitimate desires in people of the "lower orders"; it partly satisfies these desires; but it satisfies them only to the point of arousing new demands beyond its power of meeting. For society this may be irksome; for writers it is exhilarating. Gripes can be transformed into causes, ambitions cloaked as ideals. And the "angry young men" are particularly fortunate in that their complaints lead them to deal with some of the traditional materials of the novel: frustrated ambition, frozen snobbery, fake culture, decaying gentility. Through comedy they are able to *structure* their complaints. Their work touches upon sore spots in English life, hurting some people and delighting others. It threatens the Establishment, perhaps its survival, more likely its present leaders. It creates tension, opposition, a dialectic of interests. All of which is to say: it rest upon a coherent though limited vision of English social relations.

By contrast, the young men in San Francisco seem largely

a reflex of the circumstances of mass society. They are suffering from psychic and social disturbance: and as far as that goes, they are right—there is much in American life to give one a pain. But they have no clear sense of why or how they are troubled, and some of them seem opposed in principle to a clear sense of anything. The "angry young men" in England, even if their protest will prove to be entirely opportunistic and momentary, can say what it is that hurts. The San Francisco writers fail to understand, as Paul Goodman has remarked, that

> It is necessary to have some contact with institutions and people in order to be frustrated and angry. They [the San Francisco writers] have the theory that to be affectless, not to care, is the ultimate rebellion, but this is a fantasy; for right under the surface is burning shame, hurt feelings, fear of impotence, speechless and powerless tantrum, cowering before papa, being rebuffed by mama; and it is these anxieties that dictate their behavior in every crisis.

These writers, I would contend, illustrate the painful, though not inevitable, predicament of rebellion in a mass society: they are the other side of the American hollow. In their contempt for mind, they are at one with the middle class suburbia they think they scorn. In their incoherence of feeling and statement, they mirror the incoherent society that clings to them like a mocking shadow. In their yearning to keep "cool," they sing out an eternal fantasy of the shopkeeper. Feeling themselves lonely and estranged, they huddle together in gangs, create a Brook Farm of Know-Nothings, and send back ecstatic reports to the squares: Having a Wonderful Time, Having Wonderful Kicks! But alas, all the while it is clear that they are terribly lost, and what is more pitiable, that they don't even have the capacity for improvising vivid fantasies. As they race meaninglessly back and forth across the continent, veritable mimics of the American tourist, they do not have a Wonderful Time. They do not get happily drunk, many of them preferring milk shakes and tea; and their sexual revelations, particularly in Kerouac's *The Subterraneans,* are as sad as they are unintentional. They can't, that is, dream themselves out of the shapeless nightmare of California; and for that, perhaps, we should not blame them, since it is not certain that anyone can.

No wonder, then, that in Kerouac's novels one is vaguely aware that somewhere, in the unmapped beyond, a society does exist: a society with forms, requirements, burdens, injustices, duties and pleasures; but that in the space of the novels themselves we can only find a series of distraught and compulsive motions. The themes of what I have called "post-modern" fiction are reflected in the San Francisco writers as caricature and symptom; for if you shun consciousness as if it were a plague, then a predicament may ravage you but you cannot cope with it.*

Where finally does this leave us? In the midst, I hope, of the promise and confusion of American writing today. No settled ending is possible here, because the tendencies I have been noticing are still in flux, still open to many pressures and possibilities. But it may not be too rash to say that the more serious of the "post-modern" novelists—those who grapple with problems rather than merely betraying their effects—have begun to envisage that we may be on the threshold of enormous changes in human history. These changes, merely glanced by the idea of the "mass society," fill our novelists with a sense of foreboding; and through the strategy of obliqueness, they bring to bear a barrage of moral criticisms, reminders of human potentiality, and tacit exhortations.

The possibilities that appear to them are those which struck

---

* Both of these literary tendencies—the English "angries" and American "beats"—have all but disintegrated in the last few years. The achievement of the first now seems a modest one, and that of the second almost invisible. Yet the contrast made above remains, I think, a useful way of indicating how and why the English novelists have found it easier to articulate their sense of social complaint than the Americans.

at T. E. Lawrence when he returned from Arabia and discovered that he did not know how or why to live. One such possibility is that we are moving toward a quiet desert of moderation where men will forget the passion of moral and spiritual restlessness that has characterized Western society. That the human creature, no longer a Quixote or a Faust, will become a docile attendant to an automated civilization. That the "aura of the human" will be replaced by the nihilism of satiety. That the main question will no longer be the conditions of existence but existence itself. That high culture as we understand it will become increasingly problematical and perhaps reach some point of obsolescence.

But before such prospects—they form the bad dreams of thoughtful men, the nightmares our "post-modern" novelists are trying to exorcise—the mind grows dizzy and recalcitrant. It begins to solace itself with rumblings about eternal truths, and like the exacerbated judge in Faulkner's *The Hamlet,* cries out, "I can't stand no more ... This case is adjourned!"

BLACK BOYS AND NATIVE SONS

James Baldwin first came to the notice of the American literary public not through his own fiction but as author of an impassioned criticism of the conventional Negro novel. In 1949 he published in *Partisan Review* an essay called "Everybody's Protest Novel," attacking the kind of fiction, from *Uncle Tom's Cabin* to *Native Son*, that had been written about the ordeal of the American Negroes; and two years later he printed in the same magazine "Many Thousands Gone," a tougher and more explicit polemic against Richard Wright and the school of naturalistic "protest" fiction that Wright represented. The protest novel, wrote Baldwin, is undertaken out of sympathy for the Negro, but through its need to present him merely as a social victim or a mythic agent of sexual prowess, it hastens to confine the Negro to the very tones of violence he has known all his life. Compulsively re-enacting and magnifying his trauma, the protest novel proves unable to transcend it. So choked with rage has this kind of writing become, it cannot show the Negro as a unique person or locate him as a member of a community with its own traditions and values, its own "unspoken recognition of shared experience which creates a way of life." The failure of the protest novel "lies in its insistence that it is [man's] categorization alone which is real and which cannot be transcended."

Like all attacks launched by young writers against their famous elders, Baldwin's essays were also a kind of announcement of his own intentions. He wrote admiringly about Wright's courage ("his work was an immense liberation and revelation for me"), but now, precisely because Wright had prepared the way for all the Negro writers to come, he, Baldwin, would go further, transcending the sterile categories of "Negro-ness," whether those enforced by the white world or those defensively erected by the Negroes themselves. No longer mere victim or rebel, the Negro would stand free in a self-achieved humanity. As Baldwin put it some years later, he hoped "to prevent myself from becoming *merely* a Negro; or even, merely a Negro writer." The world "tends to trap and immobilize you in the role you play," and for the Negro writer, if he is to be a writer at all, it hardly matters whether the trap is sprung from motives of hatred or condescension.

Baldwin's rebellion against the older Negro novelist who had served him as a model and had helped launch his career, was not of course an unprecedented event. The history of literature is full of such painful ruptures, and the issue Baldwin raised is one that keeps recurring, usually as an aftermath to a period of "socially engaged" writing. The novel is an inherently ambiguous genre: it strains toward formal autonomy and can seldom avoid being a public gesture. If it is true, as Baldwin said in "Everybody's Protest Novel," that "literature and sociology are not one and the same," it is equally true that such statements hardly begin to cope with the problem of how a writer's own experience affects his desire to represent human affairs in a work of fiction. Baldwin's formula evades, through rhetorical sweep, the genuinely difficult issue of the relationship between social experience and literature.

Yet in *Notes of a Native Son*, the book in which his remark appears, Baldwin could also say: "One writes out of one thing only—one's own experience." What, then, was the experience of a man with a black skin, what *could* it be in this country? How could a Negro put pen to paper, how could he so much as think or breathe, without some impulsion to protest, be it harsh or mild, political or private, released or buried? The "sociology" of his existence formed a constant pressure on his literary work, and not merely in the way this might be true for any writer, but with a pain and ferocity that nothing could remove.

James Baldwin's early essays are superbly eloquent, displaying virtually in full the gifts that would enable him to become one of the great American rhetoricians. But these essays, like some of the later ones, are marred by rifts in logic, so little noticed when one gets swept away by the brilliance of the language that it takes a special effort to attend their argument.

Later Baldwin would see the problems of the Negro writer with a greater charity and more mature doubt. Reviewing in 1959 a book of poems by Langston Hughes, he wrote: "Hughes is an American Negro poet and has no choice but to be acutely aware of it. He is not the first American Negro to find the war between his social and artistic responsibilities all but irreconcilable." All but irreconcilable: the phrase strikes a note sharply different from Baldwin's attack upon Wright in the early fifties. And it is not hard to surmise the reasons for this change. In the intervening years Baldwin had been living through some of the experiences that had goaded Richard Wright into rage and driven him into exile; he too, like Wright, had been to hell and back, many times over.

II

Gawd, Ah wish all them white folks was dead.

The day *Native Son* appeared, American culture was changed forever. No matter how much qualifying the book might later need, it made impossible a repetition of the old lies. In all its crudeness, melodrama and claustrophobia of vision, Richard Wright's novel brought out into the open, as no one ever had before, the hatred, fear and violence that have crippled and may yet destroy our culture.

A blow at the white man, the novel forced him to recognize himself as an oppressor. A blow at the black man, the novel forced him to recognize the cost of his submission. *Native Son* assaulted the most cherished of American vanities: the hope that the accumulated injustice of the past would bring with it no lasting penalties, the fantasy that in his humiliation the Negro somehow retained a sexual potency—or was it a childlike good-nature?—that made it necessary to envy and still more to suppress him. Speaking from the black wrath of retribution, Wright insisted that history can be a punishment. He told us the one thing even the most liberal whites preferred not to hear: that Negroes were far from patient or forgiving, that they were scarred by fear, that they hated every moment of their suppression even when seeming most acquiescent, and that often enough they hated *us*, the decent and cultivated white men who from complicity or neglect shared in the responsibility for their plight. If such younger novelists as Baldwin and Ralph Ellison were to move beyond Wright's harsh naturalism and toward more supple modes of fiction, that was possible only because Wright had been there first, courageous enough to release the full weight of his anger.

In *Black Boy*, the autobiographical narrative he published several years later, Wright would tell of an experience he had while working as a bellboy in the South. Many times he had come into a hotel room carrying luggage or food and seen naked white women lounging about, unmoved by shame at his presence, for "blacks were not considered human beings anyway . . . I was a non-man . . . I felt doubly cast out." With the publication of *Native Son*, however, Wright forced his readers to acknowledge his anger, and in that way, if none other, he wrested for himself a sense of dignity as a man. He forced his readers to confront the disease of our culture, and to one of its most terrifying symptoms he gave the name of Bigger Thomas.

Brutal and brutalized, lost forever to his unexpended hatred and his fear of the world, a numbed and illiterate black boy stumbling into a murder and never, not even at the edge of the electric chair, breaking through to an understanding of either his plight or himself, Bigger Thomas was a part of Richard Wright, a part even of the James Baldwin who stared with horror at Wright's Bigger, unable either to absorb him into his consciousness or eject him from it. Enormous courage, a discipline of self-conquest, was required to conceive Bigger Thomas, for this was no eloquent Negro spokesman, no admirable intellectual or formidable proletarian. Bigger was drawn —one would surmise, deliberately—from white fantasy and white contempt. Bigger was the worst of Negro life accepted, then rendered a trifle conscious and thrown back at those who had made him what he was. "No American Negro exists," Baldwin would later write, "who does not have his private Bigger Thomas living in the skull."

Wright drove his narrative to the very core of American phobia: sexual fright, sexual violation. He understood that the fantasy of rape is a consequence of guilt, what the whites suppose themselves to deserve. He understood that the white man's notion of uncontaminated Negro vitality, little as it had to do with the bitter realities of Negro life, reflected some ill-formed and buried feeling that our culture has run down, lost its blood, become febrile. And he grasped the way in which the sexual issue has been intertwined with social relationships, for even as the white people who hire Bigger as their chauffeur are decent and charitable, even as the girl he accidentally kills is a liberal of sorts, theirs is the power and the privilege. "We black and they white. They got things and we ain't. They do things and we can't."

The novel barely stops to provision a recognizable social

world, often contenting itself with cartoon simplicities and yielding almost entirely to the nightmare incomprehension of Bigger Thomas. The mood is apocalyptic, the tone superbly aggressive. Wright was an existentialist long before he heard the name, for he was committed to the literature of extreme situations both through the pressures of his rage and the gasping hope of an ultimate catharsis.

Wright confronts both the violence and the cripping limitations of Bigger Thomas. For Bigger white people are not people at all, but something more, "a sort of great natural force, like a stormy sky looming overhead." And only through violence does he gather a little meaning in life, pitifully little: "he had murdered and created a new life for himself." Beyond that Bigger cannot go.

At first *Native Son* seems still another naturalistic novel: a novel of exposure and accumulation, charting the waste of the undersides of the American city. Behind the book one senses the molding influence of Theodore Dreiser, especially the Dreiser of *An American Tragedy* who knows there are situations so oppressive that only violence can provide their victims with the hope of dignity. Like Dreiser, Wright wished to pummel his readers into awareness; like Dreiser, to overpower them with the sense of society as an enclosing force. Yet the comparison is finally of limited value, and for the disconcerting reason that Dreiser had a white skin and Wright a black one.

The usual naturalistic novel is written with detachment, as if by a scientist surveying a field of operations; it is a novel in which the writer withdraws from a detested world and coldly piles up the evidence for detesting it. *Native Son*, though preserving some of the devices of the naturalistic novel, deviates sharply from its characteristic tone: a tone Wright could not possibly have maintained and which, it may be, no Negro novelist can really hold for long. *Native Son* is a work of assault rather than withdrawal; the author yields himself in part to a vision of nightmare. Bigger's cowering perception of the world becomes the most vivid and authentic component of the book. Naturalism pushed to an extreme turns here into something other than itself, a kind of expressionist outburst, no longer a replica of the familiar social world but a self-contained realm of grotesque emblems.

That *Native Son* has grave faults anyone can see. The language is often coarse, flat in rhythm, syntantically overburdened, heavy with journalistic slag. Apart from Bigger, who seems more a brute energy than a particularized figure, the characters have little reality, the Negroes being mere stock accessories and the whites either "agit-prop" villains or heroic Communists whom Wright finds it easier to admire from a distance than establish from the inside. The long speech by Bigger's radical lawyer Max (again a device apparently borrowed from Dreiser) is ill-related to the book itself: Wright had not achieved Dreiser's capacity for absorbing everything, even the most recalcitrant philosophical passages, into a unified vision of things. Between Wright's feelings as a Negro and his beliefs as a Communist there is hardly a genuine fusion, and it is through this gap that a good part of the novel's unreality pours in.

Yet it should be said that the endlessly-repeated criticism that Wright caps his melodrama with a party-line oration tends to oversimplify the novel, for Wright is too honest simply to allow the propagandistic message to constitute the last word. Indeed, the last word is given not to Max but to Bigger. For at the end Bigger remains at the mercy of his hatred and fear, the lawyer retreats helplessly, the projected union between political consciousness and raw revolt has not been achieved—as if Wright were persuaded that, all ideology apart, there is for each Negro an ultimate trial that he can bear only by himself.

Black Boy, which appeared five years after *Native Son*, is a slighter but more skillful piece of writing. Richard Wright came from a broken home, and as he moved from his helpless mother to a grandmother whose religious fanaticism (she was a Seventh-Day Adventist) proved utterly suffocating, he soon picked up a precocious knowledge of vice and a realistic awareness of social power. This autobiographical memoir, a small classic in the literature of self-discovery, is packed with harsh evocations of Negro adolescence in the South. The young Wright learns how wounding it is to wear the mask of a grinning niggerboy in order to keep a job. He examines the life of the Negroes and judges it without charity or idyllic compensation—for he already knows, in his heart and his bones, that to be oppressed means to lose out on human possibilities. By the time he is seventeen, preparing to leave for Chicago, where he will work on a WPA project, become a member of the Communist Party, and publish his first book of stories called *Uncle Tom's Children,* Wright has managed to achieve the beginnings of consciousness, through a slow and painful growth from the very bottom of deprivation to the threshold of artistic achievement and a glimpsed idea of freedom.

III

Baldwin's attack upon Wright had partly been anticipated by the more sophisticated American critics. Alfred Kazin, for examples, had found in Wright a troubling obsession with violence:

> If he chose to write the story of Bigger Thomas as a grotesque crime story, it is because his own indignation and the sickness of the age combined to make him dependent on violence and shock, to astonish the reader by torrential scenes of cruelty, hunger, rape, murder and flight, and then enlighten him by crude Stalinist homilies.

The last phrase apart, something quite similar could be said about the author of *Crime and Punishment;* it is disconcerting to reflect upon how few novelists, even the very greatest, could pass this kind of moral inspection. For the novel as a genre seems to have an inherent bias toward extreme effects, such as violence, cruelty and the like. More important, Kazin's judgment rests on the assumption that a critic can readily distinguish between the genuine need of a writer to cope with ugly realities and the damaging effect these realities may have upon his moral and psychic life. But in regard to contemporary writers one finds it very hard to distinguish between a valid portrayal of violence and an obsessive involvement with it. A certain amount of obsession may be necessary for the valid portrayal—writers devoted to themes of desperation cannot keep themselves morally intact. And when we come to a writer like Richard Wright, who deals with the most degraded and inarticulate sector of the Negro world, the distinction between objective rendering and subjective immersion becomes still more difficult, perhaps even impossible. For a novelist who has lived through the searing experiences that Wright has there cannot be much possibility of approaching his subject with the "mature" poise recommended by highminded critics. What is more, the very act of writing his novel, the effort to confront what Bigger Thomas means to him, is for such a writer a way of dredging up and then perhaps shedding the violence that society has pounded into him. Is Bigger an authentic projection of a social reality, or is he a symptom of Wright's "dependence on violence and shock?" Obviously both; and it could not be otherwise.

For the reality pressing upon all of Wright's work was a nightmare of remembrance, everything from which he had pulled himself out, with an effort and at a cost that is almost unimaginable. Without the terror of that nightmare it would have been impossible for Wright to summon the truth of the reality—not the only truth about American Negroes, perhaps not even the deepest one, but a primary and inescapable truth. Both truth and terror rested on a gross fact which Wright alone dared to confront: that violence is a central fact in the life of the American Negro, defining and crippling him with a harshness few other Americans need suffer. "No American Negro exists who does not have his private Bigger Thomas living in the skull."

Now I think it would be well not to judge in the abstract, or with much haste, the violence that gathers in the Negro's heart as a response to the violence he encounters in society. It would be well to see this violence as part of an historical experience that is open to moral scrutiny but ought to be shielded from presumptuous moralizing. Bigger Thomas may be enslaved to a hunger for violence, but anyone reading *Native Son* with mere courtesy must observe the way in which Wright, even while yielding emotionally to Bigger's deprivation, also struggles to transcend it. That he did not fully succeed seems obvious; one may doubt that any Negro writer can.

More subtle and humane than either Kazin's or Baldwin's criticism is a remark made by Isaac Rosenfeld while reviewing *Black Boy:* "As with all Negroes and all men who are born to suffer social injustice, part of [Wright's] humanity found itself only in acquaintance with violence, and in hatred of the oppressor." Surely Rosenfeld was not here inviting an easy acquiescence in violence; he was trying to suggest the historical context, the psychological dynamics, which condition the attitudes all Negro writers take, or must take, toward violence. To say this is not to propose the condescension of exempting Negro writers from moral judgment, but to suggest the terms of understanding, and still more, the terms of hesitation for making a judgment.

There were times when Baldwin grasped this point better than anyone else. If he could speak of the "unrewarding rage" of *Native Son*, he also spoke of the book as "an immense liberation." Is it impudent to suggest that one reason he felt the book to be a liberation was precisely its rage, precisely the relief and pleasure that he, like so many other Negroes, must have felt upon seeing those long-suppressed emotions finally breaking through?

The kind of literary criticism Baldwin wrote was very fashionable in America during the post-war years. Mimicking the Freudian corrosion of motives and bristling with dialectical agility, this criticism approached all ideal claims, especially those made by radical and naturalist writers, with a weary skepticism and proceeded to transfer the values such writers were attacking to the perspective from which they attacked. If Dreiser wrote about the power hunger and dream of success corrupting American society, that was because he was really infatuated with them. If Farrell showed the meanness of life in the Chicago slums, that was because he could not really escape it. If Wright portrayed the violence gripping Negro life, that was because he was really obsessed with it. The word "really" or more sophisticated equivalents could do endless service in behalf of a generation of intellectuals soured on the tradition of protest but suspecting they might be pigmies in comparison to the writers who had protested. In reply, there was no way to "prove" that Dreiser, Farrell and Wright were not contaminated by the false values they attacked; probably, since they were mere mortals living in the present society, they were contaminated; and so one had to keep insisting that such writers were nevertheless presenting actualities of modern experience, not merely phantoms of their neuroses.

If Bigger Thomas, as Baldwin said, "accepted a theology that denies him life," if in his Negro self-hatred he "*wants* to die because he glories in his hatred," this did not constitute a criticism of Wright unless one were prepared to assume what was simply preposterous: that Wright, for all his emotional involvement with Bigger, could not see beyond the limitations of the character he had created. This was a question Baldwin never seriously confronted in his early essays. He would describe accurately the limitations of Bigger Thomas and then, by one of those rhetorical leaps at which he is so gifted, would assume that these were also the limitations of Wright or his book.

Still another ground for Baldwin's attack was his reluctance to accept the clenched militancy of Wright's posture as both novelist and man. In a remarkable sentence appearing in "Everybody's Protest Novel," Baldwin wrote, "our humanity is our burden, our life; we need not battle for it; we need only to do what is infinitely more difficult—that is, accept it." What Baldwin was saying here was part of the outlook so many American intellectuals took over during the years of a post-war liberalism not very different from conservatism. Ralph Ellison expressed this view in terms still more extreme: "Thus to see America with an awareness of its rich diversity and its almost magical fluidity and freedom, I was forced to conceive of a novel unburdened by the narrow naturalism which has led after so many triumphs to the final and unrelieved despair which marks so much of our current fiction." This note of willed affirmation—as if one could *decide* one's deepest and most authentic response to society! —was to be heard in many other works of the early fifties, most notably in Saul Bellow's *Adventures of Augie March*. Today it is likely to strike one as a note whistled in the dark. In response to Baldwin and Ellison, Wright would have said (I virtually quote the words he used in talking to me during the summer of 1958) that only through struggle could men with black skins, and for that matter, all the oppressed of the world, achieve their humanity. It was a lesson, said Wright with a touch of bitterness yet not without kindness, that the younger writers would have to learn in their own way and their own time. All that has happened since, bears him out.

One criticism made by Baldwin in writing about *Native Son*, perhaps because it is the least ideological, remains important. He complained that in Wright's novel "a necessary dimension has been cut away; this dimension being the relationship that Negroes bear to one another, that depth of involvement and unspoken recognition of shared experience which creates a way of life." The climate of the book, "common to most Negro protest novels . . . has led us all to believe that in Negro life there exists no tradition, no field of manners, no possibility of ritual or intercourse, such as may, for example, sustain the Jew even after he has left his father's house." It could be urged, perhaps, that in composing a novel verging on expressionism Wright need not be expected to present the Negro world with fullness, balance or nuance; but there can be little doubt that in this respect Baldwin did score a major point: the posture of militancy, no matter how great the need for it, exacts a heavy price from the writer, as indeed from everyone else. For "Even the hatred of squalor / Makes the brow grow stern / Even anger against injustice / Makes the voice grow harsh . . ." All one can ask, by way of reply, is whether the refusal to struggle may not exact a still greater price. It is a question that would soon be tormenting James Baldwin, and almost against his will.

IV

In his own novels Baldwin hoped to show the Negro world in its diversity and richness, not as a mere spectre of protest; he wished to show it as a living culture of men and women who, even when deprived, share in the emotions and desires of common humanity. And he meant also to evoke something of the distinctiveness of Negro life in America, as evidence of its worth, moral tenacity and right to self-acceptance. How can one not sympathize with such a program? And how, precisely as one does sympathize, can one avoid the conclusion that in this effort Baldwin has thus far failed to register a major success?

His first novel, *Go Tell It on the Mountain,* is an enticing but minor work: it traces the growing-up of a Negro boy in the atmosphere of a repressive Calvinism, a Christianity stripped of grace and brutal with fantasies of submission and vengeance. No other work of American fiction reveals so graphically the way in which an oppressed minority aggravates its own oppression through the torments of religious fanaticism. The novel is also striking as a modest *Bildungsroman,* the education of an imaginative Negro boy caught in the heart-struggle between his need to revolt, which would probably lead to his destruction in the jungles of New York, and the miserly consolations of black Calvinism, which would signify that he accepts the denial of his personal needs. But it would be a mistake to claim too much for this first novel, in which a rhetorical flair and a conspicuous sincerity often eat away at the integrity of event and the substance of character. The novel is intense, and the intensity is due to Baldwin's absorption in that religion of denial which leads the boy to become a preacher in his father's church, to scream out God's word from "a merciless resolve to kill my father rather than allow my father to kill me." Religion has of course played a central role in Negro life, yet one may doubt that the special kind of religious experience dominating *Go Tell It on the Mountain* is any more representative of that life, any more advantageous a theme for gathering in the qualities of Negro culture, than the violence and outrage of *Native Son.* Like Wright before him, Baldwin wrote from the intolerable pressures of his own experience; there was no alternative; each had to release his own agony before he could regard Negro life with the beginnings of objectivity.

Baldwin's second novel, *Giovanni's Room,* seems to me a flat failure. It abandons Negro life entirely (not in itself a cause for judgment) and focusses upon the distraught personal relations of several young Americans adrift in Paris. The problem of homosexuality, which is to recur in Baldwin's fiction, is confronted with a notable courage, but also with a disconcerting kind of sentimentalism, a quavering and sophisticated submission to the ideology of love. It is one thing to call for the treatment of character as integral and unique; but quite another for a writer with Baldwin's background and passions to succeed in bringing together his sensibility as a Negro and his sense of personal trouble.

Baldwin has not yet managed—the irony is a stringent one—in composing the kind of novel he counterposed to the work of Richard Wright. He has written three essays, ranging in tone from disturbed affection to disturbing malice, in which he tries to break from his rebellious dependency upon Wright, but he remains tied to the memory of the older man. The Negro writer who has come closest to satisfying Baldwin's program is not Baldwin himself but Ralph Ellison, whose novel *Invisible Man* is a brilliant though flawed achievement, standing with *Native Son* as the major fiction thus far composed by American Negroes.

What astonishes one most about *Invisible Man* is the apparent freedom it displays from the ideological and emotional penalties suffered by Negroes in this country—I say "apparent" because the freedom is not quite so complete as the book's admirers like to suppose. Still, for long stretches *Invisible Man* does escape the formulas of protest, local color, genre quaintness and jazz chatter. No white man could have written it, since no white man could know with such intimacy the life of the Negroes from the inside; yet Ellison writes with an ease and humor which are now and again simply miraculous.

Invisible Man is a record of a Negro's journey through contemporary America, from South to North, province to city, naïve faith to disenchantment and perhaps beyond. There are clear allegorical intentions (Ellison is "literary" to a fault) but with a book so rich in talk and drama it would be a shame to neglect the fascinating surface for the mere depths. The beginning is both nightmare and farce. A timid Negro boy comes to a white smoker in a Southern town: he is to be awarded a scholarship. Together with several other Negro boys he is rushed to the front of the ballroom, where a sumptuous blonde tantalizes and frightens them by dancing in the nude. Blindfolded, the Negro boys stage a "battle royal," a free-for-all in which they pummel each other to the drunken shouts of the whites. Practical jokes, humiliations, terror—and then the boy delivers a prepared speech of gratitude to his white benefactors. At the end of this section, the boy dreams that he has opened the briefcase given him together with his scholarship to a Negro college and that he finds an inscription reading: "To Whom It May Concern: Keep This Nigger-Boy Running."

He keeps running. He goes to his college and is expelled for having innocently taken a white donor through a Negro ginmill which also happens to be a brothel. His whole experience is to follow this pattern. Strip down a pretense, whether by choice or accident, and you will suffer penalties, since the rickety structure of Negro respectability rests upon pretense and those who profit from it cannot bear to have the reality exposed (in this case, that the college is dependent upon the Northern white millionaire). The boy then leaves for New York, where he works in a white-paint factory, becomes a soapboxer for the Harlem Communists, the darling of the fellow-travelling bohemia, and a big wheel in the Negro world. At the end, after witnessing a frenzied race riot in Harlem, he "finds himself" in some not entirely specified way, and his odyssey from submission to antonomy is complete.

Ellison has an abundance of that primary talent without which neither craft nor intelligence can save a novelist: he is richly, wildly inventive; his scenes rise and dip with tension, his people bleed, his language sings. No other writer has captured so much of the hidden gloom and surface gaiety of Negro life.

There is an abundance of superbly-rendered speech: a West Indian woman inciting her men to resist an eviction, a Southern sharecropper calmly describing how he seduced his daughter, a Harlem street-vender spinning jive. The rhythm of Ellison's prose is harsh and nervous, like a beat of harried alertness. The observation is expert: he knows exactly how zootsuiters walk, making stylization their principle of life, and exactly how the antagonism between American and West Indian Negroes works itself out in speech and humor. He can accept his people as they are, in their blindness and hope: —here, finally, the Negro world does exist, seemingly apart from plight or protest. And in the final scene Ellison has created an unforgettable image: "Ras the Destroyer," a Negro nationalist, appears on a horse dressed in the costume of an Abyssinian chieftain, carrying spear and shield, and charging wildly into the police—a black Quixote, mad, absurd, unbearably pathetic.

But even Ellison cannot help being caught up with *the idea* of the Negro. To write simply about "Negro experience" with the esthetic distance urged by the critics of the fifties, is a moral and psychological impossibility, for plight and protest are inseparable from that experience, and even if less political than Wright and less prophetic than Baldwin, Ellison knows this quite as well as they do.

If *Native Son* is marred by the ideological delusions of the 'thirties, *Invisible Man* is marred, less grossly, by those of the 'fifties. The middle section of Ellison's novel, dealing with the Harlem Communists, does not ring quite true, in the way a good portion of the writings on this theme during the post-war years does not ring quite true. Ellison makes his Stalinist figures so vicious and stupid that one cannot understand how they could ever have attracted him or any other Negro. That the party leadership manipulated members with deliberate cynicism is beyond doubt, but this cynicism was surely more complex and guarded than Ellison shows it to be. No party leader would ever tell a prominent Negro Communist, as one of them does in *Invisible Man:* "You were not hired [as a functionary] to think"—even if that were what he felt. Such passages are almost as damaging as the propagandist outbursts in *Native Son*.

Still more troublesome, both as it breaks the coherence of the novel and reveals Ellison's dependence on the post-war *Zeitgeist*, is the sudden, unprepared and implausible assertion of unconditioned freedom with which the novel ends. As the hero abandons the Communist Party he wonders, "Could politics ever be an expression of love?" This question, more portentous than profound, cannot easily be reconciled to a character who has been presented mainly as a passive victim of his experience. Nor is one easily persuaded by the hero's discovery that "my world has become one of infinite possibilities," his refusal to be the "invisible man" whose body is manipulated by various social groups. Though the unqualified assertion of self-liberation was a favorite strategy among American literary people in the 'fifties, it is also vapid and insubstantial. It violates the reality of social life, the interplay between external conditions and personal will, quite as much as the determinism of the 'thirties. The unfortunate fact remains that to define one's individuality is to stumble upon social barriers which stand in the way, all too much in the way, of "infinite possibilities." Freedom can be fought for, but it cannot always be willed or asserted into existence. And it seems hardly an accident that even as Ellison's hero asserts the "infinite possibilities" he makes no attempt to specify them.

Throughout the 'fifties Richard Wright was struggling to find his place in a world he knew to be changing but could not grasp with the assurance he had felt in his earlier years. He had resigned with some bitterness from the Communist Party, though he tried to preserve an independent radical outlook, tinged occasionally with black nationalism. He became absorbed in the politics and literature of the rising African nations, but when visiting them he felt hurt at how great was the distance between an American Negro and an African. He found life in America intolerable, and he spent his last fourteen years in Paris, somewhat friendly with the intellectual group around Jean-Paul Sartre but finally a loner, a man who stood by the pride of his rootlessness. And he kept writing, steadily experimenting, partly, it may be, in response to the younger men who had taken his place in the limelight and partly because he was truly a dedicated writer.

These last years were difficult for Wright, since he neither made a true home in Paris nor kept in imaginative touch with the changing life of the United States. In the early 'fifties he published a very poor novel *The Outsider,* full of existentialist jargon applied but not really absorbed to the Negro theme. He was a writer in limbo, and his better fiction, such as the novelette "The Man Who Lived Underground," is a projection of that state.

In the late 'fifties Wright published another novel, *The Long Dream,* which is set in Mississippi and displays a considerable recovery of his powers. This book has been criticized for presenting Negro life in the South through "old-fashioned" images of violence, but one ought to hesitate before denying the relevance of such images or joining in the criticism of their use. For Wright was perhaps justified in not paying attention to the changes that have occurred in the South these past few decades. When Negro liberals write that despite the prevalence of bias there has been an improvement in the life of their people, such statements are reasonable and necessary. But what have these to do with the way Negroes feel, with the power of the memories they must surely retain? About this we know very little and would be well advised not to nourish preconceptions, for their feelings may be much closer to Wright's rasping outbursts than to the more modulated tones of the younger Negro novelists. *Wright remembered,* and what he remembered other Negroes must also have remembered. And in that way he kept faith with the experience of the boy who had fought his way out of the depths, to speak for those who remained there.

His most interesting fiction after *Native Son* is to be found in a posthumous collection of stories, *Eight Men*, written during the last 25 years of his life. Though they fail to yield any clear line of chronological development, these stories give evidence of Wright's literary restlessness, his often clumsy efforts to break out of the naturalism which was his first and, I think, necessary mode of expression. The unevenness of his writing is highly disturbing: one finds it hard to understand how the same man, from paragraph to paragraph, can be so brilliant and inept. Time after time the narrative texture is broken by a passage of sociological or psychological jargon; perhaps the later Wright tried too hard, read too much, failed to remain sufficiently loyal to the limits of his talent.

Some of the stories, such as "Big Black Good Man," are enlived by Wright's sardonic humor, the humor of a man who has known and released the full measure of his despair but finds that neither knowledge nor release matters in a world of despair. In "The Man Who Lived Underground," Wright shows a sense of narrative rhythm, which is superior to anything in his full-length novels and evidence of the seriousness with which he kept working.

The main literary problem that troubled Wright in recent years was that of rendering his naturalism a more terse and supple instrument. I think he went astray whenever he abandoned naturalism entirely: there are a few embarrassingly bad experiments with stories employing self-consciously Freudian symbolism. Wright needed the accumulated material of circumstance which naturalistic detail provided his fiction; it was as essential to his ultimate effect of shock and bruise as dialogue to Hemingway's ultimate effect of irony and loss. But Wright was correct in thinking that the problem of detail is the most vexing technical problem the naturalist writer must face, since the accumulation that makes for depth and solidity can also create a pall of tedium. In "The Man Who Lived Underground" Wright came close to solving this problem, for here the naturalistic detail is put at the service of a radical projective image—a Negro trapped in a sewer; and despite some flaws, the story is satisfying both for its tense surface and elasticity of suggestion.

Richard Wright died at 52, full of hopes and projects. Like many of us, he had somewhat lost his intellectual way but he kept struggling toward the perfection of his craft and toward a comprehension of the strange world that in his last years was coming into birth. In the most fundamental sense, however, he had done his work: he had told his contemporaries a truth so bitter, they paid him the tribute of trying to forget it.

V

Looking back to the early essays and fiction of James Baldwin, one wishes to see a little further than they at first invite: —to see past their brilliance of gesture, by which older writers could be dismissed, and past their aura of gravity, by which a generation of intellectuals could be enticed. After this hard and dismal decade, what strikes one most of all is the sheer pathos of these early writings, the way they reveal the desire of a greatly talented young man to escape the scars— and why should he not have wished to escape them? —which he had found upon the faces of his elders and knew to be gratuitous and unlovely.

Chekhov once said that what the aristocratic Russian writers assumed as their birthright, the writers who came from the lower orders had to pay for with their youth. James Baldwin did not want to pay with his youth, as Richard Wright had paid so dearly. He wanted to move, as Wright had not been able to, beyond the burden or bravado of his stigma; he wanted to enter the world of freedom, grace, and self-creation. One would need a heart of stone, or be a brutal moralist, to feel anything but sympathy for this desire. But we do not make our circumstances; we can, at best, try to remake them. And all the recent writing of Baldwin indicates that the wishes of his youth could not be realized, not in *this* country. The sentiments of humanity which had made him rebel against Richard Wright have now driven him back to a position close to Wright's rebellion.

Baldwin's most recent novel *Another Country* is a "protest novel" quite as much as *Native Son,* and anyone vindictive enough to make the effort, could score against it the points Baldwin scored against Wright. No longer is Baldwin's prose so elegant or suave as it was once; in this book it is harsh, clumsy, heavy-breathing with the pant of suppressed bitterness. In about half of *Another Country*—the best half, I would judge—the material is handled in a manner somewhat reminiscent of Wright's naturalism: a piling on of the details of victimization, as the jazz musician Rufus Scott, a sophisticated distant cousin of Bigger Thomas, goes steadily down the path of self-destruction, worn out in the effort to survive in the white man's jungle and consumed by a rage too extreme to articulate yet too amorphous to act upon. The narrative voice is a voice of anger, rasping and thrusting, not at all "literary" in the somewhat lacquered way the earlier Baldwin was able to achieve. And what that voice says, no longer held back by the proprieties of literature, is that the nightmare of the history we have made allows us no immediate escape. Even if all the visible tokens of injustice were erased, the Negroes would retain their hatred and the whites their fear and guilt. Forgiveness cannot be speedily willed, if willed at all, and before it can even be imagined there will have to be a fuller discharge of those violent feelings that have so long been suppressed. It is not a pretty thought, but neither is it a mere "unrewarding rage"; and it has the sad advantage of being true, first as Baldwin embodies it in the disintegration of Rufus, which he portrays with a ferocity quite new in his fiction, and then as he embodies it in the hard-driving ambition of Rufus' sister Ida, who means to climb up to success even if she has to bloody a good many people, whites preferably, in order to do it.

Another Country has within it another novel: a nagging portrayal of that entanglement of personal relationships—sterile, involuted, grindingly rehearsed, pursued with quasi-religious fervor, and cut off from any dense context of social life—which has come to be a standard element in contemporary fiction. The author of *this* novel is caught up with the problem of communication, the emptiness that seeps through the lives of many cultivated persons and in response to which he can only reiterate the saving value of true and lonely love. These portions of *Another Country* tend to be abstract, without the veined milieu, the filled-out world, a novel needs: as if Baldwin, once he moves away from the Negro theme, finds it quite as hard to lay hold of contemporary experience as do most other novelists. The two pulls upon his attention are difficult to reconcile, and Baldwin's future as a novelist is decidedly uncertain.

During the last few years James Baldwin has emerged as a national figure, the leading intellectual spokesman for the Negroes, whose recent essays, as in *The Fire Next Time*, reach heights of passionate exhortation unmatched in modern American writing. Whatever his ultimate success or failure as a novelist, Baldwin has already secured his place as one of the two or three greatest essayists this country has ever produced. He has brought a new luster to the essay as an art form, a form with possibilities for discursive reflection and concrete drama which make it a serious competitor to the novel, until recently almost unchallenged as the dominant literary genre in our time. Apparently drawing upon Baldwin's youthful experience as the son of a Negro preacher, the style of these essays is a remarkable instance of the way in which a grave and sustained eloquence—the rhythm of oratory, but that rhythm held firm and hard—can be employed in an age deeply suspicious of rhetorical prowess. And in pieces like the reports on Harlem and the account of his first visit South, Baldwin realizes far better than in his novel the goal he had set himself of presenting Negro life through an "unspoken recognition of shared experience." Yet it should also be recognized that these essays gain at least some of their resonance from the tone of unrelenting protest in which they are written, from the very anger, even the violence Baldwin had begun by rejecting.

Like Richard Wright before him, Baldwin has discovered that to assert his humanity he must release his rage. But if rage makes for power it does not always encourage clarity, and the truth is that Baldwin's most recent essays are shot through with intellectual confusions, torn by the conflict between his assumption that the Negro must find an honorable place in the life of American society and his apocalyptic sense, mostly fear but just a little hope, that this society is beyond salvation, doomed with the sickness of the West. And again like Wright, he gives way on occasion to the lure of black nationalism. Its formal creed does not interest him, for he knows it to be shoddy, but he is impressed by its capacity to evoke norms of discipline from followers at a time when the Negro community is threatened by a serious inner demoralization.

In his role as spokesman, Baldwin must pronounce with certainty and struggle with militancy; he has at the moment no other choice; yet whatever may have been the objective inadequacy of his polemic against Wright a decade ago, there can be no question but that the refusal he then made of the role of protest reflected faithfully some of his deepest needs and desires. But we do not make our circumstances; we can, at best, try to remake them; and the arena of choice and action always proves to be a little narrower than we had supposed. One generation passes its dilemmas to the next, black boys on to native sons.

"It is in revolt that man goes beyond himself to discover other people, and from this point of view, human solidarity is a philosophical certainty." The words come from Camus: they might easily have been echoed by Richard Wright: and today one can imagine them being repeated, with a kind of rueful passion, by James Baldwin. No more important words could be spoken in our century, but it would be foolish, and impudent, not to recognize that for the men who must live by them the cost is heavy.

A QUEST FOR PERIL: NORMAN MAILER

Whether Norman Mailer will become the great writer he candidly admits he is ambitious to become, no one can yet say. For all of his chest-thumping and bugle-tooting, he has a sharply realistic sense of the odds: he knows that a writer who sets out on a deliberate search for peril may end by paying heavily in strength and spirit. But one thing is clear, that simply as a writer he is enormously, even outrageously talented.

Anyone who wishes to see how remarkably versatile Mailer is, as well as how fiercely he has painted himself into an intellectual and literary corner, must first look at his *Advertisements for Myself*, a miscellany of stories, excerpts from novels, essays, musings and conundrums, all packed together with an italizicized running commentary which forms a rough-stroked picture of the artist as young Seeker, Rebel and Outside Dopester. At the moment this book may well be more interesting than Mailer's three novels, for in it, I think, he has packed more of his essential drives and desires. A rowdy, intense and exciting book, it assaults without equivocation almost all the decorums of liberal moderation and cultural respectability.

The running commentary, done with bravado and good

humor, as at times with an utter willingness to risk full exposure, contains some of Mailer's best writing. It is post-depressive Mailer, bouncy and high in rhythm, and full of a passionate belief that "I am imprisoned with a perception which will settle for nothing less than making a revolution in the consciousness of our time." Mailer is one of the few younger writers who has made his public self—his personality, his ideas, his claims—into a matter of legitimate interest, in a way a writer like Hemingway once did. In both the best and weakest sections of the book, one is struck by Mailer's absolute unwillingness to settle into his achievement, his impatience with a style as soon as he comes close to mastering it, his devotion to restlessness as a principle of both life and work. *Beware the death called maturity*—so runs a recurrent motif, or really a string of brotherly tips, in this rasp against adjustment.

Mailer's early stories, written in college as imitations of proletarian fiction and Dos Passos, already reveal his characteristic mixture of professional skill and a refusal of the professional stance. Several excerpts from *Barbary Shore*, which I remember as a very bad novel, are included and they read astonishingly well, with a nervous jabbing accuracy which lends some support to Mailer's claim that the book has "the air of our time, authority and nihilism stalking one another in the orgiastic hollow of this century." There follow a few war stories which illustrate his large capacity for mimetic vividness, for arranging sensory notation so that there will emerge a shaped and tacit meaning. In these pieces, as in *The Naked and the Dead*, one can also see the weaknesses which have marked Mailer's fiction until very recently: first, that his prose, betraying too strongly the influence of 'thirties journalism, is often flat and ungainly; second, that while superb at evoking an aura and springing a sequence of action, he has not yet looked into or cared about a character deeply enough so that the character can burst out of the fictional schema and into something like a life of his own.

The single best thing Mailer has written is a long story, "The Man Who Studied Yoga," which occupies a place in his writing like that of "Seize the Day" in Saul Bellow's: the one work in which the writer breaks past his self-image, to confront with absolute candor the ruins of experience. Just as "Seize the Day" makes a good part of *Augie March* seem self-indulgent, so "The Man Who Studied Yoga" makes a good part of *The Deer Park* seem willed and theoretic. Here, in transparent prose, Mailer observes the burned-out rancor, the sourness of the generation that came to maturity in the 'thirties. Tired, drained, weary of both their comforts and complaints, a few Jewish ex-radicals—a dentist, a lawyer, a comic-strip writer—spend a Sunday afternoon together in New York. They exchange bits of gossip, suffer the noise of their wives, throw off the gripes of middle age and—here Mailer makes a bold, almost allegorical leap—watch together a pornographic movie, the one stimulus that can now jerk them into a moment's vitality. At the end, again jaded and dull, the central figure "enters the universe of sleep, a man who seeks to live in such a way as to avoid pain, and succeeds merely in avoiding pleasure. What a dreary compromise is life!" Reading once more this admirable story, I can't help wondering whether Mailer's recent decision to choose extreme states of being for his central subject is, in literary terms, a wise one. Perhaps his true gift is to be a recorder of "the flat and familiar dispirit of nearly all days."

At the heart of Mailer's recent literary and intellectual adventures lies a fear which he shares with many reflective people: the fear of stasis, of an historical period ruled by functional rationality and increasingly deprived of the hunger for utopia. All of his recent writing seems to ask, Is it possible that "the smooth strifeless world" in which most cultivated Americans now live will prove to be the world of tomorrow, a glass enclosure in which there will be a minimum of courage or failure, tests or transcendence? It is a prospect invoked by the rise of mass society, and for those of us raised, or ruined, by the ethic of striving, dissatisfaction and renewal it is a disturbing prospect.

Mailer shows signs of the ideologist whose ideology has melted away. Without succumbing to the genetic fallacy or being scornful of a dilemma which in some ways I share, I can't help seeing a touch of truth in Jean Malaquais' criticism that in "The White Negro" Mailer was searching for a new "vanguard" to replace the slumbering proletariat, a new self-propelling force to jog history. What the socio-economic position of the working class was supposed to do for or to it, the hipsters' drive for self-gratification, unbroken by convention or morality and acted out in life rather than piddled away in psychoanalysis, would now do for them. But qualifications are needed. Mailer's search probably began in the political terms Malaquais suggested, and partly it may remain that; but by now it has become something else, a concern with the orgasm in its own right, a quest for a free-floating state of being in which desire satisfied and desire forever expanded become the measures of life. Some conflict seems to be involved here, between a therapeutic vision of desire and an ethic of what might be called a permanent revolution of the senses—it is a conflict between the Mailer who thinks of sexuality as a mode of health or reconciliation to the self and the Mailer who thinks of it as a strategy for social and personal revolt.

Still more recently, Mailer seems to have turned toward a generalized quest for new sources of energy, new sources of motion and rebellion, in which sexuality is in danger of becoming a mere metaphor. At one point he suggests that for man to restore his self and reaffirm his potency would mean to re-create the vital image of God, since God cannot be God until man becomes man. God becomes the name of his desperation.

This mixture of Lawrence, Emerson, Reich and some Marx carries the further implication that the achievement of sexual well-being or even a proximate version of it would have revolutionary social consequences, though I think that here Mailer's argument staggers a little. For he never succeeds in showing why the transfer of energy need take place from sexuality to sociality, other than remarking, almost as if he had lapsed into ethical culture, that "in widening the area of the possible, one widens it reciprocally for others as well." Mailer seems to be falling back upon a curious analogue to Adam Smith's invisible hand, by means of which innumerable units in conflict with each other achieve a resultant of harmony and cooperation. Here again one can see Mailer's hunger for new possibilities and modes of transcendence, even if they break forth in claustrophobic sexual images—a kind of transcendence from below, with the orgasm replacing union with the godhead, and man finding the kingdom of heaven in the darkness of night, borne aloft on the thrust of a resurrected phallus.

"The White Negro" is a remarkable display of dialectical prowess and phenomenological searchings into a new style of life; yet one may be forgiven for wondering whether the phenomenon itself is really there. The hipster, does he exist? Do living specimens, bearing the psychopathic grandeur with which Mailer invests them, actually walk the streets of our cities? Beatniks, beards, other sorry little chaps; but Mailer's brand of hipsters?

I am emboldened to ask because Mailer has had the chivalry to reprint from *Dissent,* where the discussion first appeared, not only Malaquais' criticism but also another and very effective one by Ned Polsky who argues that Mailer is romanticizing the hipster, especially when he tries to create a philosophy of Hip. Far from being a figure of violence, daring and freedom, the hipster, says Polsky, is really the ultimate in self-estrangement: inhibited, weak in feeling, driven in behavior, caring mostly to be left alone by the cops, and whatever else, hardly a force that for good or evil can shake the society in which he hides. Put another way, it seems likely that our mass society, with its astonishing capacity for absorbing friend and foe, Ph.D. and junkie, may well succeed in domesticating the hipster, if it hasn't already, and in transforming his world into a docile subculture regularly visited by social workers, anthropologists and tourists.

Meanwhile, I think Mailer is in danger of being carried away by the fertility and brilliance of his own metaphors. Using cancer as a synecdoche for the spread of social rot, he begins to talk as if he knows it to be psychosomatic in origin. Hunting for an emblem of energy in the hipster, he seems at one shocking point in "The White Negro" to be praising the violence of a hoodlum who beats up an old storekeeper. Even if one puts aside the ethical question, which certainly should not be done for long, this kind of thing can be very dangerous to writers. Professionally infatuated with language, they are prone to develop treacherous powers of self-delusion and self-incitement, as is shown only too strongly by the experience of the many twentieth century writers who have become fascinated with violence.

Mailer is trying to enter new areas of experience and feeling, and the problem will be to what extent his ideas will help him to see and to what extent they will predetermine his vision. Perhaps, as one wishes him luck, it will not seem captious to add the hope that, even as he tries to embody his new perceptions in fiction, he will also allow some play to his conventional but exceptional gifts for social observation and narrative.

I expect that in six or seven years Mailer will write a story called "The Man Who Studied Yoga, II." The plot will be simple. On a depressing Sunday afternoon, several prosperous and now middle-aged former hipsters will meet for quiet conversation. A little wistfully, they will remember the excitements of their youth and how, with time, these have gradually evaporated. Nothing can now re-create for them the kicks of the past, neither drugs nor orgy, violence nor promiscuity. By chance one of them will pick up a volume of that forgotten writer Marx and read a few apocalyptic pages—which, as people not accustomed to reading, they will find almost as stimulating as a pornographic movie would be for squares. But soon the electricity in their souls will start to flicker, and the story will end with the central figure entering "the universe of sleep. . . . What a dreary compromise is life!"

Three American poets

WALT WHITMAN: "GARRULOUS TO THE VERY LAST"

Whitman has not been very fortunate in his critics—and, one sometimes feels like blurting out, it serves him right! Seldom has a great poet engaged in such adolescent mystifications with regard to himself and his work, seldom has a poet so blatantly promoted a cult of worship in which he served as both prophet and martyr—though toward the end of his life even Whitman, in whom the promoter and the mystagogue are closely allied, grew tired of his disciples and began to mock them in a way beyond their capacity to notice. As a result of his need to think of himself in a variety of prophetic roles, Whitman became a victim of his own legend rather than a subject of critical appreciation. People with notions about cosmic consciousness, transubstantiation, indeterminate sexuality and, somewhat later, anti-fascist unity, soon attached themselves to the roomy dogmas near his books. Academicians wrote studies trying to persuade one another that they really cared whether Whitman was a neoplatonist or a pantheist or a believer in metempsychosis. And many poets and critics of the past few decades, because they didn't write like Whitman, felt they had to keep sticking pins into his reputation until it would collapse.

All this has made it extremely difficult to get at Whitman the poet and almost impossible to get at him directly: too many traps and barriers of our culture stand in the way. We have no choice but to begin with his critics, about whom Whitman once said—and here he was truly a prophet—"I will certainly elude you."

One main line of criticism has stressed Whitman as public spokesman, thereby accepting his claim to embody the collective spirit of American democracy in his rather eccentric individuality. Thereby too it has been forced into the position of placing the greatest valuation upon his more grandiose programmatic poems, a procedure that invites the embarrassment of having to take his formal ideas seriously. A second major line of criticism has exalted Whitman as a sexual champion or liberator, a sort of linsey-woolsey Lawrence—a Lawrence, that is, without the bother of Frieda.

Of inducements and provocations for seeing Whitman in these vatic postures his work offers no lack; but such critical approaches, I am convinced, obscure what is best in the poems themselves and create public images of the poet that, for good or bad, can only estrange him from the audience he deserves. That these approaches to Whitman also happen to be in violent conflict with each other makes for a fine bit of cultural comedy: the nationalist Whitmanites sniff the other way when they get to the sex poems, while the sexualist Whitmanites write as if their hero had never lived in a country.

As a national prophet Whitman now seems inadequate because he so cheerfully lacks, perhaps even refuses, a full sense of social complexity. The Jacksonian mind, admirable as it was and much as one wants to preserve something of its original vigor and bias, seems light-years away from us, almost "pastoral" in its innocence and assurance. For all that Whitman's poems often speak about city life they do not really capture its terrible *newness,* nor do they register their anticipatory awareness of the problems raised by industrialism and the mass society which helps keep the work of other nineteenth-century writers fresh and relevant. To be sure, the fact that Whitman's was a pre-industrial mind would not matter at all (it certainly doesn't matter for innumerable poets before him), were it not that in his later poems one finds frequent signs of bewilderment before the kind of America coming into existence after the Civil War.

As a sexual prophet, however, Whitman suffers from an opposite difficulty: he has done his work too well, no one is now likely to be shocked by the "Children of Adam" or "Calamus" poems. Some of them charm us, others are troubling because of the abstractness with which they celebrate the need for concrete experience, and after reading all of them one cannot help wishing that Whitman had indicated some faint awareness that the sexual liberation he proclaimed might bring new troubles of its own.

To say, however, that the dominant modes of Whitman criticism are seldom helpful is not to slight a number of fine studies. An early conservative book like Bliss Perry's has the merit of being among the first to describe, without hysteria or too great hostility, what Whitman actually wrote. Van Wyck Brooks' chapter in *America's Coming of Age*, while presenting Whitman as the American Bard, is a powerful cultural statement. Basil de Sélincourt's book, though it succumbs to the English fondness for seeing Whitman as the Great American Naïf, contains many acute remarks on his poetic technique. D. H. Lawrence in his *Studies in Classic American Literature*, despite mixed feelings toward a writer close to him in expression but alien in temperament, finally comes through by hailing Whitman as one of the great pioneers in transcending the body-mind dualism.

Yet none of these books will quite do for us now, since none of them succeeds in getting past Whitman's *persona* and into his poetry. This task is surely the most challenging that faces American criticism, but it remains neglected because most

American literary people either are indifferent to Whitman or think of him as a mere loud-mouth. The extreme version of this latter opinion comes from the powerful critic Yvor Winters, who writes that Whitman "a second-rate poet . . . had no capacity for any feeling save of the cloudiest and most general kind." As against such admirably direct wrong-headedness, there are a few signs that Whitman is again being considered by serious critics, notably a brilliant, wide-eyed essay by Randall Jarrell which simply points to Whitman's achievements in language, as if to say: *For God's sake, forget the prophecy, forget the philosophy, just look at these lines!*

Meanwhile a new outpouring of Whitman books has begun. *The Solitary Singer,* by Gay Wilson Allen, is one of those over-stuffed biographies that have recently become fashionable. The book, it can be said without hesitation, is dull enough to qualify as a definitive study. Mr. Allen manages to avoid a point of view on almost every controversial aspect of Whitman's life or writings, and this of course helps contribute to the tone of definitiveness. After having spent a lifetime studying Whitman—the jacket says twenty-five years—he is unable to write a page about the poems that has a touch of critical originality or even eccentricity. His credentials as a critic may be tested by his opinion that Whitman's verse lacks irony, a deficiency which turns out, however, to be a virtue since, he tells us, "irony results from self-pity or loss of faith." About Whitman's private life Mr. Allen writes, "he had not made up his mind or did not know whether sex meant primarily an instinctive hunger or responsible paternity"—which indicates that Mr. Allen may have a thoroughly wholesome mind but that a thoroughly wholesome mind is not the ideal qualification for a biographer of Walt Whitman. Well, the book will have to be read by graduate students in American Literature.

Milton Hindus' collection of essays *Leaves of Grass: One Hundred Years After* is another matter: it presents, whether by intention or not, a vivid picture of the schisms, disagreements and cross-currents in recent Whitman criticism. William Carlos Williams, in a characteristic prose rant, writes as if free verse were one of the inalienable rights for which the American Revolution was fought; Middleton Murry invokes the religious sense behind Whitman's democracy, but in terms so vague and grand it might as well be his own religious sense that is being honored; Kenneth Burke buries himself beneath the grassy debris of free associations on the word "leaves"; Mr. Hindus plumps for Whitman the nationalist or perhaps supernationalist, a Whitman whom he calls "Pan-American" and compares, unhappily, with Dostoevsky the pan-Slavic and Wagner the pan-German.

There are, however, two first-rate essays in the book, one by Leslie Fiedler in which he offers a witty history of Whitman's reputation, ending with a rejection of the vatic Whitman and an acceptance of the Whitman who writes of private experience, and the other by Richard Chase in which he presents the best portrait of Whitman that has yet been composed.

Fiedler's essay points the direction for a revival of serious interest in Whitman, though I think he sometimes runs wild in imposing his favorite critical tags on a writer already stuccoed with everyone else's (e.g., "Whitman's America was made in France, the Romantic notion out of Rousseau and Chateaubriand of an absolute anti-Europe, an utter anticulture made flesh, the Noble Savage as a Continent"—which is bright but hardly verifiable by Whitman's verse).

The Chase essay presents Whitman as a "divided, multiple personality, a shifting amalgam of sycophancy and sloth, of mimetic brilliance and Dionysian inspiration, of calculating common sense and philosophical insight. . . ." His Whitman—the portrait is further developed in the book Chase has since written about Whitman—is neurotic, violently energetic and profoundly indolent by turns, whimsical and witty, given to sharp transitions from manic self-assertion to painful self-doubt. Chase rejects the claim that Whitman was actively and persistently heterosexual, homosexual or both, but sees him instead as a man in whom the sexual impulse did not come to sharp expression but remained latent, diffuse and unfocused. One is reminded somewhat of Turgenev, in whom a large masculine frame was also combined with a maternal fleshiness. And like Turgenev, Whitman is a writer endowed with a curiously impersonal tenderness, a kind of pansexual empathy that is available to all objects, whether sentient or not, in the external world.

II

It is a priceless historical joke that the one poet we accept as the National Bard should lack all the accredited national virtues. Whitman himself knew this, and to recognize how aware he was of the ambiguity of his role is to gain much in reading the poetry, for then it is easier to grasp its half hidden irony and humor—Whitman staring in amusement at the sheer oddity of being Walt a *kosmos,* or Whitman announcing that "Having pried through the strata, analyz'd to a hair, counsel'd with doctors and calculated close, / I find no sweeter fat than sticks to my own bones." In his old age he once declared himself to be essentially *furtive,* a description some biographers take, perhaps rightly, to refer to his sexual history; but I think it must be applied to his life and work as a whole, to those strategies and stratagems by which he sends his assumed and hypothetical selves out into the world to discover their possibilities. Almost all American writers tend to be furtive—they have to in this country; but Whitman assumes the role with a greater consciousness of its necessity, strangeness and price.

Whitman speaks for the national ethos, the divine average, the *En Masse,* but he is actually a solitary, a secretive watcher. Whitman calls himself "one of the toughs," but the greatest esthetic pleasure of this lonely Bohemian is the opera good Americans know to be effete, and his taste in general runs toward the delicate and the rococo. Whitman puffs out his chest with the rhetoric of democracy, but his vision of the democratic life—because it involves a sexual fraternity which can only arouse the fiercest anxieties among Americans, who see in it a threat to their protective code of manliness—must be thoroughly unacceptable to the nation that fancies him its poetic spokesman. It is all a comedy of errors, and if one sometimes feels that Whitman's critics serve him right, one may also indulge the feeling that Whitman serves America right.

I have said that Whitman was a Bohemian, but not with the intention of calling to mind those desperate estrangements and eccentricities the term is likely to suggest when used about writers of our own time. American society in the nineteenth century was sufficiently loose and self-confident not merely to give most people a sense of social possibility but also to allow a margin for the survival and even the health of those who did not accept the dominant values. It was easier to be a Bohemian then, as it was easier to be a political or intellectual dissident, and by that token being a Bohemian in the 1850's did not mean a life as alienated and self-afflicting as it must often mean today. The idea of society had not yet become so overwhelming as it is with us; for long stretches of *Leaves of Grass* it seems a secondary actor, only occasionally providing that resistance to human desire which we have learned to expect from it. The writer who aspired to fulfill Emerson's prescription for the American poet—and who almost succeeded, but for the fact that he became something better—found that between America and himself there were large spaces, perhaps even wastes, and that it was this very spaciousness which allowed him to take chances in his poetry, allowed him to become a furtive experimenter and to test out variant possibilities of the self without having to worry about the pressures of society nearly as much as European writers had to worry.

This freedom, to be sure, also brought unhappy results:

it made Whitman much too cavalier toward the past of both Europe and European poetry, it tempted him into discarding literary conventions he had barely tested, let alone understood. And it made him into the first of the many American writers who would try, in the earnestness of their isolation and with the seductive beat of the national music in their ears, to force themselves into the role of folk or tribal poet. In the career of Whitman, as in the careers of Hart Crane and Sherwood Anderson and many others, this effort could lead only to a wearying oscillation between a coarse populism and a precious artiness. The price our writers have paid for trying, so to speak, to swallow the idea of America whole has almost always been a series of relapses into the shallowest kinds of estheticism. Scratch an American primitive and you often find an American decadent.

Whitman had little choice. Given the disintegrative pressures of his family background; the nature of American life and culture at the time he began to write; a scrappy education, as wide and wooly as the educations of most of our literary autodidacts—given all this, Whitman *had* to try to move back and forth between national and private themes, and the miracle is that all the while he managed to write a sizable amount of great poetry.

The most fruitful of his *personae*, the one that corresponds most to the reality of his personal and literary needs, has been described, though not of course with Whitman in mind, by the German sociologist Georg Simmel in an essay called *The Stranger.* "If wandering," writes Simmel

> . . . is the liberation from every given point in space and thus the conceptual opposite to fixation at such a point, the sociological form of the "stranger" presents the unity . . . of these two characteristics. . . . The stranger is being discussed here, not in the sense often touched upon in the past, as the wanderer who comes today and goes tomorrow. He is, so to speak, the *potential* wanderer; although he has not moved on, he has not

quite lost the freedom of coming and going. He is fixed within a particular spatial group. . . . But his position in this group is determined, essentially, by the fact that he has not belonged to it from the beginning, that he imports qualities into it. . . .

Locating the stranger as "a unity of nearness and remoteness," Simmel limits himself to examples based on a clash of cultural styles and does not consider the still more interesting case where the "strangeness" of the stranger derives not from national differences but from a fundamental divergence of outlook and value that has sprung up *within* a culture. It is in the poet-prophet such as Whitman that this divergence is most vividly dramatized, the poet-prophet whose role is made possible by his "unity of nearness and remoteness" and is sanctioned by the readiness of his culture to accept, however conditionally, his ambiguous status.

Does not Simmel's description illuminate Whitman the poet? The man who comes today and stays tomorrow, the potential wanderer whose position in the group is fixed but who imports qualities into it—is this not the author of *Song of Myself*, a poet both remarkably close to everything characteristic and indigenous in our culture and extremely alien and remote from it. The self of the poem is fluid, defined by its unwillingness to rest in definition, committed with a mixture of ingenuous faith and comic skepticism to that belief in *possibility* which is possible only to Americans. At times this self expands to the condition of a protean demigod who absorbs all creatures into his creative will yet is saved from solipsism by the grace, rather infrequent among demigods, of having a sense of humor. At times the self of the poem sinks to an almost mineral tranquillity, a torpor approaching nonidentity, a quasi-mystical dissolution of individual consciousness. The famous "oceanic" impulse which Whitman shares with other romantic poets, the "merging" impulse which disturbs many readers because it seems to blur all distinctions in quality of being, is here made acceptable and often rendered moving by the clear evidence—Whitman seldom tries to deny or hide it—that the self of the poem also acts from a deep anxiety and loneliness, a fear of annihilation which prompts its urge to cosmic identification. This cosmic straining loses much of its apparent pretentiousness once it becomes clear that it is being presented as an emblem of the poet's fears, the very fears we all know and share. Reduce it from philosophical grandiosity to a common human tremor, and Whitman's possession of all possible selves, as his corresponding withdrawal from them, becomes close and intimate.

What matters, however, is not the variety of postures the self assumes in the poem but the charm and wit and openness of passion with which they are assumed. To be sure, Whitman occasionally succumbs to rhetorical bluster and a kind of inane benignity—and who is he, one asks with an irritation all too human, to pretend to be so assured and reassuring about *our* destiny? Yet between the extremes of his cosmic megalomania and the disintegration to which the fluid self is sometimes subjected, there is the rich substance of the poem, the elegiac gravity that lends it so exquisitely dignified a tone, the quiet comedy that acts as a counter-principle to the poem's surface expansiveness. "I have no mockings or arguments, I witness and wait." "Not words, not music or rhyme I want, not custom or lecture, not even the best / Only the lull I like, the hum of your valved voice." "Speech is the twin of my vision, it is unequal to measure itself, / It provokes me forever, it says sarcastically, / *Walt you contain enough, why don't you let it out then?*" "Agonies are one of my changes of garments." "I am the man, I suffer'd, I was there."

These lines are spoken by a Stranger in the midst, a Stranger who is integral to that from which he moves apart. The poem is in this sense the most American of poems, entirely committed to the idea of freedom as something unfinished and still to be made. The self is seen as an experiment in potentiality, and Whitman, as the gayest of "pragmatists," tries on new "selves" almost as if they were new clothes—I make the comparison partly to suggest an excessively American nonchalance but I hope that after a moment it will also suggest a certain reticence and even shyness.

At his best, and in *Song of Myself* he is frequently at his best, Whitman is a master of phrasing, a master of the precise, delicate and epigrammatic statement, a master of the kind of writing which by its combination of unfamiliar elements brings us to the *surprise* of a new insight or observation. Anyone who even glances at *Song of Myself*—anyone who turns to the descriptive power with which Section 5 ends ("And mossy scabs of the worm fence, heap'd stones, elder, mullein and poke-weed") or to the very next section in which the grass is "the flag of my disposition" and then a few lines later "the beautiful uncut hair of graves" or to the final sections where death ("You bitter hug of mortality") is approached and accepted and yet parried—should see that this is the work of a poet with a great gift for language.

One of the main jobs for the Whitman critic would be to describe, with scrupulous modesty, the variety of modes and tones in which Whitman writes. Here let me simply say a word about one of them. There are passages in his long poems, and whole shorter ones, in which the struggle of the self to locate a principle of movement, or a place of rest, comes to a momentary stop. A quietness begins; the language becomes hushed and controlled; the poet, not Walt the *kosmos* but Whitman the solitary, exposes himself in all his vulnerability. It is the moment after the struggle between the self and everything that resists and hurts and destroys the self, the blessed moment when anxiety has not been suppressed or dispelled but brought to its proper subordination. He reaches such moments in occasional passages of *Song of Myself* and for almost the whole of *Crossing Brooklyn Ferry*, which seems to me his single greatest poem. One thinks of them as moments of twilight, somewhat similar to those shadowy intervals between sleeping and waking, when the unconscious is still active and free yet we are not without some capacity to extricate ourselves from it, and when the will is present to our sense of things yet is relaxed and uncensorious. These are moments of rare psychic balance, everyone knows them in one way or another, but few writers have managed to create verbal equivalents as beautiful as those of Whitman.

It is in these moments that he writes most remarkably of death. At his frequent second best and occasional worst, Whitman writes of death in the terms of late romanticism, as an adored agony he is waiting to immerse himself in. Yet even as we sense that behind his absorption with death there are pockets of the morbid, we feel that in such chants as *Crossing Brooklyn Ferry* the morbid has been, not exorcised, since it continues to have a claim upon us, but resisted, held in control, and thereby made into something other than itself. It is one of the great creative paradoxes that when Whitman here speaks of death he does so with the accent and breath of life; that when he acknowledges in *Brooklyn Ferry* the certainy of his non-being in the future it is to take on the being of those who like himself will stand and muse upon the continuity and the tragic finality of life; that when he croons his love to death in *Out of the Cradle Endlessly Rocking* it is with the assurance of gained life.

It has become customary to speak of such writings as a reflection of the religious sense. Theologians without theology try to salvage their faith by focusing upon those emotions of awe before the external world and of gratitude for being present in it for a few moments, which all sensitive human beings share. But to speak of such feelings as uniquely religious is arrogantly to pre-empt what is pervasively human. We are concerned here with the poise toward which we strain, the poise that goes beyond the triviality of "accepting" death but consists of a readiness to find a kind of peace in the determination not to accept.

The Whitman I have been presenting is an unorthodox one, and surely incomplete. I would claim nothing more than that he allows for a usable strategy for getting into the poems. Once that is done, it will no doubt be necesary to return to the other, the public Whitman.

A final note: It is generally said that Whitman declined in poetic power after the Civil War. This is true in a way, the poems of the later years being obviously more fragmentary and short-breathed than those of the earlier ones. But among the later pieces there are some with the most subtle refinement and humor. In his very old age he wrote a twelve-line poem called *After the Supper and Talk* in which he describes his reluctance to leave—we need hardly be told what it is that he must leave:

> Shunning, postponing severance—seeking to ward off the last word, ever so little . . .
> Farewells, messages lessening—dimmer the forthgoer's visage and form,
> Soon to be lost for aye in the darkness—loth, O so loth to depart!
> Garrulous to the very last.

No praise is needed, nor could any be sufficient, for the frank pathos and relaxed gaiety of that final line. This is the way a man, and a poet, should end.

ROBERT FROST: A MOMENTARY STAY

The best of Robert Frost, like the best of most writers, is small in quantity, narrow in scope and seldom the object of popular acclaim. There are a dozen or fifteen of his lyrics which register a completely personal voice, both as to subject and tone, and which it would be impossible to mistake for the work of anyone else. These lyrics mark Frost as a severe and unaccommodating writer: they are ironic, troubled and ambiguous in many of the ways modernist poems are. Despite a lamentable gift for public impersonations and for shrewdly consolidating his success in a country that cares little about poetry, Frost has remained faithful to what Yeats calls "the modern mind in search of its own meanings."

This Frost seldom ventures upon major experiments in meter or diction, nor is he as difficult in reference and complex in structure as are the great poets of the 20th Century. But as he contemplates the thinning landscape of his world and repeatedly finds himself before closures of outlook and experience, he ends, almost against his will, in the company of the moderns. With their temperament and technique he has little in common; he shares with them only a vision of disturbance. This Frost is problematic in his style of thought, quite unlike the twinkling Sage who in his last years became the darling of the nation. At his best Frost is a poet of elusiveness, wit and modesty; he does not posture in blank verse nor does he reinforce the complacence of his audience; he can even approach a hard and unmannered wisdom.

Frost has also written a small number of memorable poems in another vein: dramatic monologues and dialogues set in northern New England which present realistic vignettes of social exhaustion. While neither as original or distinguished as the best of his lyrics, they often live in one's mind, somewhat as a harshly monochromatic picture might. And that, apart from a few scattered pieces, represents the sum of his first-rate work.

To many this will seem an outrageous judgment and to others a harsh one; but it is neither. What I have said about Frost can and must be said about all but the greatest writers. Measured against the strictest critical standards, my judgment, if at all correct, should be taken as praise.

In his long poems, most of them uniting satire and didacticism, Frost is at his worst. An early long poem, "New Hampshire," foreshadows the sly folksiness that would later endear him to native moralists, lady schoolteachers, and miscellaneous middlebrows. The verse is limp; the manner coy; the thought a display of provincialism. In the least happy sense of the word, the poem is *mannered:* Frost catering to his idiosyncracies and minor virtuosities. Even when he is clever ("Lately in converse with a New York alec / About the new school of pseudo-phallic"), it is with the cleverness of a man holding fast to his limitations.

Twenty years ago Malcolm Cowley compared Frost to Hawthorne, Emerson and Thoreau and shrewdly noticed the narrowing of sensibility he had come, at his worst, to represent:

> Height, breadth and strength: he falls short in all these qualities of the great New Englanders. And the other quality for which he is often praised, his utter faithfulness to the New

England spirit, is not one of the virtues they knowingly cultivated. They realized that the New England spirit, when it stands alone, is inclined to be narrow and arithmetical. It has reached its finest growth only when cross-fertilized with alien philosophies.

Much of Frost's later work—"A Masque of Reason," "Build Soil," "A Masque of Mercy" and the bulk of "Steeple Bush"—illustrates the hardening of his public pose. It is a pose of crustiness and sometimes even heartlessness, and it reflects the feeling of a writer that he need no longer engage with the problems of his time. In such writing he is the dealer in packaged whimsies, the homespun Horace scrutinizing man, God and liberalism. Because political fashions changed during the last decades of his life, the aged Frost found himself being applauded for precisely the sententia which had previously, and with good reason, been attacked. But now his hard-shelled individualism won the admiration of readers who in their own experience had increasingly to acknowledge that it would no longer do: perhaps that is why they wished to admire it in poetry.

In these poems conversational tone slips into garrulousness, conservatism declines into smallness of mind, and public declamation ends as mere vanity of pronouncement. If this were all we had of Frost, there would be no choice but completely to accept the powerful attack launched upon him some years ago by Yvor Winters. Frost, wrote Winters, had a way of "mistaking whimsical impulse for moral choice," a kind of irrational romanticism that left him a "spiritual drifter." Reading such passages as the one in "A Masque of Reason" where God declares—

> I'm going to tell Job why I tortured him
> And trust it won't be adding to the torture.
> I was just showing off to the Devil, Job.

—one is strongly tempted to go along with Winters. Frost permits himself such mindless flippancies because he knows that by now his audience has been trained to admire his faults at the very point where they become magnified by cleverness. It is a familiar story: the writer who does not struggle to overcome his limitations will end by parodying them.

Frost the national favorite is a somewhat different figure. He is a writer of lyrics that often achieve a flawed or partial distinction: the language clear, the picture sharp, the rhythm ingratiating. "Birches," "Mending Wall," "The Death of the Hired Man," "The Pasture"—such poems are not contemptible but neither are they first-rate. They lack the urge to move past easy facilities that characterizes major writing. They depend too much on stock sentiments, especially the unconsidered respect good Americans feel obliged to show for "nature." They yield too readily to the common notion of poetic genius as an unaccountable afflatus:

> At least don't use your mind too hard,
> But trust my instinct—I'm a bard.

And they create a music too winsome and soothing:

> This saying good-by on the edge of the dark
> And the cold to an orchard so young in the bark
> Reminds me of all that can happen to harm
> An orchard away at the end of the farm.

The appeal of such poems rests upon Frost's use of what might be called a mode of false pastoral. Traditionally, pastoral poetry employs an idyllic rural setting with apparently simple characters in order to advance complex ideas and sentiments, often implying a serious criticism of the society in which the poet lives. The pastoral seems to turn away in disgust from urban or sophisticated life and to celebrate the virtues of bucolic retreat; but it does not propose that we rest with either simple characters or simple virtues. It accepts the convention of simplicity in order to demonstrate the complexity of the real; and only in an inferior kind of romantic poetry is the pretense of the pastoral taken at face value.

In his lesser poems, however, Frost comes very close to doing precisely that. He falls back upon the rural setting as a means of endorsing the common American notion that a special wisdom is to be found, and found only, among tight-lipped farmers, village whittlers and small-town eccentrics. Overwhelmingly urban, our society displays an unflagging nostalgia for the assumed benefits and beauties of country life. Between the social realities and the popular images there is a fatal split: millions of Americans who live in cities and suburbs preen themselves on homely virtues they neither possess nor could profitably employ if they did. They like to fancy themselves as good rugged country folk, or suppose they would have a better and happier life if they were. And the second-rank Frost is their poet.

He provides them with ennobling texts which both share in and reinforce the false consciousness in which they immerse themselves. He *becomes* his audience, mirroring and justifying its need for pastoral fancies. The more a magazine like *The New Yorker* influences the quality of sophisticated middle-class life, the more will many Americans feel a desire for some assuaging counter-image—woodsy, wholesome, a bit melancholic—such as Frost can provide. As a writer who bends his gift to the sincere misapprehensions of his readers, he has become a figure deeply integral to our culture; and the middle-brows who adore him must in fairness be granted the right to claim him as their own. All that can be said by way of qualification is that not the whole or best of Frost is theirs.

Matters are more complicated still. Frost is so skillful a performer that some of his most popular poems, like "Acquainted With the Night," "After Apple-Picking," and "Stopping by Woods on a Snowy Evening" are also among his finest. It might be convenient, but is also a dangerous simplification, to draw a sharp line between his popular and superior poems. The two have a way of shading into one another, as has always been the case with those major writers of the past two centuries, like Dickens, Mark Twain and Sholom Aleichem, who managed to speak both to cultivated persons and to the mass audience. And part of what Frost's ordinary readers admire or look for in his poetry they are, I think, right in wanting: a renewal of primary experience, a relatedness to the physical world, a wisdom resting on moral health.

In his dramatic poems Frost seldom falls back upon readymade pastoral. These are poems of rural realism: New England as a depressed landscape, country people who are poor and deprived, families torn apart by derangement. The best of this group, such as "Home Burial" and "Servant to Servants," are studies in frustration, often the frustration of women who can no longer bear the weight of suffering. There is no "community" behind these figures, no sustaining world in which they can move: there is no Tilbury Town or Winesburg Ohio to define social boundaries. The men and women of Frost's poems are isolated; they are figures left over by a dead or dying culture; and the world they live in has begun turning into stone.

Powerful as some of these dramatic pieces are, they share a number of faults. Frost lacks the patience, the involvement, and the deep concern with moral nuance that are essential to a writer wishing to evoke human character. He tries to conform to the hard outlines of economical portraiture and to avoid the kind of detail that would be appropriate only to a novel, but the result is often that the poems rely too much on photographic anecdote. The events they depict are supposed to speak for themselves; but events seldom do.

Precisely the shading and implication one misses in Frost's dramatic poems are what distinguish the dramatic poems of his immediate New England predecessor, Edwin Arlington Robinson. Though not nearly so brilliant a virtuoso as Frost,

Robinson writes from a fullness of experience and a tragic awareness that Frost cannot equal. No other American poet commands so rich a sense of moral life as does Robinson in "Eros Turannos," "The Wandering Jew," "Rembrandt to Rembrandt" and "The Three Taverns"—poems beside which Frost's work in the same genre seems stiff in portrayal and crude in psychology. Frost has a strong grasp on melodramatic extremes of behavior, usually extremes of loneliness and psychic exhaustion, but he lacks almost entirely Robinson's command of the middle range of experience. The life of Frost's poems is post-social, and the perspective from which it is seen a desperate one. Frost achieves a cleaner verbal surface and a purer diction, but Robinson is more abundant in moral detail and insight. Compared strictly on their performances as dramatic poets, Robinson seems a major poet and Frost a minor one. For while Frost can be a master of nuance, it is only, or almost only, when he speaks in his own voice.

And that he does when he bears down with full seriousness in his small number of distinguished lyrics. Here the archness and sentimentalism have been ruthlessly purged; he is writing for sheer life. To read these poems, as they confront basic human troubles and obliquely notice the special dislocations of our time, can be unnerving—they offer neither security nor solace. They are the work of a poet who, without the mediation of formal thought or religious sentiments, gives close and hard battle to his own experience. They seek to capture those moments when we confront experience in its bareness, observing some natural event or place with a pure sense of the dynamics of reception. They set out to record such tremors of being in their purity and isolation: as if through a critical encounter with the physical world one could move beyond the weariness of selfhood and into the repose of matter. But Frost, now supremely hard on himself, also knows that the very intensity with which these moments are felt makes certain their rapid dissolution, and that what then remains is the familiar self, once again its own prisoner. Approaching a condition in which the narrator strains to achieve a sense of oneness with the universe and thereby lose himself in the delight of merger, these lyrics return, chastened, with the necessity of shaped meaning. And in their somewhat rueful turning back to the discipline of consciousness, the effect is both painful and final. They conclude with the reflection that the central quandary of selfhood—that it must forever spiral back to its own starting point—cannot be dissolved. That Frost sees and struggles with this dilemma seems to me one reason for saying he inhabits the same intellectual climate as those modern writers whose presumed disorder is often compared unfavorably to his supposed health.

Frost's superior lyrics include: "Storm Fear," "An Old Man's Winter Night," "The Oven Bird," "Dust of Snow," "Stopping by Woods on a Snowy Evening," "Spring Pools," "Acquainted With the Night," "The Lovely Shall be Choosers," "Desert Places," "Neither Out Far Nor in Deep," "Provide, Provide," "Design," "Happiness Makes Up in Height for What It Lacks in Length," "The Most of It," "Never Again Would Bird's Song Be the Same," "Directive" and a few others.

These poems are brief, and they demand from the reader a sharp recognition of their brevity. They focus upon a moment of intense realization, a lighting-up of hope and a dimming-down to wisdom. They attempt not a full seizure of an event, but an attack upon it from the oblique. They present a scene in the natural world, sometimes one that is "purely" natural and apparently unmarred by a human observer, but more often one that brings the "I" of the poem starkly against a natural process, so that the stress falls upon a drama of encounter and withdrawal. The event or situation—how spring pools will be sucked dry by the absorptive power of trees, in "Spring Pools"; how an albino spider perched on a "white heal-all" forms a dumb-show of purposeless terror, in "Design";

how the loneliness of a winter moment encompasses an observer unawares, in "Desert Places"; how a family caught in a fearful storm may not, unaided, be able to rescue itself, in "Storm Fear"—is rendered with a desire to make a picture that will seem complete in itself, but that will also, through the very perfection of completeness, carry an aura of suggestion beyond itself. Frost allows for the sensuous pleasure of apprehending a moment in nature, but he soon cuts it short, since the point is not to linger over scene or pleasure but to move beyond them, along a line of speculation. Perhaps that is what Frost meant when he said that poetry "begins in delight and ends in wisdom."

These lyrics can be placed on a spectrum ranging from a few that seem entirely focussed upon a natural event to those which move past the event toward explicit statement. Despite the critical dogma which looks down upon statement in poetry, there is nothing inherently superior about the first of these kinds; Frost's greatest poems, as it happens, are those which end upon a coda of reflection. "Spring Pools" is an example of a poem that seems, at first, merely a snapshot of the external world:

> These pools that, though in forests, still reflect
> The total sky almost without defect,
> And like the flowers beside them, chill and shiver,
> Will like the flowers beside them soon be gone,
> And yet not out by any brook or river,
> But up by roots to bring dark foliage on.
>
> The trees that have it in their pentup buds
> To darken nature and be summer woods—
> Let them think twice before they use their powers
> To blot out and drink up and sweep away
> These flowery waters and these watery flowers
> From snow that melted only yesterday.

As a rendering of a natural event, the poem is precise, expert and complete. Exactness of description can be very moving, and so it is in "Spring Pools"; but beyond that, the poem—partly through a skillful play with prepositions in the tenth line—suggests how hard yet necessary it is that the brief loveliness of youth be sucked dry to form the strength of our prime. Where the poem moves beyond description and implication is in its problematic use of a parallelism between natural event and human experience, involving the ways in which they seem both close and ultimately distant. An implied equivalence between nature and man quickly brings a writer to the edge of the sentimental; but Frost does not cross it, for the poem, in its descriptive self-sufficiency, leaves to the reader the problem of what symbolic import to infer and how much tact he can muster in defending the poem against his inference. It is a poem about spring pools, the poignancy of youth, and problems of thinking, not in any hierarchy of value which dissolves everything into the "spiritual," but in a poised equality of perceiving.

Most of Frost's superior lyrics end with direct statement, and one measure of their success is his ability to make the statement seem an adequate climax to the remarkable descriptive writing that has preceded it. The problem is not one to be approached with *a priori* notions about the relationship between imagery and statement in verse. When Cleanth Brooks writes that "Frost does not *think* through his images; he requires statements," he is guilty of a modernist dogma to the extent that he means his remarks as an adverse criticism. Poetry has always been full of statement, even the poetry of many modernist writers who are supposed to confine themselves to symbolic indirection; and the critical problem in regard to Frost, or any other writer, hinges on the extent to which the concluding statement is related, through logical fulfillment or irony, to the texture of the poem, and the extent to which the statement is in its own right serious in thought and notable in diction.

In "Desert Places" Frost starts with a description of a natural scene and then, in a very moving way, brings in the human observer:

> Snow falling and night falling fast, oh, fast
> In a field I looked into going past,
> And the ground almost covered smooth in snow,
> But a few weeds and stubble showing last.
>
> The woods around it have it—it is theirs.
> All animals are smothered in their lairs.
> I am too absent-spirited to count;
> The loneliness includes me unawares.
>
> And lonely as it is that loneliness
> Will be more lonely ere it will be less—
> A blanker whiteness of benighted snow
> With no expression, nothing to express.

Thus far, the poem is very fine, but there follows the concluding stanza—

> They cannot scare me with their empty spaces
> Between stars—on stars where no human race is.
> I have it in me so much nearer home
> To scare myself with my own desert places.

—in which Frost collapses into the kind of coyness one has come to associate with his second-rank poems. Cut out the final stanza and "Desert Places" is a perfect small lyric; as it stands, the poem is a neat illustration of Frost's characteristic strengths and weaknesses; but the weakness of the last four lines is due not to the fact that Frost ventures a statement, but to the quality of the statement he ventures.

In most of the lyrics I have named Frost handles this problem with assurance. "The Oven Bird" presents a picture of a bird which in mid-summer sings loudly, as if in celebration of the lapsed spring:

> He says the early petal-fall is past
> When pear and cherry bloom went down in showers
> On sunny days a moment overcast;
> And comes that other fall we call the fall.

The writing here, both vivid and witty, is satisfying enough, and the theme, though treated with greater toughness, resembles that of "Spring Pools." The bird is assigned, as a pleasing conceit and not a sentimental indulgence, something of the poet's stoical resilience:

> The bird would cease and be as other birds
> But that he knows in singing not to sing.

Then come the concluding lines, in which Frost achieves a triumph of modulated rhetoric, a statement that can be regarded as an epitaph of his whole career:

> The question that he frames in all but words
> Is what to make of a diminished thing.

Many of Frost's first-rate lyrics unite with similar success a rapid passage of description and a powerful concluding statement. The familiar "Acquainted With the Night" owes a good part of its haunting quality not merely to Frost's evocation of a man walking the streets alone at night—

> I have stood still and stopped the sound of feet
> When far away an interrupted cry
> Came over houses from another street
> But not to call me back or say goodbye;

—but also to the lines that immediately follow, lines of enigmatic statement indicating an ultimate dissociation between the natural world and human desire:

> And further still at an unearthly height,
> One luminary clock against the sky
>
> Proclaimed the time was neither wrong nor right.
> I have been one acquainted with the night.

In discussing such poems it has become a commonplace to say, as W. H. Auden does, that Frost's style "approximates to ordinary speech" and that "the music is always that of the speaking voice, quiet and sensible." This does not seem an adequate way of describing Frost's lyrics, and perhaps not of any poetry worth reading a second time. Try reading "Spring Pools" or "The Most of It" in a voice approximating to ordinary speech: it cannot be done, short of violating the rhythm of the poem. Quiet these lyrics may be, "sensible" they are not. They demand a rhythm of enticement and immersion, a hastening surrender to unreflective nature—which means a rising and tensing of the voice; and then a somewhat broken or subdued return to reflectiveness. They are poems that must be read with a restrained intoning, quite different from "ordinary speech," though milder than declamation.

It is a way of reading enforced by their structure and purpose: the structure and purpose of wisdom-poems. Frost's best lyrics aim at the kind of wisdom that is struck aslant and not to be settled into the comforts of an intellectual system. It is the wisdom of a mind confessing its nakedness, caught in its aloneness. Frost writes as a modern poet who shares in the loss of firm assumptions and seeks, through a disciplined observation of the natural world and a related sequel of reflection, to provide some tentative basis for existence, some "momentary stay," as he once remarked, "against confusion." The best of his poems are neither indulgences in homely philosophy nor wanderings in romanticism. If anything, they are antipathetic to the notion that the universe is inherently good or delightful or hospitable to our needs. The symbols they establish in relation to the natural world are not, as in transcendentalist poetry, tokens of benevolence. These lyrics speak of the hardness and recalcitrance of the natural world; of its absolute indifference to our needs and its refusal to lend itself to an allegory of affection; of the certainty of physical dissolution; but also of the refreshment that can be found through a brief submission to the alienness of nature, always provided one recognizes the need to move on, not stopping for rest but remaining locked, alone, in consciousness. The lyric that best illustrates these themes is "The Most of It," which dramatizes our desire for cosmic solace and the consequence of discovering we cannot have it. I shall end by quoting this poem, because it seems best to illustrate what I have been trying to say, because it is the kind of farewell that Frost might have appreciated, and because it is one of the greatest poems ever written by an American:

> He thought he kept the universe alone;
> For all the voice in answer he could wake
> Was but the mocking echo of his own
> From some tree-hidden cliff across the lake.
> Some morning from the boulder-broken beach
> He would cry out on life, that what it wants
> Is not its own love back in copy speech,
> But counter-love, original response.
> And nothing ever came of what he cried
> Unless it was the embodiment that crashed
> In the cliff's talus on the other side,
> And then in the far distant water splashed,
> But after a time allowed for it to swim,
> Instead of proving human when it neared
> And someone else additional to him,
> As a great buck it powerfully appeared,
> Pushing the crumpled water up ahead,
> And landed pouring like a waterfall,
> And stumbled through the rocks with horny tread,
> And forced the underbush—and that was all.

WALLACE STEVENS: ANOTHER WAY OF LOOKING AT THE BLACKBIRD

> What inmost allegiance, what ultimate religion, would be proper to a wholly free and disillusioned spirit?
> —George Santayana

Gradually, under the pressure of time, the masks of Wallace Stevens are wearing away, and not because they have become obsolete or been proven deceptive but because they now seem to have figured mainly as preparations for a homelier reality. Gaudy mystifier, Crispin's pilot, flaunter of rare chromatic words, explorer of Yucatan, enemy of the day's routine, afficionado of strange hats, even the gamesman of epistemology —these roles yield to Stevens' "basic slate," an American poet reflecting upon solitary lives in a lonely age and searching for that "inmost allegiance" by which men might live out their years in thousands of Hartfords.

Stevens was the kind of poet who wrote methodically and a good deal, apparently without waiting for, though always delighted to receive, the blessings of inspiration. Writing verse seems to have become for him a means of wresting convictions of selfhood: the visible token of that which he insistently wrote about. His work is therefore very much of a piece, both in its success and failures.

After the publication of *Harmonium* in 1923, the main job of his critics was to become familiar with his decor: the exotic places, the tropical language, the cheerful jibing at bourgeois norms, the apparent *fin-de-siècle* estheticism, the flip nose-thumbing of his titles. So luxuriant did the world of his poems seem, so free of traditional moral demands, that his early admirers could hardly avoid thinking of this world as primarily a sensuous landscape. It was a view that lingered into Marianne Moore's description of Stevens as "a delicate apothecary of savors and precipitates"—though in that last word there is a hint that Miss Moore, as usual, saw more than she said.

While this was a way of reading Stevens that could yield genuine pleasures, it hardly went very far toward penetrating his deeper concerns, and even when confined to *Harmonium* it could be maintained only if one focused on the shorter poems and neglected "Sunday Morning" and "The Comedian as Letter C." In an early study of Stevens, R. P. Blackmur quickly saw that the strange cries, hoots, and words that ran through the poems, far from being mere exotica, were oblique and humorous tokens of a profoundly serious effort to grapple with the distinctively "modern" in modern experience.

Later there was a tendency to read Stevens as if he were a versifying philosopher, a misfortune for which he was himself partly to blame, since at his prolific second-best he had a way of sounding like a versifying philosopher. Stevens' poetry, now in the hands of new exegetes, was said to be about the writing of poetry, and was regarded as a series of variations on the philosophical theme of the relation between reality and imagination. Both of these statements, while true and useful, were needlessly limiting as aids toward a fuller apprehension of the poetry: the first was too narrow, the second too academic, and from neither could one gain a sense of what might be urgent or particular in Stevens' work.

Poetry written mainly about the writing of poetry—could that be the ground for any large claim as to the interest

Stevens might command from literate readers? Imagination and reality—did that not increase the peril of regarding Stevens as a shuffler of epistemological categories? Neither gambit is enough; another way is needed for looking at the blackbird.

At the base of Stevens' work, as a force barely acknowledged yet always felt, lies a pressing awareness of human disorder in our time—but an awareness radically different from that of most writers. Only rarely does it emerge in his poems as a dramatized instance or fiction; Stevens seldom tries and almost never manages to evoke the modern disorder through representations of moral conduct or social conflict. When in *Owl's Clover* he did write a poem with a relatively explicit politics, the result, as he later acknowledged, was unfortunate: rhetoric overruning thought, an assault upon a subject which as a poet Stevens was not prepared to confront.

Lacking that "novelistic" gift for portraiture-in-depth which is so valuable to a good many modern poets, Stevens does not examine society closely or even notice it directly for any length of time; he simply absorbs "the idea" of it. A trained connoisseur in chaos, he sees no need to linger before the evidence: there is enough already. And that is why it seem neither a paradox nor a conceit to say that in Stevens' poetry the social world is but dimly apprehended while a perspective upon history is brilliantly maintained: history as it filters through his consciousness of living and writing at a given time. The disorder that occupies the foreground of so much modern literature is calmly accepted by Stevens, appearing in his work not as a dominant subject but as a pressure upon all subjects.

In a somewhat similar way Stevens, though sharply responsive to the crisis of belief which has troubled so many sensitive persons in the twentieth century, is not himself directly or deeply involved in it. He knows and feels it, but has begun to move beyond it. When he writes that . . .

> The death of Satan was a tragedy
> For the imagination. A capital
> Negation destroyed him in his tenement
> And, with him, many blue phenomena . . .

the force of these lines is clearly secular, releasing an attitude of comic humaneness. Perhaps they are also a little blasphemous, since it is hard to imagine a religious writer making quite this complaint about the consequences of the death of Satan. Here, as elsewhere in Stevens, a secular imagination measures the loss that it suffers from the exhaustion of religious myths and symbols, and then hopes that emotional equivalents can be found in . . .

> One's self and the mountains of one's land,
>
> Without shadows, without magnificence,
> The flesh, the bones, the dirt, the stone.

At times, it is true, Stevens can resemble the typical intellectual of his day (or the idea of the typical intellectual) and describes himself as "A most inappropriate man / In a most unpropitious place." He can appear to regret that "The epic of disbelief / Blares oftener and soon, will soon be constant." Yet if one compares him to Eliot and the later Auden, it becomes clear that Stevens is relatively free from religious or ideological nostalgia:

> The truth is that there comes a time
> When we can mourn no more over music
> That is so much motionless sound.
>
> There comes a time when the waltz
> Is no longer a mode of desire, a mode
> Of revealing desire and is empty of shadow.

Only occasionally does one find in Stevens that intense yearning for a real or imaginary past which has become so prevalent an attitude in our century. There is instead a recognition, both sensitive and stolid, of where we happen to be. And this, in Stevens' reckoning, imposes a new burden on the poet

> . . . since in the absence of a belief in God, the mind turns to its own creations and examines them, not alone from the esthetic point of view, but for what they reveal, for what they validate and invalidate, for the support they give.

Stevens is not directly affected by the usual religious or intellectual uncertainties, at least not nearly so much as by the predicament—and possibilities—of the mind experiencing them, the mind that still moves within the orbit of some waning belief yet strives for a direction and momentum of its own. Even in those poems, such as "Sunday Morning" and "The Comedian as Letter C," which do seem to deal explicity with belief, one finds a recapitulation of a progress Stevens has already taken, not in freeing himself entirely from the crisis of belief or its emotional aftereffects (for to claim that would be impudent), but in learning to write as if in his poetic person he were a forerunner of post-crisis, post-ideological man. In "The Man With the Blue Guitar," where the guitar serves as the instrument of poetry, Stevens relates this role to an estimate, lovely in its comic modesty, of his own work:

> . . . Poetry
> Exceeding music must take the place
> Of empty heaven and its hymns,
> Ourselves in poetry must take their place,
> Even in the chatter of your guitar.

Yet Stevens is too much of a realist, too aware (as in "The Comedian as Letter C") of the sheer inertia of human existence, to suppose that the crisis of belief can be quickly overcome either by private decision or public commitment.

Accepting the condition of uncertainty and solitariness as unavoidable once man has freed himself from the gods, Stevens poses as his ultimate question not, what shall we do about the crisis of belief, but rather, how shall we live with and perhaps beyond it? And one reason for thinking of Stevens as a comic poet is that he makes this choice of questions.

How shall we live with and then perhaps beyond the crisis of belief?—it is to confront this question that Stevens keeps returning to the theme of reality and imagination. Not merely because he is interested in epistemological forays as such— though he is; nor because he is fascinated with the creative process—though that too; but because his main concern is with discovering and, through his poetry, *enacting* the possibilities for human self-renewal in an impersonal and recalcitrant age.

How recalcitrant that age can be, Stevens knew very well. The fragmentation of personality, the loss of the self in its social roles, the problem of discovering one's identity amid a din of public claims—all this, so obsessively rehearsed in modern literature, is the premise from which Stevens moves to poetry. When Stevens does write directly about such topics, it is often with lightness and humor, taking easily on a tangent what other writers can hardly bear to face. An early little poem, "Disillusionment of Ten O'Clock," is about houses that are haunted by "white night-gowns," for Stevens the uniform of ordinariness and sober nights.

> None are green,
> Or purple with green rings,
> Or green with yellow rings,
> None of them are strange,
> With socks of lace
> And beaded ceintures.

In this flat world "People are not going / To dream of baboons and periwinkles." Only here and there an old sailor, one who by age and trade stands outside the perimeter of busy dullness . . .

> Drunk and asleep in his boots,
> Catches tigers
> In red weather.

I hope it will not seem frivolous to suggest that this drunken sailor embodies a central intention of Stevens' mind, and that when Stevens in his later poems turns to such formidable matters as inquiries into the nature of reality or the relation between the perceiving eye and the perceived object, he still keeps before him the figure of that old sailor dreaming in red weather.

The elaborate conceptual maneuvers of Stevens' longer poems have as their objective not any conclusion in the realm of thought but a revelation in the realm of experience. They are written to rediscover, and help us rediscover, the human gift for self-creation; they try to enlarge our margin of autonomy; they are incitements to intensifying our sense of what remains possible even today. Each nuance of perspective noted in a Stevens poem matters not merely in its own right, but as a comic prod to animation, a nudge to the man whose eye is almost dead. And in Stevens' poetry the eye is the central organ of consciousness.

When Stevens writes about the writing of poetry, he needs to be read not only on the level of explicit statement, but also as if the idea of poetry were a synecdoche for every potential of consciousness, as if poetry were that which can help liberate us from the tyranny of mechanical life and slow dying. Stevens is a revolutionist of the imagination, neither exhorting nor needing to exhort but demonstrating through poetry the possibilities of consciousness. And he can do this, among other reasons, because in the background of his work loom the defeats and losses of the century.

Time and again Stevens turns to the clause, "It is as if

"...," for that clause charts a characteristic turning or soaring of his mind, which then is followed by another opening of perception. And these, in turn, are openings to the drama of the mind as it reaches out toward new modes of awareness and thereby "makes" its own life from moment to moment. There may be thirteen or three hundred and thirteen ways of looking at a blackbird, but what matters is that the eye, and the mind behind the eye, should encompass the life of these possible ways and the excitement of their variety. What also matters is that the mind behind the eye should remember that the blackbird, no matter how it may be seen, is always there in its mysterious tangibility.

Putting it this way I may seem to be making Stevens into a moralist of sorts: which readers awed by his urbanity of style might well take to be implausible. But in his relaxed and unhurried way Stevens is, I think, a moralist—a moralist of seeing.

Like any other convention, Stevens' use of the theme of reality and imagination as a means of reaching to his deeper concerns, can slide into formula and habit. His extraordinary gifts as a stylist aggravate rather than lessen this danger, since they allow him to keep spinning radiant phrases long after his mind has stopped moving. The reader accustomed to Stevens' habits and devices may even respond *too* well to the poems, for their characteristic inflections and themes have a way of setting off responses which are proper to Stevens' work as a whole but have not been earned by the particular poem. At other times Stevens' insistence upon human possibility can itself become mechanical, a ruthlessness in the demand for joy. And perhaps the greatest weakness in his poems is a failure to extend the possibilities of self-renewal beyond solitariness or solitary engagements with the natural world and into the life of men living together. (Yet Stevens, humorous with self-knowledge, has written some of his most poignant lines about this very limitation: "I cannot bring a world quite round, / Although I patch it as I can. / I sing a hero's head, large eye / And bearded bronze, but not a man, / Although I patch him as I can / And reach through him almost to man.")

At his best, however, Stevens transforms each variant of perception into a validation of the self. Sometimes the self is to achieve renewal by a sympathetic merger with the outer world:

> One must have a mind of winter
> To regard the frost and the boughs
> Of the pine trees crusted with snow . . .

At other times the self gains a kind of assurance from entire withdrawal, as if to grant the outer world its own being. In "Nuance on a Theme by Williams," Stevens quotes William Carlos Williams' lines, "It's a strange courage / you give me, ancient star" and then proceeds to tell the star:

> Lend no part to any humanity that suffuses
> You in its own light.
> Be no chimera of morning,
> Half-man, half-star.

The act of discovery by which sentience is regained can

> Be the finding of a satisfaction, and may
> Be of a man skating, a woman dancing, a woman
> Combing. The poem of the act of the mind.

It may be a sheer pleasure in the freshness of the physical world:

> How should you walk in that space and know
> Nothing of the madness of space,
>
> Nothing of its jocular procreations?
> Throw the lights away. Nothing must stand
>
> Between you and the shapes you take
> When the crust of shape has been destroyed.

In the "Idea of Order at Key West" the self "takes over" the outer world by endowing it with a perceptual form:

> She was the single artificer of the world
> In which she sang. And when she sang, the sea,
> Whatever self it had, became the self
> That was her song, for she was the maker . . .

And finally in Stevens' last poems the cleared mind listens for solitary sounds in winter, waiting patiently for death. These astonishing poems, like Chinese paintings in their simplicity and rightness, are Stevens' last probings, the last quiet efforts to realize life through connecting with whatever is not human. The idea of the world, now as lucid as its single sounds, becomes the final object of contemplation:

> The palm at the end of the mind,
> Beyond the last thought, rises
> In the bronze distance,
> A gold-feathered bird
> Sings in the palm, without any human meaning,
> Without human feeling, a foreign song.

Reading these last poems one encounters again the theme of discovery, the desire to transform and renew, that has given shape to all of Stevens' work. Here, if anywhere, is the answer to Santayana's question, the "ultimate religion" of our secular comedy:

> The honey of heaven may or may not come,
> But that of earth both comes and goes at once.

Some European moderns

GEORGE GISSING: POET OF FATIGUE

Some writers are born with one skin too few. The commonplace abrasions of daily life become a torment for them, and its vulgarities seem a purposeful affront. In their relationship to society they neither accept nor rebel, attack nor retreat; they simply endure.

These writers are not esthetes, nor as a rule precious. To withdraw from the troubles of human existence seems to them neither possible nor desirable. When they speak their complaint, they do so in the hope that the wounds suffered by a defenseless self are not merely haphazard accumulations of pain but have some ultimate, perhaps redeeming significance. They compose their books by registering with a petulant honesty the blows that circumstances have thrust upon them. Forever on the brink of self-pity, they seem deficient in that crude energy, that stock of animal spirits, which anyone had better have who chooses to do his work against the comforts and persuasions of the world. And sometimes, in reading their poems and novels, one feels they exemplify the notorious intuition of Thomas Hardy that in the modern era men have begun to lose the will to live: quite as if there were a thinning-out of blood which makes us creatures forever subject to the complication of our nerves.

The kind of figure I am sketching here is a distinctly "modern" one, and he finds a real-life model in George Gissing, the late-Victorian writer about whom Virginia Woolf has neatly remarked that he is "one of those imperfect novelists through whose books one sees the life of the author faintly covered by the lives of fictitious people." Respected though seldom popular during his lifetime, Gissing achieved a certain fame toward the end of his career: he was praised by literary men so different as the radical English novelist H. G. Wells and the conservative American critic Paul Elmer More. But by now he survives as little more than a name, and only one or two of his books are still in print. His fate in the histories of English literature is to be respectfully dismissed as a morose writer who turned for his material to the city poor but could not present them with the vitality and humor that had distinguished the great English novelists earlier in the century. There is some truth in this view of Gissing, but far from the whole of it.

I

During most of his forty-five years, the life of George Gissing was utterly miserable. He had a positive talent for unhappiness, perhaps the sole talent he cultivated with zest and released with abundance. His was the kind of life that could have been drawn from one of those harsh naturalistic novels that were being written all through Europe during the late nineteenth and early twentieth centuries. Indeed, the closeness between his personal experience and his literary work points to limits of imagination which, except in one book, kept Gissing from becoming a first-rate writer—for the first-rate writer can usually move beyond the narrowness, or penalties, of his own life.

George Robert Gissing was born in the town of Wakefield in Yorkshire, England, on November 22, 1857. He was the eldest son of Thomas Gissing, a pharmaceutical chemist with aspirations toward culture which a flimsy education kept him from satisfying. H. G. Wells, in a lively sketch of Gissing, has remarked that the father

> was the cardinal formative influence of his life. The tone of his father's voice, his father's gestures, never departed from him; when he read aloud, particularly if it was poetry he read, his father's voice, his father's gestures, never departed from him; and encouragement had quickened his imagination and given it its enduring bias for literary activity.

The elder Gissing was one of those earnest free-thinking autodidacts who were fairly common in mid-nineteenth-century England, and from him the novelist inherited a fierce, almost compulsive bookishness. (A recent critic, Walter Allen, has wittily complained that in his novels Gissing seems often to imply that "the sole end of life was that men and women should read.") Gissing also inherited from his father a certain feeling of superiority toward the mass of men, an aloofness from ordinary people, which took the form not so much of the usual class snobbery as of a more self-conscious and precarious kind of cultural fastidiousness. "We children," Gissing would later recall, "did not associate with the children of any other shopkeepers in Wakefield."

One result was that the boy became something of a prodigy, repeatedly winning prizes in school, and discovering in himself that love for the Greek and Latin classics which would be the only source of intellectual stability in his life. Yet it meant he would also suffer the emotions of premature loneliness that so often afflict an unusually bright boy. Gissing would always cling to the notion that between the life of the mind and the life of the senses, between a disinterested commitment to scholarship and a need to share in the common pleasures of mankind, there is an irremediable conflict.

When the boy was thirteen, his father died. The mother managed to send him to a decent Quaker school, and from there, at fifteen, he went on as a scholarship student to Owens College in Manchester. Driving himself to win honors, he led a bleak and deprived existence; his letters display a gravity beyond what can be expected from even the most serious of boys. The characteristic instabilities of his temperament were now beginning to show themselves: moments of high excitement in discovering some natural beauty or literary excellence followed by periods of depression in which he would be equally savage to his fellows and himself. It was the temperament of a boy, soon to be the temperament of a man, whose training had—in the good and bad senses—been too *fine;* so that his very growth of character, in bringing out both gifts and weaknesses, unfitted him for the world. He became, in H. G. Wells's notable phrase, a man who "had no social nerve."

Had there been money enough for Gissing to retire to the life of a gentleman-scholar producing an occasional essay on Greek metrics, he would have been spared the miseries ahead of him; in fact, he might never have written novels at all. But deformed as he was by the shabby-genteel poverty of his youth, Gissing soon found himself in the position of the educated young man no longer at home in the world of his lower-middle-class origins yet lacking those opportunities and graces that would enable him to enter the world of cultivation. It is a dilemma common enough to the England of his day and even of our own; in one of Gissing's better novels, *Born in Exile*, he describes with a notable objectivity the humiliations and embarrassments of precisely such a young man.

Made all too vulnerable by his loneliness, sufferings, and self-pity, Gissing soon fell in love—with a seventeen-year-old prostitute, Nell Harrison. Her plight stirred his imagination, to the point where he indulged himself in fantasies of rescue, and soon he was committing a series of petty thefts in the men's locker room at Owens College in order to provide Nell with money. He was caught, dismissed from school, and briefly imprisoned.

The upshot was that Gissing left England to spend a year in America, where he wandered about, earned a few dollars by writing mediocre stories for a Chicago paper, taught school in Waltham, Massachusetts, and several times approached the edge of starvation.

In 1877 he was back in London, settling to his life-long career as a writer of serious fiction and trying to make a little money on the side as a tutor. Two years later he married Nell Harrison, and after a few months of happiness their life fell into a predictable routine of quarrels and miseries. Nell proved herself a shrew, complaining over his inability to provide the popular entertainments she had been taught to desire, while Gissing could find neither energy nor language for counterattack. Wells has written shrewdly about the marriage:

> Clearly there was for him something about this woman, of which no record remains, some charm, some illusion or at any rate some specific attraction, for which he never had words. . . . His home training had made him repressive to the explosive pitch: he felt that to make love to any woman he could regard as a social equal would be too elaborate, restrained and tedious. . . .

As the domestic situation grew worse Gissing tried to continue writing, but he found that hard to do, a robust will or nervous system not being among his endowments. In a letter to his brother dated 1881, he reveals something of the outcome:

> I am getting most frightfully nervous, indeed so completely nervous that I dread the slightest variation from my humdrum life. The doorbell ringing, even, or the postman's sudden knock puts me into palpitation and head-swimming. . . . This is very greatly the consequence, I know, of home circumstances. . . . I suppose a perfectly peaceful and intellectually-active life is one of those blessings I shall only be looking forward to until there is no time left for it, and . . . "the night cometh when no man can work."

The prediction as to his future was all too accurate, yet somehow Gissing did manage to write. In 1880 he published his first novel, the amateurish but touching *Workers in the Dawn,* one of the earliest attempts by an English novelist to present the life of the working class from "the inside." The book brought him no success and little notice, but in the next decade he published seven more novels, of which one or two are still worth reading. All during these years, his life was unrelievedly hellish: a mixture of poverty, loneliness, overwork, and the torment of trying to cope with a wife who kept sinking into alcoholism and illness. After a time Nell left Gissing and returned to her old ways on the streets; and not until 1888, when he was called to a slum to claim her body, did he see her again.

How poor Gissing really was during the 1880's, whether he invited some of the miseries that came to him, and the extent to which he later exaggerated the privations of his early years in London—these are questions debated but not quite resolved by his biographers. There may have been, and undoubtedly were, elements in Gissing's character that would prompt him to compound the difficulties made inevitable by his career as a serious but unpopular writer; but the evidence also suggests that the physical hungers of Edwin Reardon and Harold Biffen, the two novelists in *New Grub Street,* were not merely imagined by Gissing but had a substantial basis in his own experience. Our addiction to psychology should not prompt us to forget that the reason some people do not eat enough is that they cannot get enough to eat.

In 1891 Gissing married again, this time Edith Underwood, a girl of poor background and scant education, who at first seemed exactly the sweet young thing Gissing thought he wanted. Soon, however, she revealed herself as a vulgar and irritable woman. Again, his characteristic mistake. Gissing was a good-looking man and intensely drawn to women, as they were to him—the power of sexuality to mold and destroy a man's ideal ambitions can be felt throughout his work. But there was also in his mind a painful confusion, perhaps a residue of Victorian morality, concerning the relations between men and women. Consciously he aspired toward ladies of intellectuality and refinement, and now and again formed friendships with women of this kind; but as a man haunted by a sense of social inadequacy and doomed to a life of poverty, he could not imagine such ladies as possible wives. To assuage his strong sexual needs and his equally strong needs for solace and companionship, he turned to poor uneducated girls, precisely the kind who at first would be awed by his cultivated manner and later become impatient, bitter, and disappointed.

By the 1890's Gissing could be described as a well-known novelist, though his income remained small. He found satisfaction in being admitted to the company and sometimes the friendship of famous writers like Thomas Hardy, George Meredith, and H. G. Wells. Yet his own life continued to be wretched, and in order to make money he kept driving himself to write more books, and books of greater length, than he should have. In the last years of his life he did find some happiness with an intelligent Frenchwoman; but happiness that comes too late has a bitter taste, and at the end Gissing was still the nervous, insecure, and self-pitying man he had always been. He died in a village in the Pyrenees in 1903.

II

By the time Gissing published his first novel in 1880, he had come to regard himself as a radical in politics and an agnostic in religion. Young, fervent, energetic, and not yet corroded by the skeptical pessimism of his later years, he could write in a letter to his brother that the purpose of *Workers in the Dawn* was to launch

> a strong (possibly *too* plain spoken) attack upon certain features of our present religious and social life which to me appear

highly condemnable. . . . I attack the criminal negligence of governments which spend their time over matters of relatively no importance, to the neglect of the terrible social evils. . . . Herein I am a mouthpiece of the advanced Radical party. As regards religious matters, I plainly seek to show the nobility of a faith dispensing with all we are accustomed to call religion, and having for its only creed a belief in the possibility of intellectual and moral progress.

In another letter to his brother, Gissing wrote with greater intensity of feeling:

I mean to bring home to people the ghastly condition (material, moral and mental) of our poor classes, to show the hideous injustice of our whole system of society, to give light upon the plan for altering it, and, above all, to preach an enthusiasm for just and high *ideals* in an age of unmitigated egotism and "shop." I shall never write a book which does not keep all these ends in view.

These sentences both echo and anticipate—not least of all in the rashness of their concluding vow—a great many statements of idealism made by young writers upon discovering the world's injustice. The radicalism of Gissing's apprentice years led him for some months to attend working-men's clubs in London where after a time he began making public speeches; but the significance of this activity should not be exaggerated, for these clubs were still vague in outlook and loose in membership, hardly resembling the kind of disciplined party that would soon be created by European socialists. Gissing's socialism was a genuine and often generous enthusiasm; but it was neither well thought out nor deeply imagined as, for example, the socialism of William Morris and George Bernard Shaw would be.

For a year or two Gissing was also drawn to Positivism, the "scientific" sociology of Auguste Comte which proposed to chart the transformations of society in objective and measurable terms, and would also, wrote Gissing, "free us, by due attention to its laws, from the state of social anarchy into which we are at present plunged." This doctrine, in Gissing's understanding of it, was closely allied to the "religion of humanity" which flourished among English writers in the latter half of the nineteenth century and which attempted to transfer the emotions of worship from the traditional ends of institutional religion to the more immediate possibilities for humanizing the life of man.

Soon enough Gissing lost his interest in political movements and philosophies of progress. A major impulse of his character—the impulse to withdraw from the threatening arena of human relationships—blotted out those sentiments of fraternity to which he had been attracted in his youth. And a certain narrowness of spirit, often to be found among disenchanted former radicals, now marked his treatment of those "just and high *ideals*" he had once said would animate all his books. Writing to his brother about *Demos*, a novel published in 1886, he said, "it will be a rather savage attack on working-class aims and capacities." That, if not much else, it certainly was. Both his character and his experience disposed him toward a conservative aloofness: —intellectually, a rather facile version of Carlyle's elitist philosophy, but temperamentally, the far more authentic despair of a sensitive man who can neither yield himself to the awards and penalties of life nor keep himself safely at a distance from them. As early as the summer of 1883 this aloofness had hardened into a crotchety kind of self-justification:

> The world is for me a collection of phenomena, which are to be studied and reproduced artistically. In the midst of the most serious complications of life, I find myself suddenly possessed with a great calm, withdrawn as it were from the immediate interests of the moment. . . . In the midst of desperate misfortune I can pause to make a note for future use, and the afflictions of others are to be material for observation. This, I rather think, is at last the final stage of my development. . . .

Brutal and egotistical it would be called by most people. What has that to do with me, if it is a fact?

A great deal, one is tempted to reply. For while apparently similar to that state of detachment most writers occasionally yearn for, what Gissing was invoking here was far more than a strategy of creative observation; it was also a personal trouble, a plight that one of his biographers would call "despersonalization," the gradual removal of affect from the surrounding world. The result was damaging to both his life and work, not least of all because he could maintain this attitude only intermittently and at large psychic cost. When we think of the detached artist as a type, we are likely to imagine a man who has achieved a measure of serenity or at least self-composure; but these Gissing could seldom reach and never long preserve. His detachment, so very different in quality from true emotional poise, was much too willed, a token of fright and suppression.

When Gissing heard that William Morris had been arrested at a socialist meeting in Hyde Park, he wrote:

> Keep apart, keep apart, and preserve one's soul. . . . It is ill to have been born in these times, but one can make a world within a world.

These lines record an abandonment of earlier opinions and display a portion of his psychic malaise, but it is only fair to add that such views could be found among many European writers at the end of the nineteenth century, partly as a recoil from the harshness and vulgarity of industrial capitalism, partly as a reaction to the growth of social radicalism among the lower classes. Gissing's skepticism, to which he clung with the tenacity, even desperation, of a man who has nothing else; his pervasive and somewhat curdled pessimism; his belief that the age in which he lived ("thoroughly mean, empty, windbaggish") marked a decline in the vigor of English life; his conviction that democracy and science would lead to a new cultural barbarism; his fear that men like himself, devoted to an "aristocracy of brains" and a style of classicism, were becoming obsolete and could not hope to check the drift of modern history—these attitudes were widespread among the intellectual classes of the day, often coming to little more than the clichés of an alarmed snobbism, but in the work of the serious writers acquiring depth and conviction. In Gissing's own books such attitudes rarely sink to the level of journalism or rise to a commanding historical vision; they show themselves largely as turns of emotional bias, *problems of literary temperament,* which make for the peculiar quality of his work.

To say this means to modify the view advanced by some of Gissing's critics that he is primarily a novelist of ideas. His intellectual development should be familiar to anyone wishing to understand his novels; it matters, however, less in its own right than as a clue to the inflections of his tone as a novelist. Virginia Woolf is right in saying that "Gissing is one of the extremely rare novelists who believes in the power of mind—who makes people think. . . ." Gissing was certainly a thoughtful man who read widely, perhaps too widely, in the social and philosophical literature of his day; but he showed little distinction or originality as a thinker and his books seldom profit from being regarded as "novels of ideas." It is with the *experience* of people who care about ideas—the troubles, embarrassments, and desires of the intellectual classes—that Gissing is concerned. His single greatest power lies in depicting the life of educated and partly educated persons who are rootless and unhappy precisely to the extent that they have managed to lift themselves out of a lower-class environment and approach the precincts of cultivation. The psychically displaced person, the declassed solitary wedged between indifferent sectors of society, the ambitious plebeian intellectual who feels himself scorned and mocked and bears the burden of his estrangement either in humiliating silence or grudging complaint—this is a central figure in Gissing's world. (One of his later novels is called *Born in Exile,* and the phrase could stand as an epigraph to both his life and work.)

This alienated figure—he will soon be appearing everywhere in modern literature—provides the perspective from which the events in Gissing's novels are seen. Sometimes the identification between Gissing and his enfeebled heroes is open, and thereby cause for that whining tone which disfigures his lesser books; sometimes, as in *New Grub Street,* the relationship between Gissing and his protagonists is wary and sophisticated, so that he can dramatize their problems without succumbing to self-pity.

The perspective of alienation, which can enclose moods ranging from the desperate to the embarrassing, is also brought to bear upon a number of other themes in Gissing's work, most notably in his treatment of women. There is hardly a Gissing novel which does not have one or two sympathetic and penetrating analyses of feminine character, analyses which seem to be done not from the rough approximations of a masculine outsider but from a close and intimate knowledge. Gissing is not at all good with the kind of women he worships as pure, noble, and beyond his grubby reach; such women are usually fantasy figures, related more to his private troubles than to the books in which they appear. But he is extremely acute in the presentation of those "odd women" (as he calls them in one of his later novels) who try painfully to reconcile feminism with their feminine natures, a budding intellectuality with constricted social roles. Somber, intelligent, and often neurotic, these women come to the forefront of English life during the last years of the nineteenth century, and Gissing is one of the first novelists to notice and describe them. But he does more than describe them. He shows a subtle intuitive grasp of their condition, almost as if he could insinuate himself into their secret thoughts and sensations. Many of their problems, as it happens, are close to his own: "it was her misfortune," he writes about a character in *Demos,* "to have feelings too refined for the position in which fate had placed her."

The kind of man who responds to women from a stance of discomfort and embarrassment—be it Gissing himself or an *alter ego* in one of his novels—can be particularly keen in his perception, for something of his own psychic make-up, some element of overwrought involvement with feminine suffering, enables him to enter the imaginative life of women far more deeply than a more "masculine" writer could. The embarrassment of the man who feels himself habitually ill at ease is nothing to envy; yet for a novelist like Gissing it does provide a compensating group of insights. Malaise too can be an opening to sensibility.

Some such view of Gissing's special quality as a novelist may help us with a problem that has vexed his critics. What finally—what *really*—is his attitude toward the poor, those somber figures trooping through his novels like squadrons of misery?

The English critic V. S. Pritchett has remarked that

> Gissing . . . went through all the phases from social indignation on behalf of the poor, to pitying and despising; climbing out of one class only to find the one above shallow, and ending by agreeing that freedom for him must mean solitude. In essence, what he looked for in his favored characters was their solitude.

This is very well said, even if some amendment is necessary: Gissing did not so much change from one attitude to another as hold all of them simultaneously, with varying degrees of confusion and stress.

A less sympathetic account is offered by Frank Swinnerton in his book on Gissing:

> He lived among the poor and "studied" them; but he lived among them by reason of the most lamentable necessity, and he studied them without ever learning their spiritual language. He was always a stranger, homeless and miserable.

It is true that Gissing was "always a stranger." But he was a stranger not merely among the poor: he could not find a place of rest anywhere in English society. It is also true that he lived among the poor "by reason of the most lamentable necessity"—but is that not precisely the reason most slum-dwellers live among the poor?

Gissing lacked certain important kinds of feeling in regard to the poor, as he lacked such feeling in regard to humanity as a whole. He had very little sense of that communal joyousness which lights up the first half of D. H. Lawrence's *Sons and Lovers*. He knew almost nothing about the pride of craft which figures importantly in Arnold Bennett's novels about the Five Towns. He would not have shared the admiration for the spirit of solidarity which such recent writers as Richard Hoggart and Raymond Williams locate in the radical tradition of English working-class life. For most of his career Gissing saw the poor not as a force within society but as a scattering of victims. He had only a faint awareness of the English workers as a socially formed class with a style and morality of its own; the poor of London, as he knew them, were lost and often degraded souls for whom the struggle to survive ate up their vital energies; and in his more charitable moments he knew that circumstances had made them what they were, it was hardly their fault, even if he himself wished desperately to escape their presence. Like George Orwell, another English writer who came to the poor as a "stranger," he would not stoop to sentimentalism. He knew that poverty brutalizes, that it drains the human spirit in a slow and relentless way. Once he had passed beyond his early radicalism, Gissing's attitude toward the poor was perhaps deficient in high-mindedness: at times distastefully snobbish and other times pitifully frightened. But it does have the supreme virtue of candor, for Gissing exposed the whole of his confusion, his mixture of sympathy and disgust, his muted wish to share in the suffering of men and his overwhelming desire to escape it. Some of the poor have themselves been known to hold similar feelings.

The experience of poverty was so painful to him that he could not settle upon a steady idea concerning it. Poverty meant, for most of his life, an *inescapable* condition; it was—to use an overworked but here quite accurate term—a trauma haunting his imagination even after he had gained some material comfort. He once wrote that for Dickens poverty, though a major formative influence, had not lasted long enough "to corrupt the natural sweetness of his mind." The same, alas, could hardly be said about Gissing, as he himself knew only too well. Life never allowed him to strike a truce with it.

In *The Private Papers of Henry Ryecroft*, a book of musings written at the end of his career, Gissing remarked: "I am no friend of the people . . . they inspire me with distrust, with fear; as a visible multitude, they make me shrink aloof, and often move me to abhorrence. . . ." That was one side, and not a very attractive side. But there was also the Gissing who could say with equal urgency: "I have hungered in the streets; I have laid my head in the poorest shelter; I know what it is to feel the heart burn with wrath and envy of 'the privileged classes.'"

Gissing's view of poverty was finally close to that of the poor themselves: he hated it and would not assent to any softening of his hatred.

III

Alone among Gissing's books *New Grub Street* survives as a classic, a work of abiding value and power. Its historical interest is large, but the claim it makes upon our attention is primarily that of a work of art. Here, one feels, Gissing's deepest emotions are objectively rendered and transformed; here, those impulses to self-pity which mar a good many of his books are subdued to the discipline of ironic observation.

New Grub Street satisfies few of the standards which modern criticism brings to the study of fiction. It is cast within the heavy frame of the three-volume Victorian novel—all too often, with Gissing, the cause of padding, but now used to present a copious portrait of English literary life. The writing itself lacks that aggressive and flaunting brilliance we often associate with modern fiction. The techniques of modern novelists—foreshortening of plot to allow for dramatic concentration, placing biased and implicated observers close to the center of action in order to make for complexity of perspective, jumbling narrative sequences to involve the reader in a struggle for the meaning of events—these do not figure in Gissing's books. They are books that move along at an even, almost sluggish pace; he relies heavily upon long patches of dialogue; and the events are usually registered through an omniscient observer standing, or pretending to stand, at a considerable remove.

Gissing's treatment of character is also conventional. While there is a strong sense of reality behind his every page, he does not provide the burrowing psychological analysis we have come to expect from modern fiction. He allows the reader to infer the inner life of his characters from what can be seen and heard of them, or he provides brief summaries of his own. His characters are usually treated as if they were fixed and synthetic entities, even if open to changes of impulse and mood; the modern tendency to dissolve character into a stream of psychological notation is not yet at work in his novels. *New Grub Street* remains in structure a Victorian novel,[1] but the subject and informing vision are post-Victorian: the setting of his drama is the modern city, that jungle of loneliness and

---

[1] Gissing was aware of the changes being wrought by the major writers of his day. In 1885 he remarked: "Thackeray and Dickens wrote at enormous length, and with profusion of detail.... Far more artistic, I think, is the later method of merely suggesting; of dealing with episodes, instead of writing biographies.... In fact, it approximates to the dramatic mode of presentment." In his own work Gissing seldom approached this "more artistic" method, and it is open to question whether his work would have been improved if he had tried to.

strife. The book is not at all difficult, it is transparent, and to subject it to a "close reading" in the current academic fashion would be tiresome. What *New Grub Street* asks from the reader is not some feat of analysis, but a considered fullness of response, a readiness to assent to, even if not agree with, its vision of defeat.

The problem of human integrity, how it may thrive or be thwarted in a range of circumstances, recurs at every crucial moment in *New Grub Street*. Like many writers to come after him, Gissing focusses upon the literary life, particularly the efforts of serious artists like Edwin Reardon and Harold Biffen to do their work decently and earn their bread honestly in an atmosphere of cant, commercialism, and corruption. It is a subject with an abiding interest for us, even if some of the details have become dated; and as we read the book it becomes clear that we are being invited to regard the struggles of men like Biffen and Reardon as instances of a problem which assaults sensitive human beings throughout the modern world. One reason the book so fully conveys the impression of "solidity" is that Gissing knew the literary and journalistic worlds of his day with a mordant precision. He knew them not merely in the factual sense which enables him to define the exact shade of malice in Clement Fadge's book reviewing, or the peculiar talent (for it *is* a talent of sorts) Jasper Milvain shows, or the combination of literary enthusiast and grinding hack to which the pedantic Alfred Yule is reduced, or the preposterous success won by Whelpdale with his plan for a magazine in which no article will be longer than two inches.[2] More important than this factual accuracy is the sense we gain from the novel that the experience it presents has been earned, absorbed, stamped with the authority of pain.

[2] Are Gissing's details really so dated? Would he find many surprises, other than technological ones, if he were to visit Manhattan? For now Jasper Milvain is a television producer transforming the classics into "spectacles," and as for Whelpdale, there can be little doubt which magazines he works for.

Gissing is a master of place, weather, atmosphere. No English novelist except Dickens so fully captures the greyness of a London winter, the greyness of lives spent under its pall, the greyness of the people who wander its streets. When Gissing describes an afternoon in which Marian Yule forces herself to work in the foggy light of the British Museum; when Marian and Jasper Milvain walk home at night through the dreary streets; when Alfred Yule meets the starving eye doctor at a cheap restaurant; when Edwin Reardon makes his way half across London to visit his estranged wife—at such moments we encounter not merely the depressing aura of a late-nineteenth-century city, but also the visible effects of that city as a social institution, an agency of inhumane human relations. An air of tiredness and staleness hangs over the world of *New Grub Street*, as if everyone were working too hard, not eating well, living badly. Among English writers Gissing is the poet of fatigue.[3]

New Grub Street is a large novel, but not a shapeless or a sprawling one. Its somber impressiveness depends on a balance struck by Gissing between the needs of dramatic representation and those of thematic rigor. Everything is controlled by Gissing's personal vision of life, yet neither characters nor events are allowed to stiffen into mere illustrations of ideas. Gissing was subject to a temptation few nineteenth-century English novelists could resist: that of crowding his pages with an excess of figures and incidents which would simulate the bustle—but, unfortunately, also the chaos—of human existence. Only a genius like Dickens could manage this without crippling losses, and even he suffers frequently from a promiscu-

---

[3] He was aware of a literary kinship with the late-eighteenth-century poet George Crabbe. In a letter to his sister dated 1888 he writes: "I have been reading Crabbe. . . . His verse stories anticipate in a remarkable way our so-called 'realistic' fiction; they deal with very low life. . . . The description of locality is minute, in a way which only modern prose writers have made common; he delights in the dreary and depressing scenery of the Suffolk coast, in squalid streets, in poverty-stricken chambers. . . ."

ous display of material. Gissing, not at all a genius, organizes his novel on more severe principles. In *New Grub Street* we are aware of the presence of a mature mind shaping the contours of the plot but also allowing the characters a measure of autonomy and idiosyncratic existence.

Throughout *New Grub Street* persons and destinies are so balanced that one stands in tragic or ironic juxtaposition to the other, and all together embody the vision of human waste which is Gissing's dominant perception. Abstractly, these contrasts may seem obvious, but Gissing handles them with an objectivity and restraint that gives the novel its aura of profound moral seriousness.

A simple contrast is that between Whelpdale and Alfred Yule. Neither a fool nor a knave, Whelpdale has a glimmer of intellectual conscience, only he never allows it to interfere with his demands upon life, and his pliability of character enables him to slide into the comforts and vulgarities of modern journalism. Irascible in manner and awkward in person, Yule is the kind of man with a positive genius for making himself disliked, yet he is also a serious if not very gifted critic: he *cares* about literature, even if with the dryness of a pedant. But this is no mere black-and-white counterposition of venality and rectitude. Gissing sees deeply enough into the destructive side of literary life—indeed of the whole social arrangement—to make clear that Yule, for all his learning, is also a hack, a compiler of encyclopedia copy who has turned his daughter into a slavey. Character and conviction may seem to pit Whelpdale against Yule, but circumstance erects a troubling parallel between them.

A more deep-going contrast is that between Edwin Reardon and Jasper Milvain, the contrast between a man of slender but genuine talent, who values the idea of excellence even if he cannot quite attain it, and a man who regards himself as a commodity for sale on the market. This counterposition, too, is not a simple moralistic one. Reardon is weak, petulant, without those reserves of combativeness his vocation requires: something within his character moves steadily toward self-destruction. Milvain is facile and mediocre but hardly a villain, for his ambitions are those of the vast majority of ordinary men and his methods for attaining them no worse than the common run. Reardon allows his conscience to work upon him, Milvain works upon his conscience. Reardon exposes himself to the blows and pressures of the world, Milvain proclaims his opportunism as a gesture of apparent candor which enables him to be all the more cynical. Gissing would seem to be suggesting here an important and difficult observation: that once men have made a fundamental choice of vocation, traits of character matter a good deal less than we would like to suppose. One either drifts with the world or struggles against its current, floats as a Milvain or goes under as a Reardon. The problem of integrity is, of course, related to human character, but in Gissing's view, what character mainly does is to determine the fortitude and persistence with which a man keeps to a course already taken.

Reardon is obviously the figure in *New Grub Street* with whom Gissing is most intimately involved, and therefore the figure who presents for him the greatest risks. At very few points, however, does Gissing slacken his critical judgment of Reardon, and one may even say that to the extent that Gissing brings out the feebleness of Reardon's will, so does he manage to win a growing sympathy for his failure. This sympathy rests not on any illusion as to Reardon's power to endure or a concealed identification with his weakness; it is the response we make, at an appropriate distance, to Gissing's success in rendering him as a figure of need and vulnerability. And one reason Gissing brings this off is that beside Reardon he has placed the likeable and quixotic Harold Biffen. The two characters represent complementary aspects of Gissing's self-awareness, and the assignment of a pure-spirited idealism and humane stoicism to Biffen removes for Gissing the temptation to shower pity on Reardon. Gissing can now fall back upon Biffen for the demonstration of his cultural and moral positives, and as a result he need not rush, as otherwise he might, to Reardon's defense.

Such contrasts and balances of character help create the over-all "architecture" of the book. Its local vividness of portrayal, chapter by chapter, is due to something else: the remarkable, almost Hardyesque tolerance, a blend of accurate judgment and humane forbearance, Gissing shows toward his characters. It is the tolerance not of a writer who has compromised his standards or surrendered to a sleazy sort of worldliness, but of a writer with a profound reserve of experience behind him, which enables him to grasp how *difficult* it is for men simply to get by. Only novelists who know something about the enormity of social pain are likely to preserve a decent restraint in moral judgment. And because in this book Gissing commands both the knowledge and restraint, his treatment of character is admirably free and plastic.

Jasper Milvain, for example, is finally odious, yet he displays touches of consideration for those about him and we are ready to accept his claim that with a somewhat higher income he would be a reasonably decent man. (That is just the point: what he is prepared to do for the higher income.) Alfred Yule is an ill-tempered bully, yet there are moments when he reveals those discomforts of conscience we recognize as the mark, or brand, of the human.

Perhaps the most admirable examples of Gissing's capacity for plastic characterization are the two young women, Marian Yule and Amy Reardon. Endlessly touching in her eagerness for love ("Are you sorry I wear my hair short?" she asks Milvain, and this innocent question seems to plunge to the very heart of injustice), Marian is a figure repeatedly caught in the delicate motions of her feelings. Amy Reardon we are invited to dislike, and for very good reasons; yet she too is presented not as a female monster but as a woman of mixed qualities and motives. With somewhat better circumstances she would make Reardon a satisfactory wife; they are separated not primarily because of her wickedness or his weakness, but because they live by different assumptions of value. Good will cannot bridge these assumptions; money, it is painful to admit, might. Amy is to be judged, she is often detestable, yet she too is human—it takes considerable vanity or self-assurance not to see in oneself at least a trace of Amyism. When Reardon comes to Brighton to visit their dying child, her remorse, for the moment, is genuine. "Hers was the kind of penitence," writes Gissing in one of his caustic sentences, "which is forced by sheer circumstances on a nature which resents any form of humiliation; she could not abandon herself to unreserved grief for what she had done or omitted, and the sense of this defect made a great part of her affliction." Yes, for the moment her remorse is genuine; and it is precisely the kind that will soon enough lead her to the arms of Jasper Milvain.

One last word about Gissing's capacities as a novelist. Somewhat like Hardy, he commands in *New Grub Street* a notable gift for symbolic condensation through fragments of incident, bits and pieces of action, that seem to contain the meaning of the book in a few words or gestures. One thinks of the moment when Reardon has just been left by Amy: "he sat reading a torn portion of a newspaper, and became quite interested in the report of a commercial meeting in the City, a thing he would never have glanced at under ordinary circumstances." This is a sign of the novelist's true power: to notice so accurately the mechanical gestures of a man left numb by sorrow. Or there is the moment following Marian's protest of her father's abuse, when Yule replies with genuine dignity, except that, as Gissing finely remarks, "between the beginning and the end of his speech he softened into a sort of self-satisfied pathos." The last phrase tells us a very great deal about men like Yule. Or there is the moment, soon after Reardon's death, when Amy and Milvain meet in London and without saying anything explicit, merely by the hint of a smile, quite "understand" each other.

Such details are put to the service of the vision that works its way through the whole of the novel, concluding in the bitter ironies of the scene in which Amy and Milvain, no longer troubled by the memory of Reardon, bask and coo in their genteel success. It is a vision of disenchantment with the values of modern life and, more deeply, it asserts the power of that "injustice which triumphs so flagrantly in the destinies of men." This, to be sure, is far from all of the human story, just as Gissing is far from the only kind of novelist we should accept. But from the limits of what he saw, Gissing drew that power of rejection which makes *New Grub Street* a work approaching greatness. There was much in our existence he did not see; about suffering he was seldom wrong.

CÉLINE: THE SOD BENEATH THE SKIN

The underground man, both as literary figure and social type, first enters European awareness in the nineteenth century. As rebel against the previously secure Enlightenment, he rejects the claims of science, the ordered world-view of the rationalists, the optimism of the radicals. He speaks in the accents of romanticism, but a romanticism gone sour and turned in upon itself. He is tempted neither by knowledge, like Faust, nor glory, like Julien Sorel; he is beyond temptation of any sort. The idea of ambition he regards as a derangement of ego, and idealism as the most absurd of vanities. He hopes neither to reform nor to cure the world, only to escape from beneath its pressures. For he believes—it is the one thing he believes entirely—that the world is intent upon crushing him, and he takes a spiteful pleasure in delaying its victory. That in the end it will crush him, he never doubts.

A creature of the city, he has no fixed place among the social classes; he lives in holes and crevices, burrowing beneath the visible structure of society. Elusive and paranoid, he plays a great many parts yet continues to be recognizable as a type through his unwavering rejection of official humanity: the humanity of decorum, moderation and reasonableness. Even while tormenting himself with reflections upon his own insignificance, the underground man hates still more—hates more than his own hateful self—the world above ground.

He refuses definition, fixity, coherence. Meek and arrogant, dialectically resourceful and derisive of intellect, starved for love and scornful of those who offer it, he lives in a chaos of subterranean passions. Beneath each layer of his being there quivers another, in radical conflict with the first. He can move in quick succession from satanic pride to abject humility and then recognize, with mocking self-approval, that the humility is no more than a curtain for his pride. Nor need the sequel of exposure end there; it could go on forever. From a conviction of his inferiority he abases himself toward everyone: —toward everyone but the men of ordinary decent sentiments who seem to have escaped the abyss of suffering and are therefore regarded by him as objects of contempt. Yet to say this is also to notice his conviction of superiority, for at heart he is gratified by the stigmata of his plight and regards his pain as evidence of distinction. Gratified, he indulges in a vast self-pity; but this psychic quick-change artist can also be mercilessly ironic about that self-pity. Above all else, he is a master of parody.

The assumption that man is rational, so important to Western society, and the assumption that his character is definable, so important to Western literature, are both threatened when the underground man appears on the historical scene. His emergence signifies the end of the belief that the human being can be understood by means of a static psychology, and in accordance with the modernist spirit, he is seen not as a person with a unique ensemble of traits but as a history of experiences that often are impenetrable and gratuitous.

Brilliantly anticipated in Diderot's fiction, *Rameau's Nephew*, the underground man first appears full face in Dostoevsky's novels. Here he assumes his most exalted guise, as a whole man suffering the burdens of consciousness. In *Notes from the Underground* he scrutinizes his motives with a kind of phenomenological venom; and then, as if to silence the moralists of both Christianity and humanism who might urge upon him a therapeutic commitment to action, he enters a few relationships with other people, relationships that are commonplace yet utterly decisive in revealing the impossibility of escape from his poisoned self.

In the twentieth century the underground man comes into his own and, like a rise of pus, breaks through the wrinkled skin of tradition. Thus far, at least, it is his century. He appears everywhere in modern literature, though seldom with the intellectual resources and intensity of grandeur that Dostoevsky accorded him. In France, during the thirties, the half-forgotten writer Louis-Ferdinand Céline published several novels in which he expressed with exuberant completeness the underground man's revulsion from the modern world. And if the underground man as portrayed by Dostoevsky could be taken as the product of an overwrought imagination, now his historical reality is beyond dispute. Author, central character and chorus, he is running the whole show.

II

Louis-Ferdinand Céline was born in Paris in 1894. His life was shaped primarily by his sufferings in the first world war, during which he was severely wounded and had to undergo several operations on his skull. Throughout his remaining years he was tormented by migraines. "My own trouble's lack of sleep," he once wrote, "I should never have written a line if I'd been able to sleep." Working as a doctor in a poor neighborhood of Paris, Céline wrote and published in 1932 his first novel, *Journey to the End of the Night* (*Voyage Au Bout De La Nuit*), in which he picked up the story of his life at the close of adolescence and carried it through his middle years. The book was an immediate critical success, with figures as various as André Gide, Ramon Fernandez and Leon Trotsky saluting its irascible vitality.

Journey to the End of the Night is composed as a series of loosely-related episodes, a string of surrealist burlesques, fables of horror and manic extravaganzas, each following upon the other with energy and speed. While the sort of novel Céline wrote—a wandering first-person narrative, picaresque in structure and expressionist in manner—presupposes an intimate relationship between author and central character, he was describing less the actual events of his life than their hallucinatory echoes, the distended memories of sleepless nights. The material in these novels is frequently appalling, yet the voice of the narrator is not at all what we have come to expect in the contemporary literature of exposure and shock. It is not a voice of cultivated sensibility, nor of moral anguish, and only on occasion does it rise to an unqualified indignation. Céline writes in a tone of cheerful nausea, a tone largely beyond bitterness or protest, as if he had decided to leave behind the metaphysics of Dostoevsky and the emotions of romanticism. Especially important here is the comparison with Dostoevsky, for it suggests how radically the underground man has experienced a change of character. Dostoevsky's underground man trembles in fright and despair before the possibility of nihilism; Céline's no longer regards a valueless existence as anything but a fact of life to be taken for granted.

The prose of *Journey to the End of the Night* is drawn from Parisian argot, and even those with a command of literary French find it difficult. For just as the hero of his novels is utterly unheroic ("I wasn't very wise myself but I'd grown sensible enough to be definitely a coward forever"), so is the style of these novels the opposite of literary and academic conventions. Fierce, sputtering, brawling, sometimes on the verge of hysteria, it is an "anti-style," a deliberate nose-thumbing at classical decorum. "To resensitize the language," Céline has written, "so that it pulses more than it reasons—that was my goal." As a statement of intention this is far less original than he supposes, but in its very familiarity it fits perfectly with the general impulse of modern literature. Like most modern writers Céline does not hesitate to sacrifice composure to vividness, unity of effect to ferocity of expression. He neither cares about a fixed literary tradition nor worries about such tiresome souvenirs as formal tidiness. His aim is to burst out, to launch the diatribe of a Parisian who is at one and the same time a miserable sod and an outraged man. Psychological refinements, introspective turns of self-analysis, romantic agonies—Céline will have none of these. The underground man who moves through his novels is beyond the promethean gesture; he looks upon modern society as a blend of asylum and abbatoir; so it is, so it must be; and meanwhile, with a jovial toughness, he acts out the slogan of the declassed and disabused: *Je m'en fiche.*

The "I" of the novel is something of a louse, quite indifferent to the cautions of morality, yet a man who can lay claim to one virtue: he dislikes lying to himself. Not that he is infatuated with notions about the sacredness of truth. It is simply that in weighing his own feelings he wants an honest measure: he intends to be sincere with himself, even if with no one else. In one of his infrequent moments of contemplativeness, he tells himself:

> The greatest defeat, in anything, is to forget, and above all to forget what it is that has smashed you, and to let yourself be smashed without ever realizing how thoroughly devilish men can be. When our time is up, we people mustn't bear malice, but neither must we forget . . .

Sincerity is one of the few values to which Céline is genuinely—one almost says, sincerely—attached. Not by chance, it is also a dominant motif in modern literature, a token of that "psychology of exposure" through which the nineteenth century unmasked itself and the twentieth shivers in self-contempt. The triumph of literary modernism is signalled by a turn from truth to sincerity, from the search for objective law to a desire for personal response. The first involves an effort to apprehend the nature of the universe, and can lead to metaphysics, suicide, revolution and God; the second involves an effort to discover our demons within, and makes no claim upon the world other than the right to publicize the aggressions of candor. Sincerity becomes the last-ditch defense for men without belief, and in its name absolutes can be toppled, morality dispersed and intellectual systems dissolved. Sincerity of feeling and exact faithfulness of language—which now means a language of fragments, violence and exasperation—becomes the ruling passion of Céline's narrator. In the terrible freedom it allows him, sincerity is a bomb shattering the hypocricies of the Third Republic; in the lawlessness of its abandonment, a force of darkness and anti-intelligence.

The dominant motif of the book is undirected flight. From its opening pages, in which the narrator casually volunteers for the army (why not?), he is constantly running from the terrors and apparitions of his world. Céline, or as he now calls himself in the novel, Bardamu, is trapped in the first world war and unable to think about it; he refuses to take it seriously, even to the point of opposition. The pages describing the war-time experiences of Bardamu, in their reduction of official glory to nihilist farce, are among the most scathing ever composed on this theme. Bardamu prepares to go off to war; Poincaré president of the Republic, prepares "to open a show of lapdogs;" *Vive la France!* Bardamu learns, soon enough, that bullets whistle and he must run. For a while he serves as runner to a senile, delicate and rose-loving general, and his reward—Bardamu's, not the general's—is that his feet smell. Running for the general, Bardamu comes to a major decision: if he is to survive he will have to stop running for generals and begin running from them. Heroism is for Sundays; meanwhile the Bardamus must exploit the resources of their cowardice.

And so he runs: from the army to the rear; from one hospital to another; from France to a fantastic trading post in a rotting African jungle; from the African jungle to the industrial jungle of America, first as a bum and then as a worker on the Detroit assembly lines; from America back to France, where, still running up and down stairs to earn a few francs, he becomes an indigent doctor. The one peaceful spot he finds is a post in an insane asylum. For ". . . when people are well, there is no way of getting away from it, they're rather frightening . . . When they can stand up, they're thinking of killing you. Whereas when they're ill, there's no doubt about it, they're less dangerous."

Throughout the book Bardamu keeps looking for a strange character named Robinson, his down-at-the-heels and laconic double. Go to the edge of hopelessness and there you will find Robinson: in the front lines, where he proposes a scheme for desertion; in Africa, where he is getting ready to run off with the company's funds; in Detroit, where he provides tips on brothels. Repeated through the book as a mock-ritual, these meetings between underground man and shameless alter-ego lead to nothing, for here all quests are futile, even one so modest as Bardamu's for Robinson. When Robinson dies there is nothing more to look for, and the concluding words of the book, a virtual manifesto of disgust, are: "Let's hear no more of all of this."

Images of death streak the novel. The African episode is a journey to the death of archaic tribalism, the American a journey to the death of industrial civilization. Backward or forward, it's all the same, "a great heap of worm-eaten sods like me, bleary, shivering and lousy." Céline is obsessed not merely with the inexorability of death but even more with the vision of putrefaction: ". . . three feet below ground I . . . will be streaming with maggots, stinking more horribly than a heap of bank-holiday dung, all my disillusioned flesh absurdly rotting."

The algebra of our century: flight from death equals flight to death. But is there in this wild and rasping novel perhaps something more, perhaps a flicker of positive vision? Doesn't the enormity of Céline's hatred indicate some hidden yearning for the good which he himself can hardly express? In principle it is hard to deny such a possibility. Céline too has his humanities, and can be lavish with bottom-dog compassion; some yearning for the good, one might suppose, is indispensible if he is to summon the energy needed for so vindictive an outburst against "man's viciousness." But the particular truth about this novel is less ennobling, less assuaging. As a force within the book, this presumptive yearning for good is hard to discover, perhaps because it is buried beneath the debris of disillusion. Beneath that debris there may well be a misshapen core of moral sentiment, but it can seldom compete for attention with Céline's rich provisioning of symptoms of disorder and sensations of disgust.

III

In *Death on the Installment Plan* (*Mort à Crédit*) Céline returned to his childhood and adolescence in order to complete the record of his experience. An even grizzlier testimony than *Journey to the End of the Night,* Céline's second novel is written in a fitful and exuberant prose, and its tone is one of joyous loathing at having to turn back in memory to the miasma of youth. The misanthropy of the earlier novel ripens into outright paranoia: but with such bubbling energy, such a bilious and sizzling rhetoric, such a manic insistence upon dredging up the last recollection of filth! *Death on the Installment Plan* is a prolonged recital of cheating, venality and betrayal: the child as victim of the world. Still a boy, he learns to hate the whole social order: "It made me choke to think of it . . . of all the treachery of things! . . . all the swinishness! . . . the whole collection of ordures! Yes, God Almighty, I'd had my bellyful."

Two linked motifs control the book: the richest account of retching in modern literature and a profound yearning for solitude. Both are sequels to the running motif in *Journey to the End of the Night:* one runs from the filth and hopes to find a corner of quiet and a bit of peace. When Céline describes retching, he is an absolute virtuoso: "She brings up the lot . . . right into the wind . . . and I get it full in my face, the whole stinking stew that's been gurgling in her throat . . . I, who haven't so much as a crumb to bring up! Ah, now, yes, I find I have, after all . . . my stomach gives one more turn . . ." Vomit links with Céline's fruitless effort to disgorge the whole of his experience, as he runs through the darkness of the night. If only he could start afresh, with nothing on his stomach, and be rid of the rubbish of the past . . . but it cannot be done, there is always one more crumb of recollection.

The yearning for solitude is poignantly developed in *Death on the Installment Plan*. All a paranoid ever wants is "to be let alone," a wish that to be satisfied on his terms would require nothing less than a reconstruction of the universe. In one section of the novel, a set-piece displaying Céline's gifts at their best, he describes a stay in an English country-school, where he finds a happiness of sorts through taking long walks with a little idiot boy and an unobtrusive woman teacher, neither of whom troubles him by attempts at conversation. With the dumb and gentle he finds a paradise of muteness; here defenses can be lowered and nerves unravelled. And in this solitude it is also possible to enjoy the modest pleasures of masturbation. The adolescent hero of *Death on the Installment Plan* masturbates systematically, not with the excited curiosity of a youth but with the tameness of an old man. Pleasure can come only from himself, and only when alone with himself. And who knows, perhaps for the underground man as secret sharer of his potency, this is a kind of good faith, an act of sincerity.

IV

There are writers in whose work a literary theme can barely be kept apart from a personal obsession, and psychological illness, through some perverse dynamic, becomes the source of a boundless creative energy. Céline is one of these.

The Nose and the Mound. Céline depicts a severed universe: on one side, he himself, the big nose, and on the other, the world at large, an enormous mound of *merde*. Maestro of bad smells, Céline learns that his nose is the one organ he can trust implicitly: it is the organ that remains sincere, and by it one can know women, cities, nations, destinies. "It's by smells that people, places and things come to their end. A whiff up one's nostrils is all that remains of past experience." His journey to America is a prolonged exploit in olefactory revulsion, climaxed by a visit to an underground urinal in New York, where he is simply awe-stricken—Cortez before the Pacific! —by "its joyous communion of filth."

Forever exposing himself to the multiplicity of *merde*, Céline reacts not merely to the hideousness of our social arrangements but even more, to the very conditions of existence itself, which dictate the stupidity of death, intolerable enough, and the prolonged stench of dying, still more intolerable. In *Journey to the End of the Night* he declares himself "appalled by my realization of biological ignominy," the last two words of this clause breaking forth as the very source of Céline's inspiration. He flinches before the sensual attributes of the least offensive body, and every time he sees a man engaging in the physiological functions he seethes with rage. Lusting after Lola, the sweet American nurse with piquant buttocks, he shudders in his lust: worms will reign over that flesh too. Had Céline lived in the early Christian era, he would have found himself a Manichean sect and spat upon sensual appetite as the taste of the devil. Being a twentieth century Parisian, he submits to the most humiliating debaucheries precisely from his fury at being unable to avoid decay. Sartre and Camus may be students in the metaphysic of nausea, but what, by comparison with Céline, do they know about its actual qualities? In the art of nausea they are mere theoretic specialists, while Céline is an empiric master.

Perhaps we can now understand somewhat better the running motif of *Journey to the End of the Night*. Céline is running not merely from society but from the sight of every living creature, and running, he trips over the knowledge that it is from himself he would flee, the self that is alone inescapable. In *Death on the Installment Plan* he often befouls himself as a child, an act which at first seems the physical equivalent of his readiness to abandon self-respect as a luxury too dangerous for this world, but which after a time comes also to signify a recognition that even he is hopelessly implicated in the physicality against which he rages. One thinks of Swift, whose balked sense of purity melts into a fascination with filth, but there is a notable difference: Swift's writings almost always chart a descent from idea to matter, there is a wracking struggle of opposed life-principles, while in Céline rot is sovereign and flesh serves as argument for a gargantuan cosmic deception.

The Cheat of Language. Where finally can the compulsion to sincerity, to the last shameless self-revelation, lead but to silence? Céline writes: "I grow foul as soon as anyone talks to me; I hate it when they prattle." Or again: "The very idea made me howl with terror. Having to talk again—oh, Gawd." Anything beyond the reach of the nose is to be distrusted; all talk about human life is mere drivel unless it begins and ends with the breviary: "I am ... thou art ... all of us are despoilers, cheats, slobs." But once that has been said and said again and again, once Céline has spent the virtuosity of his rhetoric upon the denunciation of language, what then remains?

Comedy and Nausea. Cut away from its context in the novels, Céline's outlook upon life is narrow-spirited and tiresome. What saves him as a writer is that he so enjoys roaring his invective from the sewers, he makes his nausea into something deeply comic. In *Journey to the End of the Night*, talking about the war, he solemnly observes that "horses are lucky. They go through the war, like us, but they're not asked to . . . seem to believe in it. In this business they are unfortunate but free." During his visit to Africa, after suffering the afflictions of the jungle, he remarks that he is especially misfortunate because, as it happens, he "does not like the country." In *Death on the Installment Plan* his boss, a bogus scientist, launches a typical Célinesque diatribe after having failed in a piece of chicanery: "I'll get them right this time . . . Their bellies, Ferdinand! Not their heads, but their bellies. Their digestions shall be my customers . . . I'm through with the spirit for keeps! We're onto the bowels now, Ferdinand, the grand alimentary canal."

It is this perspective of comic nausea that accounts for the vividness of Céline's novels. His hatred and fear of abstraction lead him to stake everything on the specific incident. With noisy verbs and cascades of adjectives, he assaults nose, ear, eye, creating a carnival of sensations. But precisely this vividness soon reveals Céline's limitation as a writer, for it tends to be monolithic and exhausting. Strictly speaking, Céline is not a satirist in the sense that Swift was, despite the remarkable energy of disgust the two writers share; Céline is neither intelligent nor discriminating enough to be a true satirist. His metier is a kind of savage burlesque. The nausea that makes him recoil from experience is linked to the comedy that makes him relish the experience of recoil—beyond that he cannot go.

Philistine and Genius. Halfway, both of Céline's novels begin to lag, for they are really more like a vaudeville, a grab-bag of skits, than coherently developed fictions. In terms of sheer *performance* they contain pages rivalling Dickens, yet once the climax of a skit is known there is seldom much point in waiting either for its conclusion or repetition. By its very nature, the skit cannot be sustained over a long period of time: it is essentially a virtuoso device and virtuosity holds one's attention largely through initial shock or brilliance. This is a technical difficulty, but as always, the technical difficulty reflects a deeper problem in literary intelligence. The opening of a Céline novel is so seductively vigorous in manner and conclusive in meaning that little remains for further development. A mere accumulation of misfortunes, even when rendered with comic genius, becomes enervating unless the misfortunes are controlled by some principle of selection, some idea of greater scope than the probability of further misfortune.

One comes at times to suspect that Céline writes from a total emptiness, that his show of energy hides a void, that he is really without any genuine attitude or values. At such points his novels seem like charades in which the gestures of life are enacted but the content has been lost. Driven by his simplistic ethics and his raging indiscriminateness of feeling to always greater assertions of cynicism, he falls, predictably, into the opposite error of sentimentalism. When he falls in love, it is with an embarrassing callowness. Let a Detroit prostitute show him an ounce of kindness or an inch of thigh, and he moons like a schoolboy.

The ultimate limitation in Céline's work is a limitation of intelligence. He does not know what to do with his outpourings, except to multiply them; he cannot surmount his brilliant monomania. He is unable to distinguish among the kinds and degrees of loathesomeness, between a speck of dust and a mound of filth. Irritation and outrage, triviality and betrayal grate on his nerves almost equally. Except on grounds of radical incompleteness, it would be difficult to quarrel with Céline's description of twentieth century experience; but there is something exasperating, at times even stupid, about a writer who roars with the same passion against nuisance and disaster. So overwhelmed is he by his demon of dirt, so infatuated with the invective he sends hurtling through his pages, he seems unable to think—and in the kind of novels he wrote, thought can be postponed but not dismissed. For all his authentic sense of affliction and all his gift for comedy, Céline remains something of a philistine, a philistine blessed with genius but a philistine nonetheless.

V

Shortly after the appearance of *Journey to the End of the Night* there appeared a striking critical essay by Leon Trotsky praising the novel—"Céline walked into great literature as other men walk into their own homes"—and predicting that Céline "will not write a second book with such an aversion for the lie and such a disbelief in the truth. The dissonance must resolve itself. Either the artist will make his peace with the darkness or he will perceive the dawn."

Trotsky's timing was a little off, and what he meant by "the dawn" need not concern us here. Céline did manage to write a second novel with the same attitudes as those in *Journey to the End of the Night*, but essentially the prediction of Trotsky was correct. In 1936 Céline, by now a famous writer, took a trip to Russia and shortly thereafter wrote a little book called *Mea Culpa* in which, together with some shrewd observations about the Stalin dictatorship, he indulged himself in a wild harangue against the inherent bestiality of mankind. Apart from the humor and inventiveness of his novels, Céline's reflections served only to reveal the radical limitations of the kind of modern novelist who presents his intellectual incapacity as a principled anti-intellectualism.

There now begins a visible disintegration of Céline as both writer and person. In 1938 he published a book entitled *Trifles for a Massacre* (*Bagatelles pour un Massacre*), a dreary tract in which he blamed the Jews for everything from the defeat of Napoleon to the rise of surrealism, the corruption of the French language and the Sino-Japanese war. André

Gide, reviewing the book, took it to be a satire on the assumption that it was impossible that a writer of Céline's gifts could mean what he said; but now it seems obvious that Céline did in fact mean what he said.

During the second world war Céline played a dishonorable role, living at peace with the Nazi occupation forces and expressing admiration for the Vichy collaborators. (See the preface to *Guignol's Band*, a late fiction that has almost no literary value but some pathological interest.) After the war the French government accused Céline of having been a collaborator and he, self-exiled to Denmark, offered the sad reply that he had merely been an "abstentionist." Tried by the French authorities *in absentia*, he was convicted, sentenced, but not required to serve his time in prison. During the last decade of his life—he died in 1961—Céline was allowed to return to France, where he lived in semi-retirement, a lonely and embittered man. Young readers in the late fifties and early sixties who have come to admire Beckett, Genet and Burroughs seem hardly to know that behind these writers, both as predecessor and possible influence, stands the disheveled but formidable figure of Louis-Ferdinand Céline.

His career, like that of Ezra Pound, is a classical instance of how a writer suffers in his purely literary work when his powers of mind are unequal to his powers of imagination. From the depths of the underground man's soul Céline brought forth all its effluvia, so that the world could see what was simmering there. His two novels, in all their brilliant imperfection, seem likely to survive the sickness of their inspiration. But at the end, unable to transcend the foulness which was his authentic and entirely legitimate subject, he made "his peace with the darkness." And not he alone.

SHOLOM ALEICHEM: VOICE OF OUR PAST

Fifty or sixty years ago the Jewish intelligentsia, its head buzzing with Zionist, Socialist and Yiddishist ideas, tended to look down upon Sholom Aleichem. His genius was acknowledged, but his importance skimped. To the intellectual Jewish youth in both Warsaw and New York he seemed old-fashioned, lacking in complexity and rebelliousness—it is even said that he showed no appreciation of existentialism. Sh. Niger, the distinguished Yiddish critic, tried to explain this condescension by saying that laughter, the characteristic effect of Sholom Aleichem's stories, is for children and old people, not the young. Perhaps so; the young are notoriously solemn. But my own explanation would be that the Jewish intellectuals simply did not know what to make of Sholom Aleichem: they did not know how to respond to his moral poise and his invulnerability to ideological fashions.

With the passage of the years embarrassment has been replaced by indifference. Soon we shall be needing an historical expedition, armed with footnotes, to salvage his work. Even today we cannot be quite certain that our affection for him rests upon a strict regard for the words he put on the page, rather than a parochial nostalgia.

It has been customary to say that Sholom Aleichem speaks

for a whole people, but saying this we might remember that his people have not spoken very well for him. The conventional estimate—that Sholom Aleichem was a folksy humorist, a sort of jolly gleeman of the *shtetl*—is radically false. He needs to be rescued from his reputation, from the quavering sentimentality which keeps him at a safe distance.

When we say that Sholom Aleichem speaks for a whole culture, we can mean that in his work he represents all the significant levels of behavior and class in the *shtetl* world, thereby encompassing the style of life of the east European Jews in the nineteenth century. In that sense, however, it may be doubted that he does speak for the whole *shtetl* culture. For he does not command the range of a Balzac or even a Faulkner, and he does not present himself as the kind of writer who is primarily concerned with social representation. The ambition, or disease, of literary "scope" leaves him untouched.

Nor can we mean, in saying that Sholom Aleichem speaks for a whole culture, that he advances the conscious program of that culture. Toward the dominant Jewish ideologies of his time Sholom Aleichem showed a characteristic mixture of sympathy and skepticism, and precisely this modesty enabled him to achieve a deeper relation to the *folksmassen* than any Jewish political leader. He never set himself up as cultural spokesman or institution, in the style of Thomas Mann at his worst; he had no interest in boring people.

Sholom Aleichem speaks for the culture of the east European Jews because he embodies—not represents—its essential values in the very accents and rhythm of his speech, in the inflections of his voice and the gestures of his hands, in the pauses and suggestions between the words even more than the words themselves. To say that a writer represents a culture is to imply that a certain distance exists between the two. But that is not at all the relationship between Sholom Aleichem and the culture of the east European Jews: it is something much more intimate and elusive, something for which, having so little experience of it, we can barely find a name. In Sholom Aleichem everything that is deepest in the ethos of the east European Jews is brought to fulfillment and climax. He is, I think, the only modern writer who may truly be said to be a culture-hero, a writer whose work releases those assumptions of his people, those tacit gestures of bias, which undercut opinion and go deeper into communal life than values.

II

In his humorous yet often profoundly sad stories, Sholom Aleichem gave to the Jews what they instinctively felt was the right and true judgment of their experience: a judgment of love through the medium of irony. Sholom Aleichem is the great poet of Jewish humanism and Jewish transcendence over the pomp of the world. For the Jews of Eastern Europe he was protector and advocate; he celebrated their communal tradition; he defended their style of life and constantly underlined their passionate urge to dignity. But he was their judge as well: he ridiculed their pretensions, he mocked their vanity, and he constantly reiterated the central dilemma, that simultaneous tragedy and joke, of their existence—the irony of their claim to being a Chosen People, indeed, the irony of their existence at all.

Sholom Aleichem's Yiddish is one of the most extraordinary verbal achievements of modern literature, as important in its way as T. S. Eliot's revolution in the language of English verse or Berthold Brecht's infusion of street language into the German lyric. Sholom Aleichem uses a sparse and highly controlled vocabulary; his medium is so drenched with irony that the material which comes through it is often twisted and elevated into direct tragic statement—irony multiples upon itself to become a deep winding sadness. Many of his stories are monologues, still close to the oral folk tradition, full of verbal by-play, slow in pace, winding in direction, but always immediate and warm in tone. His imagery is based on an absolute mastery of the emotional rhythm of Jewish life; describing the sadness of a wheezing old clock, he writes that it was "a sadness like that in the song of an old, worn-out cantor toward the end of Yom Kippur"—and how sad that is only someone who has heard such a cantor and therefore knows the exquisite rightness of the image can really say.

The world of Sholom Aleichem is bounded by three major characters, each of whom has risen to the level of Jewish archetype: Tevye the Dairyman; Menachem Mendel the *luftmensch*; and Mottel the cantor's son, who represents the loving, spontaneous possibilities of Jewish childhood. Tevye remains rooted in his little town, delights in displaying his uncertain Biblical learning, and stays close to the sources of Jewish survival. Solid, slightly sardonic, fundamentally innocent, Tevye is the folk voice quarreling with itself, criticizing God from an abundance of love, and realizing in its own low-keyed way all that we mean, or should mean, by humaneness.

Tevye represents the generation of Jews that could no longer find complete deliverance in the traditional God yet could not conceive of abandoning Him. No choice remained, therefore, but to celebrate the earthly condition: poverty and hope. For if you had become skeptical of deliverance from above and had never accepted the heresy of deliverance from below, what could you do with poverty but celebrate it? "In Kasrilevke," says Tevye, "there are experienced authorities on the subject of hunger, one might say specialists. On the darkest night, simply by hearing your voice, they can tell if you are hungry and would like a bite to eat, or if you are really starving." Tevye, like the people for whom he speaks, is constantly assaulted by outer forces. The world comes to him, most insidiously, in the form of undesired sons-in-law: one who is poverty-stricken but romantic; another who is a revolutionist and ends in Siberia; a third—could anything be worse?—who is a gentile; and a fourth—this *is* worse—who is a Jew but rich, coarse, and unlearned.

Menachem Mendel, Tevye's opposite, personifies the element of restlessness and soaring, of speculation and fancy-free idealization, in Jewish character. He has a great many occupations: broker, insurance agent, matchmaker, coal dealer, and finally—it is inevitable—writer; but his fundamental principle in life is to keep moving. The love and longing he directs toward his unfound millions are the love and longing that later Jews direct toward programs and ideologies. He is the utopian principle of Jewish life; he is driven by the modern demon. Through Tevye and Menachem Mendel, flanked by little Mottel, Sholom Aleichem creates his vision of the Yiddish world.

There is a strong element of fantasy, even surrealism, in Sholom Aleichem. Strange things happen: a tailor becomes enchanted, a clock strikes thirteen, money disappears in the synagogue during Yom Kippur, a woman's corpse is dragged across the snow, a timid little Jew looks at himself in the mirror and sees the face of a Czarist officer. Life is precarious, uncertain, fearful, yet always bound by a sense of community and affection.

III

Sholom Aleichem came at a major turning point in the history of the east European Jews: between the unquestioned dominance of religious belief and the appearance of modern ideologies, between the past of traditional Judaism and the future of Jewish politics, between a totally integrated culture and a culture that by a leap of history would soon plunge into the midst of modern division and chaos. Yet it was the mark of Sholom Aleichem's greatness that, coming as he did at this point of transition, he betrayed no moral imbalance or uncertainty of tone. He remained unmoved by the fanaticisms of his time, those that were Jewish and those that were not; he lost himself neither to the delusions of the past nor the delusions of the future. His work is the fulfillment—pure, relaxed, humane—of that moment in the history of the Jews in which a people lives securely with itself, untroubled by any dualism, hardly aware of a distinction, between the sacred and secular.

The world he presented was constantly precarious and fearful, yet the vision from which it was seen remained a vision of absolute assurance. It was a vision controlled by that sense of Jewish humaneness which held the best of—even as it transcended—both the concern with the other world that had marked the past and the eagerness to transform this world that would mark the future. His work abounds in troubles, but only rarely does it betray anxiety.

In reading Sholom Aleichem one seldom thinks to wonder about his opinions. He stands between the age of faith and the age of ideology, but I doubt that there has ever been a reader naive enough to ask whether Sholom Aleichem *really* believed in God. For him it was not a living question, no more than it was for the people who read him. To say that he believed in God may be true, but it is also irrelevant. To say that he did not believe in God is probably false, but equally irrelevant.

What Sholom Aleichem believed in was the Jews who lived with him and about him, most of them Jews still believing in God. Or perhaps he believed in those Jews who lived so completely in the orbit of their fathers—fathers who had surely believed in God—that there was no need for them to ask such questions.

In Sholom Aleichem's stories God is there, not because He is God, not because there is any recognition or denial of His heavenly status, but simply because He figures as an actor in the life of the Jews. God becomes absorbed into the vital existence of the people, or to put it more drastically: God is there because Tevye is there.

But Tevye, does *he* believe in God? Another hopeless

question. Tevye believes in something more important than believing in God; he believes in talking to God. And Tevye talks to God as to an old friend whom one need not flatter or assuage: Tevye, as we say in American slang, gives Him an earful.

Tevye, we may assume, makes God extremely uncomfortable—though also a little proud at the thought that, amid the countless failures of His world, He should at least have created a Tevye who can make him so sublimely uncomfortable. And how does Tevye do this? By telling God the complete truth. It is not a pretty truth, and if God would care to dispute anything Tevye has told him, Tevye is entirely prepared to discuss it with Him further. But whatever other mistakes He may have made, God is too clever to get into an argument with Tevye. God knows that Tevye does not fear Him: a Jew is afraid of people, not of God. So perhaps you can see how absurd it is to ask whether Sholom Aleichem *really* believed in God: —Sholom Aleichem who created a character to serve as the conscience of God.

All this comes through in Sholom Aleichem's stories as a blend of rapture and the absurd, sublimity and household ordinariness. Nor is it confined to Sholom Aleichem alone. In the poems of Jacob Glatstein, one of the great living Yiddish writers, there is a whole series of loving and estranged monologues to God. Glatstein writes: "I love my sorrowful God/ My companion . . . I love to sit with Him upon a stone/ And to pour out all my words . . . And there He sits with me, my friend, my companion, clasping me/ And shares His last bite of food with me.". Later, in the same poem, Glatstein adds: "The God of my unbelief is magnificent . . . My God sleeps and I watch over him/ My weary brother dreams the dream of my people."

Had Tevye lived through the events of the past thirty years, that is how he would have felt.

IV

Sholom Aleichem believed in Jews as they embodied the virtues of powerlessness and the healing resources of poverty, as they stood firm against the outrage of history, indeed, against the very idea of history itself. Whoever is unable to conceive of such an outlook as at least an extreme possibility, whoever cannot imagine the power of a messianism turned away from the apocalyptic future and inward toward a living people, cannot understand Sholom Aleichem or the moment in Jewish experience from which he stems.

It is here that the alien reader may go astray. He may fail to see that for someone like Tevye everything pertaining to Jewishness can be a curse and an affliction, a wretched joke, a source of mockery and despair, but that being a Jew is nevertheless something to be treasured. Treasured, because in the world of Tevye there was a true matrix of human sociability.

The stories Sholom Aleichem told his readers were often stories they already knew, but then, as the Hasidic saying goes, they cared not for the words but the melody. What Sholom Aleichem did was to give back to them the very essence of their life and hope, in a language of exaltation: the exaltation of the ordinary.

When Tevye talked to his horse, it was the same as if he were talking to his wife. When he talked to his wife, it was the same as if he were talking to God. And when he talked to God, it was the same as if he were talking to his horse. That, for Tevye, was what it meant to be a Jew.

Kierkegaard would never have understood it.

V

Between Sholom Aleichem and his readers there formed a community of outcasts: *edele kaptzunim*. Millions of words flowed back and forth, from writer to reader and reader to writer, for no people has ever talked so much in all recorded history; yet their companionship did not rest upon or even require words.

The last thing I wish to suggest here is an image of the sweetly pious or sentimental. Sholom Aleichem did not hesitate to thrust his barbs at his readers, and they were generous at reciprocating. Having love, they had no need for politeness. But the love of which I speak here is sharply different from that mindless ooze, that collapse of will, which the word suggests to Americans. It could be argumentative, fierce, bitter, violent; it could be ill-tempered and even vulgar; only one thing it could not be: lukewarm.

The Jews never fooled Sholom Aleichem. Peretz, I think, was sometimes deceived by the culture of the east European Jews, and Sholem Asch tried to deceive it at the end of his career. But with Sholom Aleichem, even as he was the defender of the Jews and their culture, there was always a sly wrinkle near his eyes which as soon as Jews saw it, they said to themselves: *Im ken men nisht upnaren,* him you cannot deceive. That is why, when you go through his stories, you find so little idealization, so little of that cozy self-indulgence and special pleading which is the curse of Jewish life. Between Sholom Aleichem and his readers there is a bond of that wary respect which grows up among clever men who recognize each other's cleverness, enjoy it and are content.

Middleton Murry once said of Thomas Hardy that "the contagion of the world's slow stain has not touched him." This magnificent remark must have referred to something far more complex and valuable than innocence, for no one could take Hardy to be merely innocent; it must have referred to the artist's final power, the power to see the world as it is, to love it and yet not succumb to it; and that is the power one finds in Sholom Aleichem.

THE FICTION OF ANTI-UTOPIA

"I feel sometimes as though the whole modern world of capitalism and Communism and all were rushing toward some enormous efficient machine-made doom of the true values of life."

This sentence was written in 1922 by Max Eastman, then a prominent intellectual defender of the Russian Revolution. It contains the crux of what would later fill volumes of disenchantment; and the need to speak it constitutes one reason why the intellectual experience of our time has been so full of self-distrust and self-assault. For some decades there had already been present a tradition in which conservative thinkers assaulted the idea of utopia as an impious denial of the limitations of the human lot, or a symptom of political naïveté, or a fantasy both trivial and boring—this last view finding a curious echo in Wallace Stevens' dismissal of the utopia called heaven: "does ripe fruit never fall?" But the kind of fiction I have in mind and propose to call anti-utopian does not stem from the conservative tradition, even when wryly borrowing from it.

Eastman's sentence would not seem remarkable if spoken by G. K. Chesterton or Hilaire Belloc; its continuing power to shock depends upon our knowledge that it came from a man of the left. And anti-utopian fiction, as it seeks to embody the sentiments expressed by Eastman, also comes primarily from men of the left. Eugene Zamiatin (*We*) is a dissident from Communism; George Orwell (*1984*) a heterodox socialist; Aldous Huxley (*Brave New World*) a scion of liberalism. The peculiar intensity of such fiction derives from the writer's discovery that in facing the prospect of a future he had been trained to desire, he finds himself struck with horror. The work of these writers is a systematic release of trauma, a painful turning upon their own presuppositions. It is a fiction of urgent yet reluctant testimony, forced by profoundly serious men from their own resistance to fears they cannot evade.

What they fear is not, as liberals and radicals always have, that history will suffer a miscarriage; what they fear is that the long-awaited birth will prove to be a monster. Not many Americans are able to grasp this experience: few of us having ever cultivated the taste for utopia, fewer still have suffered the bitter aftertaste of anti-utopia. For Europeans, however, it all comes with the ferocity of shock. Behind the anti-utopian novel lies not merely the frightful vision of a totalitarian world, but something that seems still more alarming. To minds raised on the assumptions, whether liberal or Marxist, of 19th-Century philosophies of history—assumptions that the human enterprise has a purposive direction, or *telos,* and an upward rhythm, or progress—there is also the churning fear that history itself has proved to be a cheat. And a cheat not because it has turned away from our expectations, but because it betrays our hopes precisely through an inverted fulfillment of those expectations. Not progress denied but progress realized, is the nightmare haunting the anti-utopian novel. And behind this nightmare lies a crisis of thought quite as intense as that suffered by serious 19th Century minds when they discovered that far more painful than doubting the existence of God was questioning the validity of his creation.

Whether to distinguish literary genres or sub-genres through purely formal characteristics or to insist upon the crucial relevance of subject, theme and intellectual content, is something of a problem for theorists of criticism. It is all the more so in regard to fiction, which is less a genre than a menagerie of genres. I am inclined to think that in regard to prose fiction strictly formal characteristics will never suffice, even while remaining necessary, for proper description; and so I shall note here some of the main intellectual premises shaping anti-utopian fiction and then a few of those formal properties by which it may be distinguished from the familiar kinds of novel.

The first of the intellectual premises I have already re-marked upon: what might be called the disenchantment with history, history both as experience and idea. The second is closely related. It is the vision of a world foreseen by a character in Dostoevsky's *The Possessed* who declares his wish for a mode of existence in which "only the necessary is necessary." Zamiatin's *We*, the first and best of the anti-utopian novels, portrays a "glass paradise" in which all men live in principled unprivacy, without a self to hide or a mood to indulge. Zamiatin thus reflects, as Orwell later would in his "telescreen" and Charlie Chaplin in a sequence of *Modern Times*, the fear that the historical process, at breakneck-speed and regardless of our will, is taking us toward a *transparent universe* in which all categories are fixed, the problematic has been banished, unhappiness is treason and the gratuitous act beyond imagining. In *Brave New World* docile human creatures are produced in a hatchery: the ideal of man's self-determination, so important to Western liberalism, becomes a mocking rationale for procreation by norm. One of the "disturbed" characters in *We* remarks to one of the well-adjusted: "You want to encircle the infinite with a wall" and shifting from the metaphysical to the psychological, adds: "We are the happy arithmetical mean. As you would put it, the integration from zero to infinity, from imbeciles to Shakespeare."

This world of total integration is deprived of accident, contingency and myth; it permits no shelter for surprise, no margin for novelty, no hope for adventure. The rational raised to an irrational power becomes its god. Reality, writes Orwell in *1984*, "is not external. Reality exists in the human mind and nowhere else . . . whatever the Party holds to be truth *is* truth." Reality is not an objective fact to be acknowledged or transformed or resisted; it is the culminating fabrication produced by the *hubris* of rationalism.

But a certain kind of rationalism, I must hasten to add; since none of the anti-utopian novelists, at least in their novels, has anything to do with invoked mysticism. The sociologist Karl Mannheim distinguishes between two kinds of rationality, "substantial" and "functional." Substantial rationality is "an act of thought which reveals intelligent insight into the interrelations of events in a given situation." Functional rationality, the parallel in conduct to the process of industrial rationalization, consists of

> . . . a series of actions . . . organized in such a way that it leads to a previously defined goal, every element in this series of actions receiving a functional position and role. . . . It is by no means characteristic, however, of functional organization that . . . the goal itself be considered rational. . . . One may strive to attain an irrational eschatological goal, such as salvation, by so organizing one's ascetic behavior that it will lead to this goal. . . .

And Mannheim remarks:

> The violent shocks of crises and revolutions have uncovered a tendency which has hitherto been working under the surface, namely the paralyzing effect of functional rationalization on the capacity for rational judgment.

In his abstract way Mannheim hits upon the nightmare-vision of the anti-utopian novelists: that what men do and what they are become unrelated; that a world is appearing in which technique and value have been split apart, so that technique spins forward with a mad fecundity while value becomes debased to a mere slogan of the state. This kind of "technicism," Spengler has remarked, is frequently visible in a society that has lost its self-assurance. And in his preface to *Brave New World* Huxley shows a keen awareness of the distinction between "substantial" and "functional rationality" when he remarks that "The people who govern the Brave New World may not be sane . . . but they are not madmen, and their aim is not anarchy but social stability." They live, that is, by the strict requirements of functional rationality.

All three of our writers have a lively appreciation of the need felt by modern men to drop the burden of freedom, that need crystalized in the remark of the 19th Century anarchist Michael Bakunin, "I do not want to be I, I want to be We." The schema of the anti-utopian novel requires that in one or two forlorn figures, sports from the perfection of adjustment, there arise once more a spontaneous appetite for individuality. In *Brave New World* it takes the form of historical nostalgia; in *1984*, a yearning for a personal relationship that will have no end other than its own fulfillment; and in *We*, a series of brilliant forays into self-consciousness. The narrator of *We* discloses the ethos of his world when he remarks that the half-forgotten Christians "knew that resignation is virtue and pride a vice; [and almost as if echoing Bakunin] that 'We' is from 'God,' and 'I' from the devil." But as a deviant from the deadening health of his society, he engages in a discovery of selfhood through a realization of how strange, how thoroughly artificial, the very notion of selfhood is:

> Evening . . . the sky is covered with a milky-golden tissue, and one cannot see what is there, beyond, on the heights. The ancients "knew" that the greatest, bored skeptic—their god— lived there. We know that crystalline, blue, naked, indecent Nothing is there. . . . I had firm faith in myself; I believed

that I knew all about myself. But then . . . I look in the mirror. And for the first time in my life, yes, for the first time in my life, I see clearly, precisely, consciously and with surprise, I see myself as some "him!" I am "he.". . . And I know surely that "he" with his straight brows is a stranger. . . .

The idea of the personal self, which for us has become an indispensable assumption of existence, is seen by Zamiatin, Orwell and Huxley as a *cultural* idea. It is a fact within history, the product of the liberal era, and because it is susceptible to historical growth and decline, it may also be susceptible to historical destruction. All three of our anti-utopian novels are dominated by an overwhelming question: can human nature be manufactured? Not transformed or manipulated or debased, since these it obviously can be; but manufactured by will and decision.

When speaking about the historical determinants of human nature, one tacitly assumes that there *is* a human nature, and that for all of its plasticity it retains some indestructible core. If Zamiatin, Orwell and Huxley wrote simply from the premise of psychological relativism, they would deprive themselves of whatever possibilities for drama their theme allows, for then the very idea of a limit to the malleability of human nature would be hard to maintain. They must assume that there are strivings in men toward candor, freedom, truth and love which cannot be suppressed indefinitely; yet they have no choice but to recognize that at any particular historical moment these strivings can be suppressed effectively, surviving for men of intelligence less as realities to be counted on than as potentialities to be nurtured. Furthermore, in modern technology there appears a whole new apparatus for violating human nature: brainwashing and torture in *1984,* artificial biological selection in *Brave New World,* and an operation similar to a lobotomy in *We.* And not only can desire be suppressed and impulse denied; they can be transformed into their very opposites, so that people sincerely take slavery to be freedom and learn, in *Brave New World,* that "the secret of happiness and virtue is liking what you've got to like."

Ultimately the anti-utopian novel keeps returning to the choice posed by Dostoevsky's legend of the Grand Inquisitor in *The Brothers Karamazov:* the misery of the human being who must bear his burden of independence against the contentment of the human creature at rest in his obedience. But what now gives this counterposition of freedom and happiness a particularly sharp edge is the fact that through the refinements of technology Dostoevsky's speculation can be realized in social practice. In a number of intellectual and literary respects *Brave New World* is inferior to *1984* and *We,* but in confronting this central question it is bolder and keener, for Huxley sees that the problem first raised by Dostoevsky—will the satisfaction of material wants quench the appetite for freedom?—relates not only to totalitarian dictatorships but to the whole of industrial society. Like so many other manifestations of our culture, the anti-utopian novel keeps rehearsing the problems of the 19th Century: in this instance, not merely Dostoevsky's prophetic speculation but also the quieter fear of Alexis de Tocqueville that "a kind of virtuous materialism may ultimately be established in the world which would not corrupt but enervate the soul, and noiselessly unbend its springs of action."

The main literary problem regarding anti-utopian fiction is to learn to read it according to its own premises and limits, which is to say, in ways somewhat different from those by which we read ordinary novels.

Strictly speaking, anti-utopian fictions are not novels at all. Northrop Frye has usefully distinguished among kinds of fiction in order to remind us that we have lost in critical niceness by our habit of lumping all prose fiction under the heading of the novel. He is right of course, but I suspect that for common usage the effort to revive such distinctions is a lost cause, and that it may be better to teach readers to discriminate among kinds of novels. If we do for the moment accept Frye's categories it becomes clear that books like *We, 1984,* and *Brave New World* are not really novels portraying a familiar social world but what he calls Menippean satire, a kind of fiction that

> ... deals less with people as such than with mental attitudes ... The Menippean satire thus resembles the confession in its ability to handle abstract ideas and theories, and differs from the novel in its characterization, which is stylized rather than naturalistic, and presents people as mouthpieces of the ideas they represent.... At its most concentrated the Menippean satire presents us with a vision of the world in terms of a single intellectual pattern.

Accept this description and the usual complaints about the anti-utopian novel come to seem irrelevant. By its very nature the anti-utopian novel cannot satisfy the expectations we hold, often unreflectively, about the ordinary novel: expectations that are the heritage of 19th Century romanticism with its stress upon individual consciousness, psychological analysis and the scrutiny of intimate relations. When the English critic Raymond Williams complains that the anti-utopian novel lacks "a substantial society and correspondingly substantial persons," he is offering a description but intends it as a depreciation, quite as if a critic complained that a sonnet lacks a complex dramatic plot. For the very premise of anti-utopian fiction is that it projects a world in which such elements—"substantial society ... substantial persons"—have largely been suppressed and must now be painfully recovered, if recovered at all.

One might even speculate that it would be a mistake for the author of an anti-utopian novel to provide the usual complement of three-dimensional characters such as we expect in ordinary fiction, or to venture an extended amount of psychological specification. For these books try to present a world in which individuality has become obsolete and personality a sign of subversion. The major figures of such books are necessarily grotesques: they resemble persons who have lost the power of speech and must struggle to regain it; Winston Smith and Julia in *1984* are finally engaged in an effort to salvage the idea of the human *as an idea*, which means to experiment with the possibilities of solitude and the risks of contemplation. The human relations which the ordinary novel takes as its premise, become the possibilities toward which the anti-utopian novel strains. What in the ordinary novel appears as the tacit assumption of the opening page is now, in the anti-utopian novel, a wistful hope usually unrealized by the concluding page. That the writer of anti-utopian fiction must deal with a world in which man has been absorbed by his function and society by the state, surely places upon him a considerable quota of difficulties. But this is the task he sets himself, and there can be no point in complaining that he fails to do what in the nature of things he cannot do.

The anti-utopian novel lacks almost all the usual advantages of fiction: it must confine itself to a rudimentary kind of characterization, it cannot provide much in the way of psychological nuance, it hardly pretends to a large accumulation of suspense. Yet, as we can all testify, the anti-utopian novel achieves its impact, and this it does through a variety of formal means:

1) *It posits a "flaw" in the perfection of the perfect.* This "flaw," the weakness of the remembered or yearned-for human, functions dramatically in the anti-utopian novel quite as the assumption of original sin or a socially-induced tendency toward evil does in the ordinary novel. The "flaw" provides the possibility and particulars of the conflict, while it simultaneously insures that the outcome will be catastrophic. Since the ending of the anti-utopian novel is predictable and contained,

so to say, within its very beginning, the tension it creates depends less on a developed plot than on an overpowering conception. Leading to—

2) *It must be in the grip of an idea at once dramatically simple and historically complex: an idea that has become a commanding passion.* This idea consists, finally, in a catastrophic transmutation of values, a stoppage of history at the expense of its actors. In reading the anti-utopian novel we respond less to the world it projects than to the urgency of the projection. And since this involves the dangers of both monotony and monomania—

3) *It must be clever in the management of its substantiating detail.* Knowing all too well the inevitable direction of things, we can be surprised only by the ingenuity of local detail. And here arises a possible basis for comparative valuations among anti-utopian novels. Orwell's book is impressive for its motivating passion, less so for its local composition. Huxley's is notably clever, but too rationalistic and self-contained: he does not write like a man who feels himself imperilled by his own vision. Zamiatin is both passionate and brilliant, clever and driven. His style, an astonishing mosaic of violent imagery, sustains his vision throughout the book in a way that a mere linear unfolding of his fable never could. But since the anti-utopian novel must satisfy the conflicting requirements of both a highly-charged central idea and cleverness in the management of detail, it becomes involved with special problems of verisimilitude. That is—

4) *It must strain our sense of the probable while not violating our attachment to the plausible.* To stay too close to the probable means, for the anti-utopian novel, to lose the very reason for its existence; to appear merely implausible means to surrender its power to shock. Our writers meet this difficulty by employing what I would call the dramatic strategy and the

narrative psychology of "one more step." Their projected total state is one step beyond our known reality—not so much a picture of modern totalitarian society as an extension, by just one and no more than one step, of the essential pattern of the total state.

5) *In presenting the nightmare of history undone, it must depend on the ability of its readers to engage in an act of historical recollection.* This means, above all, to remember the power that the idea of utopia has had in Western society. "The Golden Age," wrote Dostoevsky, "is the most unlikely of all the dreams that have been, but for it men have given up their life and all their strength . . . Without it the people will not live and cannot die." Still dependent on this vision of the Golden Age, the anti-utopian novel thus shares an essential quality of all modern literature: it can realize its values only through images of their violation. The enchanted dream has become a nightmare, but a nightmare projected with such power as a validate the continuing urgency of the dream.

Politics and culture

IMAGES OF SOCIALISM
(with Lewis Coser)

"God," said Tolstoy, "is the name of my desire." This remarkable sentence could haunt one a lifetime, it reverberates in so many directions. Tolstoy may have intended partial assent to the idea that, life being insupportable without some straining toward "transcendence," a belief in God is a psychological necessity. But he must also have wanted to turn this rationalist criticism into a definition of his faith. He must have meant that precisely because his holiest desires met in the vision of God he was enabled to cope with the quite unholy realities of human existence. That God should be seen as the symbolic objectification of his desire thus became both a glorification of God and a strengthening of man, a stake in the future and a radical criticism of the present.

Without sanctioning the facile identification that is frequently made between religion and socialist politics, we should like to twist Tolstoy's remark to our own ends: *socialism is the name of our desire.* And not merely in the sense that it is a vision which, for many people throughout the world, provides moral sustenance, but also in the sense that

---

This essay was written in 1954.

it is a vision which objectifies and gives urgency to their criticism of the human condition in our time. It is the name of our desire because the desire arises from a conflict with, and an extension from, the world that is; nor could the desire survive in any meaningful way were it not for this complex relationship to the world that is.

At so late and unhappy a moment, however, can one still specify what the vision of socialism means or should mean? Is the idea of utopia itself still a tolerable one?

I

The impulse to imagine "the good society" probably coincides with human history, and the manner of constructing it —to invert what exists—is an element binding together all pre-Marxist utopias. These dreamers and system-makers have one thing in common: their desire to storm history.

The growth of the modern utopian idea accompanies the slow formation of the centralized state in Europe. Its imagery is rationalistic, far removed from the ecstatic visions that accompany the religiously inspired rebellions agitating feudal society in its last moments. As the traditional patchwork of autonomous social institutions in Western Europe was replaced, in the interests of efficiency, by an increasingly centralized system of rule, men began to conceive of a society that would drive this tendency to its conclusion and be governed completely by rationality. But not only the increasing rationality of political power inspired the thinking of social philosophers; they were stirred by the growth of a new, bourgeois style of life that emphasized calculation, foresight and efficiency, and made regularity of work an almost religious obligation.

As soon as men began to look at the state as "a work of art," as "an artificial man, created for the protection and salvation of the natural man" (Hobbes, "Leviathan"), it took but one more step to imagine that this "work of art" could be rendered perfect through foresight and will. Thomas Campanella, a rebellious Calabrian monk of the 17th Century, conceived in his "City of the Sun" of such a perfect work of art. In Campanella's utopia, unquestionably designed from the most idealistic of motives, one sees the traits of many pre-Marxist utopias. Salvation is *imposed*, delivered from above; there is an all-powerful ruler called the Great Metaphysicus (surely no more absurd than the Beloved Leader); only one book exists in the City of the Sun, which may be taken as an economical image of modern practice: naturally, a book called Wisdom. Sexual relations are organized by state administrators "according to philosophical rules," the race being "managed for the good of the commonwealth and not of private individuals. . . ." Education is conceived along entirely rationalistic lines, and indeed it must be, for Campanella felt that the Great Metaphysicus, as he forces perfection upon history, has to deal with recalcitrant materials: the people, he writes in a sentence that betrays both his bias and his pathos, is "a beast with a muddy brain."

And here we come upon a key to utopian thought: the galling sense of a chasm between the scheme and the subjects, between the plan, ready and perfect, and the people, mute and indifferent. (Poor Fourier, the salesman with Phalanxes in his belfry, comes home daily at noon, to wait for the one capitalist, he needs no more than one, who will finance utopia.) Intellectuals who cannot shape history try to rape it, either through actual violence, like the Russian terrorists, or imagined violence, the sudden seizure of history by a utopian claw. In his City of the Sun Campanella decrees—the utopian never hesitates to decree—that those sentenced to death for crimes against the Godhead, liberty and the higher magistrates are to be rationally enlightened, before execution, by special functionaries, so that in the end they will acquiesce in their own condemnation. Let no one say history is unforeseen.

Two centuries after Campanella, Etienne Cabet, a disciple of Robert Owen and Saint-Simon, envisaged the revolutionary dictatorship of Icar, an enlightened ruler who refuses to stay in power longer than is necessary for establishing the new society; he no doubt means it to wither away. Meanwhile Icaria has only one newspaper, and the republic has "revised all useful books which showed imperfections and it has burned all those which we judged dangerous and useless."

The point need not be overstressed. The utopians were not —or not merely—the unconscious authoritarians that hostile critics have made them out to be. No doubt, some did harbor strong streaks of authoritarian feeling which they vicariously released through utopian images; but this is far from the whole story. Robert Owen wanted a free cooperative society. Decentralization is stressed in Morelly's utopia, "Floating Islands." The phalanxes of Fourier are to function without any central authority and if there must be one, it should be located as far from France as possible, certainly no nearer than Constantinople.

But it is not merely a question of desirable visions. In the most far-fetched and mad fantasies of the utopians there are imbedded brilliant insights. The same Fourier who envisaged the transformation of brine into an agreeable liquid and the replacement of lions and sharks by mildly domestic "anti-lions" and "anti-sharks" also writes with the deepest understanding of the need for both the highest specialization of labor in modern society and the greatest variety and alternation of labor in order to overcome the monotony of specialization. Puzzling over the perennial teaser set before socialists— "Who'll do the dirty work?"—Fourier comes up with the shrewd psychological observation that it is children who most enjoy dirt and. . . .

The authoritarian element we find in the utopians is due far less to psychological malaise or power-hunger (most of them were genuinely good people) than to the sense of desperation that frequently lies beneath the surface of their fantasying. All pre-Marxist utopian thinking tends to be ahistorical, to see neither possibility nor need for relating the image of the good society to the actual workings of society as it is. For Fourier it is simply a matter of discovering the "plan" of God, the ordained social order that in realizing God's will ensures man's happiness. (Socialism for Fourier is indeed the name of his desire—but in a very different sense from that which we urge!) The imagined construction of utopia occurs *outside* the order or flux of history: it comes through fiat. Once utopia is established, history grinds to a standstill and the rule of rationality replaces the conflict of class or, as the utopians might have preferred to say, the conflict of passions. In his "Socialism, Utopian and Scientific" Frederick Engels describes this process with both sympathy and shrewdness:

> Society presented nothing but wrongs; to remove these was the task of reason. It was necessary, then, to *impose this upon society from without* by propaganda and, whenever possible, by the example of model experiments. These new social systems were foredoomed as utopian; the more completely they were worked out in detail, the more they could not avoid drifting off into pure phantasies. . . .
>
> We can leave it to the literary small fry to solemnly quibble over these phantasies, which today only make us smile, and to crow over the superiority of their own bald reasoning, as compared with such 'insanity.' As for us, we delight in the stupendously great thoughts and germs of thought that everywhere break out through their phantastic covering. . . . (Emphasis added.)

Given the desire to impose utopia upon an indifferent history, a desire which derives, in the main, from a deep sense of alienation from the flow of history, it follows logically enough that the utopians should for the most part think in terms of elite politics. Auguste Comte specifies that in the "State of Positive Science," society is to be ruled by an elite of intellectuals. The utopia to be inaugurated by the sudden triumph of reason over the vagaries and twists of history—what other recourse could a lonely, isolated utopian have but the elite, the small core of intellect that, like himself, controls and guides? Saint-Simon, living in the afterglow of the French Revolution, begins to perceive the mechanics of class relations and the appearance for the first time in modern history of the masses as a decisive force. But in the main our generalization holds: reformers who lack some organic relationship with major historical movements must almost always be tempted into a more or less benevolent theory of a ruling elite.

II

Utopia without egalitarianism, utopia dominated by an aristocracy of mind, must quickly degenerate into a vision of useful slavery. Hence, the importance of Marx's idea that socialism is to be brought about, in the first instance, by the activities of a major segment of the population, the workers. Having placed the drive toward utopia not beyond but squarely—perhaps a little too squarely—within the course of history, and having found in the proletariat that active "realizing" force which the utopians could nowhere discern on the social horizon, Marx was enabled to avoid the two major difficulties of his predecessors: ahistoricism and the elite theory. He had, to be sure, difficulties of his own, but not these.

Marx was the first of the major socialist figures who saw the possibility of linking the utopian desire with the actual development of social life. By studying capitalism both as an "ideal" structure and a "real" dynamic, Marx found the sources of revolt within the self-expanding and self-destroying rhythms of the economy itself. The utopians had desired a revolt against history but they could conduct it, so to speak, only from the space-platform of the imaginary future; Marx gave new power to the revolt against history by locating it, "scientifically," within history.

The development of technology, he concluded, made possible a society in which men could "realize" their humanity, if only because the brutalizing burden of fatigue, that sheer physical exhaustion from which the great masses of men had never been free, could now for the first time be removed. This was the historic option offered mankind by the Industrial Revolution, as it is now being offered again by the Atomic Revolution. Conceivably, though only conceivably, a society might have been established at any point in historical time which followed an equalitarian distribution of goods; but there would have been neither goods nor leisure enough to dispense with the need for a struggle over their distribution; which means bureaucracy, police, an oppressive state; and in sum, the destruction of equalitarianism. Now, after the Industrial Revolution, the machine might do for all humanity what the slaves had done for the Greek patriciate.

Marx was one of the first political thinkers to see that both industrialism and "the mass society" were here to stay, that all social schemes which ignored or tried to controvert this fact were not merely irrelevant, they weren't even interesting. It is true, of course, that he did not foresee—he could not—a good many consequences of this tremendous historical fact. He did not foresee that "mass culture" together with social atomization (Durkheim's *anomie*) would set off strong tendencies of demoralization working in opposition to those tendencies that made for disciplined cohesion in the working class. He did not foresee that the rise of totalitarianism might present mankind with choices and problems that went beyond the capitalist/socialist formulation. He did not foresee that the nature of leisure would become, even under capitalism, as great a social and cultural problem as the nature of work. He did not foresee that industrialism would create problems which, while not necessarily insoluble, are likely to survive the span of capitalism. But what he did foresee was crucial: that the great decisions of history would now be made in a mass society, that the "stage" upon which this struggle would take place had suddenly, dramatically been widened far beyond its previous dimensions.

And when Marx declared the proletariat to be the active social force that could lead the transition to socialism, he was neither sentimentalizing the lowly nor smuggling in a theory of the elite, as many of his critics have suggested. Anyone who has read the chapter in *Capital* on the Working Day or Engels' book on the conditions of the English workers knows that they measured the degradation of the workers to an extent precluding sentimentality. As for the idea of the proletariat as an elite, Marx made no special claim for its virtue or intelligence, which is the traditional mode of justifying an elite; he merely analyzed its peculiar *position* in society, as the class most driven by the workings of capitalism to both discipline and rebellion, the class that come what may, utopia or barbarism, would always remain propertyless.

There is another indication that Marx did not mean to favor an elite theory by his special "placing" of the proletariat. His theory of "increasing misery"—be it right, wrong or vulgarized—implied that the proletariat would soon include the overwhelming bulk of the population. The transition to socialism, far from being assigned to a "natural" elite or a power group, was seen by Marx as the task of the vast "proletarianized" majority. Correct or not, this was a fundamentally democratic point of view.

Concerned as he was with the mechanics of class power, the "laws of motion" of the existing society, and the strategy of social change, Marx paid very little attention to the description of socialism. The few remarks to be found in his early work and in such a later book as *The Critique of the Gotha Program* are mainly teasers, formulations so brief as to be cryptic, which did not prevent his disciples from making them into dogmas. An interesting division of labor took place. Marx's predecessors, those whom he called the "utopian socialists," had devoted themselves to summoning pictures of the ideal future, perhaps in lieu of activity in the detested present; Marx, partly as a reaction to their brilliant day-dreaming, decided to focus on an analysis of those elements in the present that made possible a strategy for reaching the ideal future. And in the meantime, why worry about the face of the future, why create absurd blueprints? As a response to Fourier, Saint-Simon and Owen there was much good sense in this attitude; given the state of the European labor movements in the mid-19th century it was indispensable to turn toward practical problems of national life (Germany) and class organization (England.) But the Marxist movement, perhaps unavoidably, paid a price for this emphasis.

As the movement grew, the image of socialism kept becoming hazier and hazier, and soon the haziness came to seem a condition of perfection. The "revisionist" Social Democrat Eduard Bernstein could write that the goal is nothing, the movement everything; as if a means could be intelligently chosen without an end in view! In his *State and Revolution* Lenin, with far greater fullness than Marx, sketched a vision of socialism profoundly democratic, in which the mass of humanity would break out of its dumbness, so that cooks could become cabinet ministers, and even the "bourgeois principle of equality" would give way to the true freedom of non-measurement: "from each according to his ability and to each according to his need." But this democratic vision did not sufficiently affect his immediate views of political activity, so that in his crucial pamphlet *Will the Bolsheviks Retain State Power?* written in 1917, Lenin, as if to brush aside the traditional Marxist view that the socialist transformation requires a far greater popular base than any previous social change, could say that "After the 1905 Revolution Russia was ruled by 130,000 landowners. . . . And yet we are told that Russia will not be able to be governed by the 240,000 members of the Bolshevik Party—governing in the interests of the poor and against the rich."

What happened was that the vision of socialism—would it not be better to say the *problem* of socialism?—grew blurred in the minds of many Marxists because they were too ready to entrust it to History. The fetishistic use of the word "scientific," than which nothing could provide a greater sense of assurance, gave the Marxist movement a feeling that it had finally penetrated to the essence of History, and found there once and for all its true meaning. The result was often a deification of History: what God had been to Fourier, History became to many Marxists—a certain force leading to a certain goal. And if indeed the goal was certain, or likely enough to be taken as certain, there was no need to draw up fanciful blueprints, the future would take care of itself and require no advice from us. True enough, in a way. But the point that soon came to be forgotten was that it is we, in the present, who need the image of the future, not those who may live in it. And the consequence of failing to imagine creatively the face of socialism—which is not at all the same as an absurd effort to paint it in detail—was that it tended to lapse into a conventional and lifeless "perfection."

III

Perfection, in that the image of socialism held by many Marxists—the image which emerged at the level of implicit belief—was one of a society in which tension, conflict and failure had largely disappeared. It would be easy enough to comb the works of the major Marxists in order to prove this statement, but we prefer to appeal to common experience, to our own knowledge and memories as well as to the knowledge and memories of others. In the socialist movement one did not worry about the society one wanted: innumerable and, indeed, inconceivable subjects were discussed but almost never the idea of socialism itself, for History, Strategy and The Party (how easily the three melted into one!) had eliminated that need. Socialism was the Future—and sometimes a future made curiously respectable, the middle-class values that the radicals had violently rejected now being reinstated, unwittingly, in their vision of the good society. There could hardly be a need to reply to those critics who wondered how some of the perennial human problems could be solved under socialism: one *knew* they would be. In effect, the vision of socialism had a way of declining into a regressive infantile fantasy, a fantasy of protection.

Our criticism is not that the Marxist movement held to a vision of utopia: that it did so was entirely to its credit, a life without some glimmer of a redeeming future being a life cut off from the distinctively human. Our complaint is rather that the vision of utopia grew slack and static. Sometimes it degenerated into what William Morris called "the cockney dream" by which efficiency becomes a universal solvent for all human problems; sometimes it slipped off, beyond human reach, to the equally repulsive vision of a society in which men become rational titans as well-behaved and tedious as Swift's Houhynhnms. Only occasionally was socialism envisaged as a society with its own rhythm of growth and tension, change and conflict.

Marx's contribution to human thought is immense, but except for some cryptic if pregnant phrases, neither he nor his disciples have told us very much about the society in behalf of which they called men into battle. This is not quite so fatal a criticism as it might seem, since what probably mattered most was that Marxism stirred millions of previously dormant people into historical action, gave expression to their claims and yearnings, and lent a certain form to their desire for a better life. But if we want sustained speculations on the shape of this better life we have to turn to radical mavericks, to the anarchists and libertarians, to the Guild Socialists. And to such a writer as Oscar Wilde, whose *The Soul of Man Under Socialism* is a small masterpiece. In his paradoxical and unsystematic way Wilde quickly comes to a sense of what the desirable society might be like. The great advantage of socialism, he writes, is that it "would relieve us from that sordid necessity of living for others which, in the present condition of things, presses so hard upon almost everybody." By focusing upon "the unhealthy and exaggerated altruism" which capitalist society demands from people, and by showing how it saps individuality, Wilde arrives at the distinctive virtue of Socialism: that it will make possible what he calls Individualism.

IV

We do not wish to succumb to that which we criticize. Blueprints, elaborate schemes do not interest us. But we think it may be useful to suggest some of the qualities that can make the image of socialism a serious and mature goal, as well as some of the difficulties in that goal:

• Socialism is not the end of human history, as the deeply-held identification of it with perfection must mean. There is no total fulfillment, nor is there an "end to time." History is a process which throws up new problems, new conflicts, new questions; and socialism, being within history, cannot be expected to solve all these problems or, for that matter, to raise humanity at every point above the level of achievement of previous societies.* As Engels remarked, there is no final syn-

---

* In his book *Entretiens* the French surrealist Andre Breton records a dialogue in which he, Diego Rivera and Leon Trotsky took part. Trotsky, writes Breton, "suffered visibly when one of us stopped to caress pre-Columbian pottery; I still see the look of blame he fixed on Rivera when Rivera stated that the art of design had declined since the epochs of the cave, and how he exploded one evening when we let ourselves go by speculating out loud that once the classless society was installed, new causes of bloody conflict—that is, causes other than economic—might not fail to appear. . . ." Breton, to be sure, like most surrealists, is rather too liberal with other people's blood, but that apart, his implied criticism of Trotsky has a point.

thesis, only contiuued clash. What socialists want is simply to do away with those sources of conflict which are the cause of material deprivation and which, in turn, help create psychological and moral suffering. Freedom may then mean that we can devote ourselves to the pursuit of more worthwhile causes of conflict. The hope for a conflictless society is reactionary, as is a reliance upon some abstract "historical force" that will conciliate all human strife.

• The aim of socialism is to create a society of cooperation, but not necessarily, or at least not universally, of harmony. Cooperation is compatible with conflict, is indeed inconceivable without conflict, while harmony implies a stasis.

• Even the "total abolition" of social classes, no small or easy thing, would not or need not mean the total abolition of social problems.

• In a socialist society there would remain a whole variety of human difficulties that could not easily be categorized as social or non-social; difficulties that might well result from the sheer friction between the human being and society, *any* society—from, say, the process of "socializing" those recalcitrant creatures known as children. The mere existence of man is a difficulty, a problem, with birth, marriage, pain and death being only among the more spectacular of his crises. To be sure, no intelligent radical has ever denied that *such* crises would last into a socialist society, but the point to be stressed is that with the elimination of our major material troubles, these other problems might rise to a new urgency, so much so as to become *social* problems leading to new conflicts.

V

But social problems as we conceive of them today would also be present in a socialist society.

Traditionally, Marxists have lumped all the difficulties posed by critics and reality into that "transitional" state that is to guide, or bump, us from capitalism to socialism, while socialism itself they have seen as the society that would transcend these difficulties. This has made it a little too easy to justify some of the doings of the "transitional" society, while making it easier still to avoid considering—not what socialism *will* be like—but what our image of it should be. Without pretending to "solve" these social problems as they might exist under socialism, but intending to suggest a bias or predisposition, we list here a few of them:

1) *Bureaucracy*

Marxists have generally related the phenomenon of bureaucratism to social inequality and economic scarcity. Thus, they have seen the rise of bureaucracy in Leninist Russia as a consequence of trying to establish a workers' state in an isolated and backward country which lacked the economic prerequisites for building socialism. Given scarcity, there arises a policeman to supervise the distribution of goods; given the policeman, there will be an unjust distribution. Similarly, bureaucratic formations of a more limited kind are seen as parasitic elites which batten upon a social class yet, in some sense, "represent" it in political and economic conflicts. Thus bureaucratism signifies a deformation, though not necessarily a destruction, of democratic processes.

This view of bureaucratism seems to us invaluable. Yet it would be an error to suppose that because a class society is fertile ground for bureaucracy, a classless society would automatically be free of bureaucracy. There are other causes for this social deformation; and while in a socialist society these other causes might not be aggravated by economic inequality and the ethos of accumulation as they are under capitalism, they would very likely continue to operate. One need not accept Robert Michels' "Iron Law of Oligarchy" in order to see this. (Michels' theory is powerful but it tends to boomerang:

anyone convinced by it that socialism is impossible will have a hard time resisting the idea that democracy is impossible.) Thus the mere presence of equality of wealth in a society does not necessarily mean an equality of power or status: if Citizen A were more interested in the politics of his town or the functioning of his factory than Citizen B, he would probably accumulate more power and status; hence, the *possibility* of misusing them. (Socialists have often replied, But why should Citizen A want to misuse his power and status when there is no pressing economic motive for doing so? No one can answer this question definitively except by positing some theory of "human nature," which we do not propose to do; all we can urge is a strong wariness with regard to any theory which discounts in advance the possibility that non-economic motives can lead to human troubles.) Then again, the problem of sheer size in economic and political units is likely to burden a socialist society as much as it burdens any other society; and large political or economic units, because they require an ever increasing delegation of authority, often to "experts," obviously provide a setting in which bureaucracy can flourish. But most important of all is the sheer problem of representation, the fact that as soon as authority is delegated to a "representative" there must follow a loss of control and autonomy.

Certain institutional checks can, of course, be suggested for containing bureaucracy. The idea of a division of governmental powers, which many Marxists have dismissed as a bourgeois device for thwarting the popular will, would deserve careful attention in planning a socialist society, though one need not suppose that it would have to perpetuate those elements of present-day parliamentary structure which do in fact thwart the popular will. Similarly, the distinction made in English political theory, but neglected by Marxists, between democracy as an expression of popular sovereignty and democracy as a pattern of government in which the rights of minority groups are especially defended, needs to be honored. In general, a society that is pluralist rather than unitary in emphasis, that recognizes the need for diversification of function rather than concentration of authority—this is the desired goal.

And here we have a good deal to learn from a neglected branch of the socialist movement, the Guild Socialists of England, who have given careful thought to these problems. G. D. H. Cole, for example, envisages the socialist society as one in which government policy is a resultant of an interplay among socio-economic units that simultaneously cooperate and conflict. Cole also puts forward the provocative idea of "functional representation," somewhat similar to the original image of the Soviets. Because, he writes, "a human being, as an individual, is fundamentally incapable of being represented," a man should have "as many distinct, and separately exercised, votes, as he has distinct social purposes or interests," voting, that is, in his capacity of worker, consumer, artist, resident, etc.*

But such proposals can hardly be expected to bulk very large unless they are made in a culture where the motives for private accumulation and the values sanctioning it have significantly diminished. If, as we believe, the goal of socialism is to create the kind of man who, to a measurable degree, ceases to be a manipulated object and becomes a motivated subject, then the growth of socialist consciousness must prove an important bulwark against bureaucracy. A society that stresses cooperation can undercut those prestige factors that make for bureaucracy; a society that accepts conflict, and pro-

---

* A serious objection to this idea is that it seems to put a premium on "activity," so that the good socialist citizen who prefers to raise begonias may be relegated to a secondary status by comparison with the one who prefers to attend meetings. Cole seems to follow in the unattractive tradition of "the life of the member" party, whereby the movement swallows up the whole life of those who belong to it. (Cf. *In the Twilight of Socialism*, by Joseph Buttinger)

vides a means for modulating it, will encourage those who combat bureaucracy.

2) *Planning and Decentralization*

Unavoidably, a great deal of traditional socialist thought has stressed economic centralization as a prerequisite for planning, especially in the "transitional" state between capitalism and socialism. Partly, this was an inheritance from the bourgeois revolution, which needed a centralized state; partly, it reflected the condition of technology in the nineteenth century, which required centralized units of production; partly, it is a consequence of the recent power of Leninism, which stressed centralism as a means of confronting the primitive chaos of the Russian economy but allowed it to become a dogma in countries where it had no necessary relevance. Whatever the historical validity of these emphases on centralism, they must now be abandoned. According to the famous economist Colin Clark, the new forms of energy permit an economical employment of small decentralized industrial units. Certainly, every impulse of democratic socialism favors such a tendency. For if mass participation—by the workers, the citizens, the people as a whole—in the economic life of the society is to be meaningful, it must find its most immediate expression in relatively small economic units. Only in such small units is it possible for the non-expert to exercise any real control.

From what we can learn about Stalinist "planning," we see that an economic plan does not work, it quickly breaks down, if arbitrarily imposed from above and hedged in with rigid specifications which allow for none of the flexibility, none of the economic *play*, that a democratic society requires. Social planning, if understood in democratic terms—and can there really be social planning, as distinct from economic regulation, without a democratic context?—requires only a loose guiding direction, a general pointer from above. The rest, the actual working out of variables, the arithmetic fulfillment of algebraic possibilities, must come from below, from the interaction, cooperation and conflict of economic units participating in a democratic community.

All of this implies a considerable modification of the familiar socialist emphasis on nationalization of the means of production, increase of productivity, a master economic plan, etc. —a modification but not a total rejection. To be sure, socialism still presupposes the abolition of private property in the basic industries, but there is hardly a branch of the socialist movement, except the more petrified forms of Trotskyism, which places any high valuation on nationalization of industry per se. Almost all socialists now feel impelled to add that what matters is the use to which nationalization is put and the degree of democratic control present in the nationalized industries. But more important, the idea of nationalization requires still greater modification: there is no reason to envisage, even in a "transitional" society, that all basic industries need be owned by the state. The emphasis of the Guild Socialists upon separate Guilds of workers, each owning and managing their own industries, summons no doubt a picture of possible struggles within and between industries; all the better! Guilds, cooperatives, call them what you will—these provide possible bulwarks against the monster Leviathan, the all-consuming state, which it is the sheerest fatuity to suppose would immediately cease being a threat to human liberty simply because "we" took it over. The presence of numerous political and economic units, living together in a tension of cooperation-and-conflict, seems the best "guarantee" that power will not accumulate in the hands of a managerial oligarchy—namely, that the process already far advanced in capitalist society will not continue into socialism. Such autonomous units, serving as buffers between government and people, would allow for various, even contradictory, kinds of expression in social life.* The conflicts that might break out among them would be a healthy social regulator, for while the suppression of conflict makes for an explosive accumulation of hostility, its normalization means that a society can be "sewn-together" by non-cumulative struggles between component groups. And even in terms of "efficiency," this may prove far more satisfactory than the bureaucratic state regulation of Stalinist Russia.

Only if an attempt is made to encompass the total personality of the individual into one or another group is conflict likely to lead to social breakdown. Only then would conflicts over relatively minor issues be elevated into "affairs of state." So long as the dogma of "total allegiance"—a dogma that has proven harmful in both its Social Democratic and Leninist versions—is not enforced, so long as the individual is able to participate in a variety of groupings without having to commit himself totally to any of them, society will be able to absorb a constant series of conflicts.

Nor would the criterion of efficiency be of decisive importance in such a society. At the beginning of the construction of socialism, efficiency is urgently required in order to provide the material possibility for a life of security and freedom. But efficiency is needed in order, so to speak, to transcend efficiency.

Between the abstract norms of efficiency and the living needs of human beings there may always be a clash. To speak in grandiose terms, as some anarchists do, of Efficiency vs. Democracy is not very valuable, since living experience always requires compromise and complication. All one can probably say is that socialists are not concerned with efficiency as such but with that type of efficiency which does not go counter to

---

* In the famous "trade union" dispute between Lenin and Trotsky that took place in the early 1920's, Lenin clearly understood, as Trotsky did not, that even, and particularly, in a workers' state—or, as Lenin more realistically called it, a deformed workers' state—the workers need agencies of protection, in this case trade unions, against their "own" state. That the dispute remained academic is another matter.

key socialist values. Under socialism there are likely to be many situations in which efficiency will be consciously sacrificed, and indeed one of the measures of the success of a socialist society would be precisely how far it could afford to discard the criterion of efficiency. This might be one of the more glorious ideas latent in Engels' description of socialism as a "reign of freedom."

These remarks are, of course, scrappy and incomplete, as we intend them to be, for their usefulness has a certain correlation with their incompleteness; but part of what we have been trying to say has been so well put by R. H. S. Crossman that we feel impelled to quote him:

> The planned economy and the centralization of power are no longer socialist objectives. They are developing all over the world as the Political Revolution [the concentration of state powers] and the process is accelerated by the prevalence of war economy. The main task of socialism today is to prevent the concentration of power in the hands of *either* industrial management *or* the state bureaucracy—in brief, to distribute responsibility and so to enlarge freedom of choice. This task was not even begun by the Labour Government. On the contrary, in the nationalized industries old managements were preserved almost untouched.
>
> In a world organized in ever larger and more inhuman units, the task of socialism is to prevent managerial responsibility degenerating into privilege. This can only be achieved by increasing, even at the cost of "efficiency," the citizen's right to participate in the control not only of government and industry, but of the party for which he voted. . . . After all, it is not the pursuit of happiness but the enlargement of freedom which is socialism's highest aim.

3) *Work and Leisure*

No Marxist concept has been more fruitful than that of "alienation." As used by Marx, it suggests the psychic price of living in a society where the worker's "deed becomes an alien power." The division of labor, he writes, makes the worker "a cripple . . . forcing him to develop some highly specialized dexterity at the cost of a world of productive impulses. . . ." The worker becomes estranged from his work, both as process and product; his major energies must be expended upon tasks that have no organic or creative function within his life; the impersonality of the social relationships enforced by capitalism, together with the sense of incoherence and discontinuity induced by the modern factory, goes far toward making the worker a dehumanized part of the productive process rather than an autonomous human being. It is not, of course, to be supposed that this is a description of a given factory; it is a "lead" by which to examine a given factory. This theory is the starting point of much speculation on the nature of modern work, as well as upon the social and psychological significance of the industrial city; and almost all the theorizing on "mass culture," not to mention many of the efforts to "engineer" human relations in the factory, implicitly acknowledge the relevance and power of Marx's idea.

But when Marx speaks of alienation and thereby implies the possibility of non-alienation, it is not always clear whether he has in mind some pre-capitalist society in which men were presumably not alienated or whether he employs it as a useful "fiction" derived by a process of abstraction from the observable state of society. If he means the former, he may occasionally be guilty of romanticizing, in common with many of his contemporaries, the life of pre-capitalist society; for most historians of feudalism and of that difficult-to-label era which spans the gap between feudalism and capitalism, strongly imply that the peasant and even the artisan was not quite the unalienated man that some intellectuals like to suppose. Nonetheless, as an analytical tool and a reference to future possibilities, the concept of alienation remains indispensable.

So long as capitalism, in one form or another, continues to exist, it will be difficult to determine to what degree it is the social setting and to what degree the industrial process that makes so much of factory work dehumanizing. That a great deal of this dehumanization is the result of a social structure which deprives many men of an active sense of participation or decision-making and tends to reduce them to the level of controlled objects, can hardly be doubted at so late a moment.

We may consequently suppose that in a society where the democratic ethos had been reinforced politically and had made a significant seepage into economic life, the problem of alienation would be alleviated. But not solved.

In his *Critique of the Gotha Program* Marx speaks of the highest stage of the new society as one in which "the enslaving subordination of individuals in the division of labor has disappeared, and with it also the antagonism between mental and physical labor; labor has become not only a means of living, but itself the first necessity of life. . . ." Remembering that Marx set this as a *limit* toward which to strive and not as a condition likely to be present even during the beginning of socialism, let us then suppose that a society resembling this limit has been reached. The crippling effects of the division of labor are now largely eliminated because people are capable of doing a large variety of social tasks; the division between physical and mental labor has been largely eliminated because the level of education has been very much raised; and—we confess here to being uncertain as to Marx's meaning—labor has become "the first necessity of life." But even now the problem of *the nature of work* remains. Given every conceivable improvement in the social context of work; given a free and healthy society; given, in short, all the desiderata Marx lists— even then there remains the uncreativeness, the tedium, what frequently must seem the meaninglessness, of the jobs many people have to perform in the modern factory.

It may be said that in a socialist society people could live creatively in their leisure; no doubt. Or that people would have to do very little work because new forms of energy would be developed; quite likely. But then the problem would be for men to find an outlet for their "productive impulses" not in the way Marx envisaged but in another way, not in work but in leisure. Except for certain obviously satisfying occupations, and by this we do *not* mean only intellectual occupations, work might now become a minor part of human life. The problem is whether in any society it would now be possible to create—given our irrevocable commitment to industrialism—the kind of "whole man" Marx envisaged, the man, that is, who realizes himself through and by his work.

It is not as a speculation about factory life in a socialist society that this problem intrigues us, but rather as an entry into another problem about which Marx wrote very little: what we now call "mass culture." Socialists have traditionally assumed that a solution to economic problems would be followed by a tremendous flowering of culture; and this may happen, we do not know. But another possible outcome might be a population of which large parts were complacent and self-satisfied, so that if hell is now conceived as a drawing room, utopia might soften into a suburb. In any case, we are hardly likely to feel as certain about the cultural consequences of social equality as Trotsky did when he wrote in *Literature and Revolution* that under socialism men might reach the level of Beethoven and Goethe. This seems implausibly romantic, since it is doubtful that the scarcity of Beethovens and Goethes can be related solely to social inequality; and what is more it does not even seem very desirable to have a society of Beethovens and Goethes.

Between the two extreme forecasts there is the more likely possibility that under socialism a great many people would inevitably engage in work which could not release "a world of productive impulses" but which would be brief and light enough to allow them a great deal of leisure. The true problem of socialism might then be to determine the nature, quality and variety of leisure. Men, that is, would face the full and terrifying burden of human freedom, but they would be more prepared to shoulder it than ever before.

VI

"The past and present," wrote Pascal, "are our means; the future alone our end." Taken with the elasticity that Pascal intended—he surely did not mean to undervalue the immediacy of experience—this is a useful motto for what we have called utopian thinking, the imaginative capacity for conceiving of a society that is qualitatively better than our own yet no mere fantasy of static perfection.

Today, in an age of curdled realism, it is necessary to assert the utopian image. But this can be done meaningfully only if it is an image of social striving, tension, conflict; an image of a problem-creating and problem-solving society.

In his *Essay on Man* Ernst Cassirer has written almost all that remains to be said:

> A Utopia is not a portrait of the real world, or of the actual political or social order. It exists at no moment of time and at no point in space; it is a "nowhere." But just such a conception of a nowhere has stood the test and proved its strength in the development of the modern world. It follows from the nature and character of ethical thought that it can never condescend to accept the "given." The ethical world is never given; it is forever in the making.

Some time ago one could understandably make of socialism a consoling day-dream. Now, when we live in the shadow of defeat, to retain, to will the image of socialism is a constant struggle for definition, almost an act of pain. But it is the kind of pain that makes creation possible.

THIS AGE OF CONFORMITY

Intellectuals have always been partial to grandiose ideas about themselves, whether of an heroic or masochistic kind, but surely no one has ever had a more grandiose idea about the destiny of modern intellectuals than the brilliant economist Joseph Schumpeter. Though he desired nothing so much as to be realistic and hard-boiled, Schumpeter had somehow absorbed all those romantic notions about the revolutionary potential and critical independence of the intellectuals which have now and again swept through the radical and bohemian worlds. Marx, said Schumpeter, was wrong in supposing that capitalism would break down from inherent economic contradictions; it broke down, instead, from an inability to claim people through ties of loyalty and value. "Unlike any other type of society, capitalism inevitably . . . creates, educates and subsidizes a vested interest in social unrest." The intellectuals, bristling with neurotic aspirations and deranged by fantasies of utopia made possible by the very society they would destroy, become agents of discontent who infect rich and poor, high and low. In drawing this picture Schumpeter hardly meant to praise the intellectuals, yet until a few years ago many of them would have accepted it as both truth and

---

This essay was written in 1954.

tribute, though a few of the more realistic ones might have smiled a doubt as to their capacity to do *all that*.

Schumpeter's picture of the intellectuals is not, of course, without historical validity, but at the moment it seems spectacularly, even comically wrong. And wrong for a reason that Schumpeter, with his elaborate sense of irony, would have appreciated: he who had insisted that capitalism is "a form or method of economic change and not only never is but never can be stationary" had failed sufficiently to consider those new developments in our society which have changed the whole position and status of the intellectuals. Far from creating and subsidizing unrest, capitalism in its most recent stage has found an honored place for the intellectuals; and the intellectuals, far from thinking of themselves as a desperate "opposition," have been enjoying a return to the bosom of the nation. Were Archibald MacLeish again tempted to play Cato and chastize the Irresponsibles, he could hardly find a victim. We have all, even the handful who still try to retain a glower of criticism, become responsible and moderate.

II

In 1932 not many American intellectuals saw any hope for the revival of capitalism. Few of them could support this feeling with any well-grounded theory of society; many held to a highly simplified idea of what capitalism was; and almost all were committed to a vision of the *crisis* of capitalism which was merely a vulgarized model of the class struggle in Europe. Suddenly, with the appearance of the New Deal, the intellectuals saw fresh hope: capitalism was not to be exhausted by the naive specifications they had assigned it, and consequently the "European" policies of the Roosevelt administration might help dissolve their "Europeanized" sense of crisis. So that the more American society became Europeanized, adopting measures that had been common practice on the Continent for decades, the more the American intellectuals began to believe in . . . American uniqueness. Somehow, the major capitalist power in the world would evade the troubles afflicting capitalism as a world economy.

The two central policies of the New Deal, social legislation and state intervention in economic life, were not unrelated, but they were separable as to time; in Europe they had not always appeared together. Here, in America, it was the simultaneous introduction of these two policies that aroused the enthusiasm, as it dulled the criticism, of the intellectuals. Had the drive toward bureaucratic state regulation of a capitalist economy appeared by itself, so that one could see the state becoming a major buyer and hence indirect controller of industry, and industries on the verge of collapse being systematically subsidized by the state, and the whole of economic life being rationalized according to the long-run needs, if not the immediate tastes, of corporate economy—had all this appeared in isolation, the intellectuals would have reacted critically, they would have recognized the trend toward "state capitalism" as the danger it was. But their desire for the genuine social reforms that came with this trend made them blind or indifferent to the danger. Still, one may suppose that their enthusiasm would have mellowed had not the New Deal been gradually transformed into a permanent war economy; for whatever the theoretical attractions of the Keynesian formula for salvaging capitalism, it has thus far "worked" only in times of war or preparation for war. And it was in the war economy, itself closely related to the trend toward statification, that the intellectuals came into their own.

Statification, war economy, the growth of a mass society and mass culture—all these are aspects of the same historical process. The kind of society that has been emerging in the West, a society in which bureaucratic controls are imposed upon (but not fundamentally against) an interplay of private interests, has need for intellectuals in a way the earlier, "traditional" capitalism never did. It is a society in which ideology plays an unprecedented part: as social relations become more abstract and elusive, the human object is bound to the state with ideological slogans and abstractions—and for this chore intellectuals are indispensable, no one else can do the job as well. Because industrialism grants large quantities of leisure time without any creative sense of how to employ it, there springs up a vast new industry that must be staffed by intellectuals and quasi-intellectuals: the industry of mass culture. And because the state subsidizes mass education and our uneasy prosperity allows additional millions to gain a "higher" education, many new jobs suddenly become available in the academy: some fall to intellectuals. Bohemia gradually disappears as a setting for our intellectual life, and what remains of it seems willed or fake. Looking upon the prosperous ruins of Greenwich Village, one sometimes feels that a full-time bohemian career has become as arduous, if no as expensive, as acquiring a Ph.D.

Bohemia, said Flaubert, was "the fatherland of my breed." If so, his breed, at least in America, is becoming extinct. The most exciting periods of American intellectual life tend to coincide with the rise of bohemia, with the tragic yet liberating rhythm of the break from the small town into the literary roominess of the city, or from the provincial immigrant family into the centers of intellectual experiment. Given the nature of contemporary life, bohemia flourishes in the city—but that has not always been so. Concord too was a kind of bohemia, sedate, subversive and transcendental all at once. Today, however, the idea of bohemia, which was a strategy for bringing artists and writers together in their struggle with and for the world—this idea has become disreputable, being rather nastily associated with kinds of exhibitionism that have only an incidental relationship to bohemia. Nonetheless, it is the disintegration of bohemia that is a major cause for the way intellectuals feel, as distinct from and far more important than what they say or think. Those feelings of loneliness one finds among so many American intellectuals, feelings of damp dispirited isolation which undercut the ideology of liberal optimism, are partly due to the break-up of bohemia. Where young writers would once face the world together, they now sink into suburbs, country homes and college towns. And the prices they pay for this rise in social status is to be measured in more than an increase in rent.

It is not my purpose to berate anyone, for the pressures of conformism are at work upon all of us, to say nothing of the need to earn one's bread; and all of us bend under the terrible weight of our time—though some take pleasure in learning to enjoy it. Nor do I wish to indulge in the sort of good-natured condescension with which Malcolm Cowley recently described the younger writers as lugubrious and timid long-hairs huddling in chill academies and poring over the gnostic texts of Henry James—by contrast, no doubt, to Cowley's own career of risk-taking. Some intellectuals, to be sure, have "sold out" and we can all point to examples, probably the same examples. But far more prevalent and far more insidious is that slow attrition which destroys one's ability to stand firm and alone: the temptations of an improved standard of living combined with guilt over the historical tragedy that has made possible our prosperity; one's sense of being swamped by the rubbish of a reactionary period together with the loss of those earlier certainties that had the advantage, at least, of making resistance easy. Nor, in saying these things, do I look forward to any sort of material or intellectual asceticism. Our world is neither to be flatly accepted nor rejected: it must be engaged, resisted and—who knows, perhaps still—transformed.

All of life, my older friends often tell me, is a conspiracy against that ideal of independence with which a young intellectual begins; but if so, wisdom consists not in premature surrender but in learning when to evade, when to stave off and when to oppose head-on. Conformity, as Arthur Koestler said some years ago, "is often a form of betrayal which can be carried out with a clear conscience." Gradually we make our peace with the world, and not by anything as exciting as a secret pact; nowadays Lucifer is a very patient and reasonable fellow with a gift for indulging one's most legitimate desires; and we learn, if we learn anything at all, that betrayal may consist of a chain of small compromises, even while we also learn that in this age one cannot survive without compromise. What is most alarming is not that a number of intellectuals have abandoned the posture of iconoclasm: let the *Zeitgeist* give them a jog and they will again be radical, all too radical. What is most alarming is that the whole idea of the intellectual vocation—the idea of a life dedicated to values that cannot possibly be realized by a commercial civilization—has gradually lost its allure. And it is this, rather than the abandonment of a particular program, which constitutes our rout.

In a recent number of *Perspectives* Lionel Trilling addressed himself to some of these problems; his perspective is sharply different from mine. Mr. Trilling believes that "there is an unmistakable improvement in the American cultural situation of today over that of, say, thirty years ago," while to me it seems that any comparison between the buoyant free-spirited cultural life of 1923 with the dreariness of 1953, or between their literary achievements, must lead to the conclusion that Mr. Trilling is indulging in a pleasant fantasy. More important, however, is his analysis of how this "improvement" has occurred: "In many civilizations there comes a point at which wealth shows a tendency to submit itself, in some degree, to the rule of mind and imagination, to apologize for its existence by a show of taste and sensitivity. In America the signs of this submission have for some time been visible. . . . Intellect has associated itself with power, perhaps as never before in history, and is now conceded to be in itself a kind of power."

Such stately terms as "wealth" and "intellect" hardly make for sharp distinctions, yet the drift of Mr. Trilling's remarks is clear enough—and, I think, disastrous.

It is perfectly true that in the government bureaucracy and institutional staff, in the mass-culture industries and the academy, intellectuals have been welcomed and absorbed as never before. It is true, again, that "wealth" has become far more indulgent in its treatment of intellectuals, and for good reasons: it needs them more than ever, they are tamer than ever, and its own position is more comfortable and expansive than it has been for a long time. But if "wealth" has made a mild bow toward "intellect" (sometimes while picking its pocket) then "intellect" has engaged in some undignified prostrations before "wealth." Thirty years ago "wealth" was on the defensive, and twenty years ago it was frightened, hesitant, apologetic. "Intellect" was self-confident, aggressive, secure in its belief or, if you wish, delusions. Today the ideology of American capitalism, with its claim to a unique and immaculate destiny, is trumpeted through every medium of communication: official propaganda, institutional advertising and the scholarly writings of people who, until a few years ago, were its major opponents. Marx-baiting, that least risky of occupations, has become a favorite sport in the academic journals; a whining genteel chauvinism is widespread among intellectuals; and the bemoaning of their own fears and timidities a constant theme among professors. Is this to be taken as evidence that "wealth" has subordinated itself to "intellect"? Or is the evidence to be found in the careers of such writers as Max Eastman and James Burnham? To be sure, culture has acquired a more honorific status, as restrained ostentation has replaced conspicuous consumption: wealthy people collect more pictures or at least more modern ones, they endow foundations with large sums—but all this is possible because "intellect" no longer pretends to challenge "wealth."

What has actually been taking place is the absorption of

large numbers of intellectuals, previously independent, into the world of government bureaucracy and public committees; into the constantly growing industries of pseudo-culture; into the adult education business, which subsists on regulated culture-anxiety. This process of bureaucratic absorption does not proceed without check: the Eisenhower administration has recently dismissed a good many intellectuals from government posts. Yet it seems likely that such stupidity will prove temporary and that one way or another, in one administration or another, the intellectuals will drift back into the government: they must, they are indispensable.

Some years ago C. Wright Mills wrote an article in which he labeled the intellectuals as "powerless people." He meant, of course, that they felt incapable of translating their ideas into action and that their consequent frustration had become a major motif in their behavior. His description was accurate enough; yet we might remember that the truly powerless people are those intellectuals—the new realists—who attach themselves to the seats of power, where they surrender their freedom of expression without gaining any significance as political figures. For it is crucial to the history of the American intellectuals in the past few decades—as well as to the relationship between "wealth" and "intellect"—that whenever they become absorbed into the accredited institutions of society they not only lose their traditional rebelliousness but to one extent or another *they cease to function as intellectuals.* The institutional world needs intellectuals *because* they are intellectuals but it does not want them *as* intellectuals. It beckons to them because of what they are but it will not allow them, at least within its sphere of articulation, either to remain or entirely cease being what they are. It needs them for their knowledge, their talent, their inclinations and passions; it insists that they retain a measure of these endowments, which it means to employ for its own ends, and without which the intellectuals would be of no use to it whatever. A simplified but useful equation suggests itself: the relation of the institutional world to the intellectuals is as the relation of middlebrow culture to serious culture. The one battens on the other, absorbs and raids it with increasing frequency and skill, subsidizes and encourages it enough to make further raids possible—at times the parasite will support its victim. Surely this relationship must be one reason for the high incidence of neurosis that is supposed to prevail among intellectuals. A total estrangement from the sources of power and prestige, even a blind unreasoning rejection of every aspect of our culture, would be far healthier if only because it would permit a free discharge of aggression.

I do not mean to suggest that for intellectuals all institutions are equally dangerous or disadvantageous. Even during the New Deal, the life of those intellectuals who journeyed to Washington was far from happy. The independence possible to a professor of sociology is usually greater than that possible to a writer of television scripts, and a professor of English, since the world will not take his subject seriously, can generally enjoy more intellectual leeway than a professor of sociology. Philip Rieff, a sociologist, has caustically described a major tendency among his colleagues as a drift from "science" to "policy" in which "loyalty, not truth, provides the social condition by which the intellectual discovers his new environment." It is a drift "from the New School to the Rand Corporation."

There is, to be sure, a qualitative difference between the academy and the government bureau or the editorial staff. The university is still committed to the ideology of freedom, and many professors try hard and honestly to live by it. If the intellectual cannot subsist independently, off his work or his relatives, the academy is usually his best bet. But no one who has a live sense of what the literary life has been and might still be, either in Europe or this country, can accept the notion that the academy is the natural home of intellect. What seems so unfortunate is that the whole *idea* of independence is losing its traditional power. Scientists are bound with chains of official secrecy; sociologists compete for government research chores; foundations become indifferent to solitary writers and delight in "teams"; the possibility of living in decent poverty from moderately serious literary journalism becomes more and more remote. Compromises are no doubt necessary, but they had better be recognized for what they are.

Perhaps something should be said here about "alienation," a subject on which intellectuals have written more self-humiliating nonsense than any other, except several. Involved, primarily, is a matter of historical fact. During most of the bourgeois epoch, the European intellectuals grew increasingly alienated from the social community because the very ideals that had animated the bourgeois revolution were now being violated by bourgeois society; their "alienation" was prompted not by bohemian willfulness or socialist dogmatism but by a loyalty to Liberty, Fraternity, Equality, or to a vision of a preindustrial society that, by a trick of history, came pretty much to resemble Liberty, Fraternity, Equality. Just as it was the triumph of capitalism which largely caused this sense of estrangement, so it was the expansion of capitalism that allowed the intellectuals enough freedom to express it. As Philip Rahv has put it: "During the greater part of the bourgeois epoch . . . [writers] preferred alienation from the community to alienation from themselves." Precisely this choice made possible their strength and boldness, precisely this "lack of roots" gave them their speculative power. Almost always, the talk one hears these days about "the need for roots" veils a desire to compromise the tradition of intellectual independence, to seek in a nation or religion or party a substitute for the tenacity one should find in oneself. Isaac Rosenfeld's remark that "the ideal society . . . cannot afford to include many deeply rooted individuals" is not merely a clever *mot* but an important observation.

It may be that the issue is no longer relevant; that, with the partial submission of "wealth" to "intellect," the clash between a business civilization and the values of art is no longer as urgent as we once thought; but if so, we must discard a great deal, and mostly the best, of the literature, the criticism and the speculative thought of the twentieth century. For to deny the historical fact of "alienation" (as if that would make it any the less real!) is to deny our heritage, both as burden and advantage, and also, I think, to deny our possible future as a community.

Much of what I have been describing here must be due to a feeling among intellectuals that the danger of Stalinism allows them little or no freedom in their relations with bourgeois society. This feeling seems to me only partly justified, and I do not suffer from any inclination to minimize the Stalinist threat. To be sure, it does limit our possibilities for action—if, that is, we still want to engage in any dissident politics—and sometimes it may force us into political alignments that are distasteful. But here a crucial distinction should be made: the danger of Stalism may require temporary expedients in the area of *power* such as would have seemed compromising some years ago, but there is no reason, at least no good reason, why it should require compromise or conformity in the area of *ideas,* no reason why it should lead us to become partisans of bourgeois society, which is itself, we might remember, heavily responsible for the Stalinist victories.

III

"In the United States at this time liberalism is not only the dominant but even the sole intellectual tradition." This sentence of Lionel Trilling's contains a sharp insight into the political life of contemporary America. If I understand him correctly, he is saying that our society is at present so free from those pressures of conflicting classes and interests which make for sharply defined ideologies, that liberalism colors, or perhaps the word should be, bleaches all political tendencies. It becomes a loose shelter, a poncho rather than a program; to call oneself a liberal one doesn't really have to believe in anything. In such a moment of social slackness, the more extreme intellectual tendencies have a way, as soon as an effort is made to put them into practice, of sliding into and becoming barely distinguishable from the dominant liberalism. Both conservatism and radicalism can retain, at most, an intellectual recalcitrance, but neither is presently able to engage in a sustained practical politics of its own; which does not mean they will never be able to.

The point is enforced by looking at the recent effort to affirm a conservative ideology. Mr. Russell Kirk, who makes this effort with some earnestness, can hardly avoid the eccentricity of appealing to Providence as a putative force in American politics: an appeal that suggests both the intensity of his conservative desire and the desperation behind the intensity. Mr. Peter Viereck, a friskier sort of writer, calls himself a conservative, but surely this is nothing more than a mystifying pleasantry, for aside from the usual distinctions of temperament and talent it is hard to see how his conservatism differs from the liberalism of Arthur Schlesinger, Jr. For Viereck conservatism is a shuffling together of attractive formulas, without any effort to discover their relationship to deep *actual* clashes of interest: he fails, for example, even to consider that in America there is today neither opportunity nor need for conservatism (since the liberals do the necessary themselves) and that if an opportunity were to arise, conservatism could seize upon it only by acquiring a mass, perhaps reactionary dynamic, that is, by "going into the streets." And that, surely, Mr. Viereck doesn't want.

If conservatism is taken to mean, as in some "classical" sense it should be, a principled rejection of industrial economy and a yearning for an ordered, hierarchical society that is not centered on the city, then conservatism in America is best defended by a group of literary men whose seriousness is proportionate to their recognition that such a politics is now utterly hopeless and, in any but a utopian sense, meaningless. Such a conservatism, in America, goes back to Fenimore Cooper, who anticipates those implicit criticisms of our society which we honor in Faulkner; and in the hands of serious imaginative writers, but hardly in the hands of political writers obliged to deal with immediate relations of power, it can become a myth which, through abrasion, profoundly challenges modern experience. As for the "conservatism" of the late Senator Taft, which consists of nothing but Liberal economics and wounded nostalgia, it lacks intellectual content and, more important, when in power it merely continues those "statist" policies it had previously attacked.

This prevalence of liberalism yields, to be sure, some obvious and substantial benefits. It makes us properly skeptical of the excessive claims and fanaticisms that accompany ideologies. It makes implausible those "aristocratic" rantings against democracy which were fashionable in some literary circles a few years ago. (So that when a charlatan like Wyndham Lewis is revived and praised for his wisdom, it is done, predictably, by a Hugh Kenner in the *Hudson Review*.) And it allows for the hope that any revival of American radicalism will acknowledge not only its break from, but also its roots in, the liberal tradition.

At the same time, however, the dominance of liberalism contributes heavily to our intellectual conformity. Liberalism dominates, but without confidence or security; it knows that its victories at home are tied to disasters abroad; and for the *élan* it cannot summon, it substitutes a blend of complacence and anxiety. It makes for an atmosphere of blur in the realm of ideas, since it has a stake in seeing momentary concurrences as deep harmonies. In an age that suffers from incredible catastrophes it scoffs at theories of social apocalypse—as if any *more* evidence were needed; in an era convulsed by war, revolution and counter-revolution it discovers the virtues of "moderation." And when the dominant school of liberalism, the school of *realpolitik*, scores points in attacking "the ritualistic liberals," it also betrays a subterranean desire to retreat into the caves of bureaucratic caution. Liberalism is an ideology, as "the haunted air," has never been stronger in this country; but can as much be said of the appetite for freedom?

Sidney Hook discovers merit in the Smith Act: he was not for its passage but doubts the wisdom of its repeal. Mary McCarthy, zooming to earth from never-never land, discovers in the American war economy no less than paradise: "Class barriers disappear or tend to become porous; the factory worker is an economic aristocrat in comparison to the middle-class clerk. . . . The America . . . of vast inequalities and dramatic contrasts is rapidly ceasing to exist." Daniel Boorstin —he cannot be charged with the self-deceptions peculiar to idealism—discovers that "the genius of American politics" consists not in the universal possibilities of democracy but in a uniquely fortunate geography which, obviously, cannot be exported. David Riesman is so disturbed by Veblen's rebelliousness toward American society that he explains it as a projection of father-hatred; and what complex is it, one wonders, which explains a writer's assumption that Veblen's view of America is so inconceivable as to require a home-brewed psychoanalysis? Irving Kristol writes an article minimizing the threat to civil liberties and shortly thereafter is chosen to be public spokesman for the American Committee for Cultural Freedom. And in the Committee itself, it is possible for serious intellectuals to debate—none is *for* McCarthy—whether the public activities of the Wisconsin hooligan constitute a serious menace to freedom.

One likes to speculate: suppose Simone de Beauvoir and Bertrand Russell didn't exist, would not many of the political writers for *Commentary* and the *New Leader* have to invent them? It is all very well, and even necessary, to demonstrate that Russell's description of America as subject to "a reign of terror" is malicious and ignorant, or that de Beauvoir's picture of America is a blend of Stalinist clichés and second-rate literary fantasies; but this hardly disposes of the problem of civil liberties or of the justified alarm many sober European intellectuals feel with regard to America. Between the willfulness of those who see only terror and the indifference of those who see only health, there is need for simple truth: that intellectual freedom in the United States is under severe attack and that the intellectuals have, by and large, shown a painful lack of militancy in defending the rights which are a precondition of their existence.[1]

It is in the pages of the influential magazine *Commentary* that liberalism is most skillfully and systematically advanced as a strategy for adapting to the American *status quo*. Until the last few months, when a shift in editorial temper seems to have occurred, the magazine was more deeply preoccupied, or preoccupied at deeper levels, with the dangers to freedom stemming from people like Freda Kirchwey and Arthur Miller than the dangers from people like Senator McCarthy. In March 1952 Irving Kristol, then an editor of *Commentary*, could write that "there is one thing the American people know about Senator McCarthy: he, like them, is unequivocally anti-Communist. About the spokesmen for American liberalism, they feel they know no such thing. And with some justification." In September 1952, at the very moment when McCarthy had become a central issue in the presidential campaign,

[1] It must in honesty be noted that many of the intellectuals least alive to the problem of civil liberties are former Stalinists or radicals; and this, more than the vast anti-Marxist literature of recent years, constitutes a serious criticism of American radicalism. For the truth is that the "old-fashioned liberals" like John Dewey and Alexander Meiklejohn, at whom it was once so fashionable to sneer, have displayed a finer sensitivity to the need for defending domestic freedoms than the more "sophisticated" intellectuals who leapt from Marx to Machiavelli.

Elliot Cohen, the senior editor of *Commentary*, could write that McCarthy "remains in the popular mind an unreliable, second-string blowhard; his *only* support as a great national figure is from the fascinated fears of the intelligentsia." (My emphasis—I.H.) As if to blot out the memory of these performances, Nathan Glazer, still another editor, wrote an excellent analysis of McCarthy in the March 1953 issue; but at the end of his article, almost as if from another hand, there again appeared the magazine's earlier line: "All that Senator McCarthy can do on his own authority that someone equally unpleasant and not a Senator can't, is to haul people down to Washington for a grilling by his committee. It is a shame and an outrage that Senator McCarthy should remain in the Senate; yet I cannot see that it is an imminent danger to personal liberty in the United States." It is, I suppose, this sort of thing that is meant when people speak about the need for replacing the outworn formulas and clichés of liberalism and radicalism with *new ideas*.

IV

To what does one conform? To institutions, obviously. To the dead images that rot in one's mind, unavoidably. And almost always, to the small grating necessities of day-to-day survival. In these senses it may be said that we are all conformists to one or another degree. When Sidney Hook writes, "I see no specific virtue in the attitude of conformity or nonconformity," he is right if he means that no human being can, or should, entirely accept or reject the moral and social modes of his time. And he is right in adding that there are occasions, such as the crisis of the Weimar republic, when the non-conformism of a Stefan George or an Oswald Spengler can have unhappy consequences.

But Professor Hook seems to me quite wrong in supposing that his remark applies significantly to present-day America. It would apply if we lived in a world were ideas could be weighed in free and delicate balance, without social pressures or contaminations, so that our choices would be made solely from a passion for truth. As it happens, however, there are tremendous pressures in America that make for intellectual conformism and consequently, in this tense and difficult age, there are very real virtues in preserving the attitude of critical skepticism and distance. Even some of the more extreme antics of the professional "Bohemians" or literary anarchists take on a certain value which in cooler moments they might not have.[2]

What one conforms to most of all—despite and against one's intentions—is the *Zeitgeist*, that vast insidious sum of pressures and fashions; one drifts along, anxious and compliant, upon the favored assumptions of the moment; and not a soul in the intellectual world can escape this. Only, some resist and some don't. Today the *Zeitgeist* presses down upon us with a greater insistence than at any other moment of the century. In the 1930's many of those who hovered about the *New Masses* were mere camp-followers of success; but the conformism of the party-line intellectual, at least before 1936, did sometimes bring him into conflict with established power: he had to risk something. Now, by contrast, established power and the dominant intellectual tendencies have come together in a harmony such as this country has not seen since the Gilded Age; and this, of course, makes the temptations of conformism all the more acute. The carrots, for once, are real.

Real even for literary men, who these days prefer to meditate upon symbolic vegetables. I would certainly not wish to suggest any direct correlation between our literary assumptions and the nature of our politics; but surely some of the recent literary trends and fashions owe something to the more general intellectual drift toward conformism. Not, of course,

[2] It may be asked whether a Stalinist's "non-conformism" is valuable. No, it isn't; the Stalinist is anything but a non-conformist; he has merely shifted the object of his worship, as later, when he abandons Stalinism, he usually shifts it again.

that liberalism dominates literary life, as it dominates the rest of the intellectual world. Whatever practical interest most literary men have in politics comes to little else than the usual liberalism, but their efforts at constructing literary ideologies —frequently as forced marches to discover values our society will not yield them—result in something quite different from liberalism. Through much of our writing, both creative and critical, there run a number of ideological motifs, the importance of which is hardly diminished by the failure of the men who employ them to be fully aware of their implications. Thus, a major charge that might be brought against some New Critics is not that they practice formal criticism but that they don't; not that they see the work of art as an object to be judged according to laws of its own realm but that, often unconsciously, they weave ideological assumptions into their writings.[3] Listening last summer to Cleanth Brooks lecture on Faulkner, I was struck by the deep hold that the term "orthodox" has acquired on his critical imagination, and not, by the way, on his alone. But "orthodox" is not, properly speaking, a critical term at all, it pertains to matters of religious or other belief rather than to literary judgment; and a habitual use of such terms can only result in the kind of "slanted" criticism Mr. Brooks has been so quick, and right, to condemn.

Together with "orthodox" there goes a cluster of terms which, in their sum, reveal an implicit ideological bias. The

[3] This may be true of all critics, but is most perilous to those who suppose themselves free of ideological coloring. In a review of my Faulkner book—rather favorable, so that no ego wounds prompt what follows— Mr. Robert Daniel writes that "Because of Mr. Howe's connections with . . . the *Partisan Review*, one might expect his literary judgments to be shaped by political and social preconceptions, but that does not happen often." Mr. Daniel is surprised that a critic whose politics happen to be radical should try to keep his literary views distinct from his nonliterary ones. To be sure, this is sometimes very difficult, and perhaps no one entirely succeeds. But the one sure way of not succeeding is to write, as Mr. Daniel does, from no very pressing awareness that it is a problem for critics who appear in the *Sewanee Review* quite as much as for those who appear in *Partisan Review*.

word "traditional" is especially tricky here, since it has legitimate uses in both literary and moral-ideological contexts. What happens, however, in much contemporary criticism is that these two contexts are either taken to be one or to be organically related, so that it becomes possible to assume that a sense of literary tradition necessarily involves and sanctions a "traditional" view of morality. There is a powerful inclination here—it is the doing of the impish *Zeitgeist*—to forget that literary tradition can be fruitfully seen as a series of revolts, literary but sometimes more than literary, of generation against generation, age against age. The emphasis on "tradition" has other contemporary implications: it is used as a not very courageous means of countering the experimental and the modern; it can enclose the academic assumption—and this is the curse of the Ph.D. system—that the whole of the literary past is at every point equally relevant to a modern intelligence; and it frequently includes the provincial American need to be more genteel than the gentry, more English than the English. Basically, it has served as a means of asserting conservative or reactionary moral-ideological views not, as they should be asserted, in their own terms, but through the refining medium of literary talk.

In general, there has been a tendency among critics to subsume literature under their own moral musings, which makes for a conspicuously humorless kind of criticism.[4] Morality is assumed to be a sufficient container for the floods of experience, and poems or novels that gain their richness from the complexity with which they dramatize the incommensurability between man's existence and his conceptualizing, are

---

[4] Writing about *Wuthering Heights* Mr. Mark Schorer solemnly declares that "the theme of the moral magnificence of unmoral passion is an impossible theme to sustain, and the needs of her temperament to the contrary, all personal longing and reverie to the contrary, Emily Brontë teaches herself that this was indeed not at all what her material must mean as art." What is more, if Emily Brontë had lived a little longer she would have been offered a Chair in Moral Philosophy.

thinned, pruned and allegorized into moral fables. Writers who spent—in both senses of the word—their lives wrestling with terrible private demons are elevated into literary dons and deacons. It is as if Stendhal had never come forth, with his subversive wit, to testify how often life and literature find the whole moral apparatus irrelevant or tedious, as if Lawrence had never written *The Man Who Died,* as if Nietzsche had never launched his great attack on the Christian impoverishment of the human psyche. One can only be relieved, therefore, at knowing a few critics personally: how pleasant the discrepancy between their writings and their lives!

But it is Original Sin that today commands the highest prestige in the literary world. Like nothing else, it allows literary men to enjoy a sense of profundity and depth—to relish a disenchantment which allows no further risk of becoming enchanted—as against the superficiality of *mere* rationalism. It allows them to appropriate to the "tradition" the greatest modern writers, precisely those whose values and allegiances are most ambiguous, complex and enigmatic, while at the same time generously leaving, as Leslie Fiedler once suggested, Dreiser and Farrell as the proper idols for that remnant benighted enough to maintain a naturalist philosophy. To hold, as Dickens remarks in *Bleak House,* "a loose belief that if the world go wrong, it was, in some off-hand manner, never meant to go right," this becomes the essence of wisdom. (Liberals too have learned to cast a warm eye on "man's fallen nature," so that one gets the high comedy of Arthur Schlesinger, Jr. interrupting his quite worldly political articles with uneasy bows in the direction of Kierkegaard.) And with this latest dispensation come, of course, many facile references to the ideas supposedly held by Rousseau[5] and Marx, that man is

---

[5] Mr. Randall Jarrell, who usually avoids fashionable cant: "Most of us know, now, that Rousseau was wrong; that man, when you knock his chains off, sets up the death camps." Which chains were knocked off in Germany to permit the setting-up of death camps? And which chains must be put up again to prevent a repetition of the death camps?

"perfectible" and that progress moves in a steady upward curve.

I say, facile references, because no one who has troubled to read Rousseau or Marx could write such things. Exactly what the "perfectibility of man" is supposed to mean, if anything at all, I cannot say; but it is not a phrase intrinsic to the *kind* of thought one finds in the mature Marx or, most of the time, in Rousseau. Marx did not base his argument for socialism on any view that one could isolate a constant called "human nature"; he would certainly have agreed with Ortega that man has not a nature, but a history. Nor did he have a very rosy view of the human beings who were his contemporaries or recent predecessors: see in *Capital* the chapter on the Working Day, a grisly catalogue of human bestiality. Nor did he hold to a naive theory of progress: he wrote that the victories of progress "seem bought by the loss of character. At the same pace that mankind masters nature, man seems to become enslaved to other men or to his own infamy."

As for Rousseau, the use of even a finger's-worth of historical imagination should suggest that the notion of "a state of nature" which modern literary people so enjoy attacking, was a political metaphor employed in a pre-revolutionary situation, and not, therefore, to be understood outside its context. Rousseau explicitly declared that he did not suppose the "state of nature" to have existed in historical time; it was, he said, "a pure idea of reason" reached by abstraction from the observable state of society. As G. D. H. Cole remarks, "in political matters at any rate, the 'state of nature' is for [Rousseau] only a term of controversy . . . he means by 'nature' not the original state of a thing, nor even its reduction to the simplest terms; he is passing over to the conception of 'nature' as identical with the full development of [human] capacity. . . ." There are, to be sure, elements in Rousseau's thought which one may well find distasteful, but these are not the elements commonly referred to when he is used in literary talk as a straw man to be beaten with the cudgels of "orthodoxy."

What then is the significance of the turn to Original Sin among so many intellectuals? Surely not to inform us, at this late moment, that man is capable of evil. Or is it, as Cleanth Brooks writes, to suggests that man is a "limited" creature, limited in possibilities and capacities, and hence unable to achieve his salvation through social means? Yes, to be sure; but the problem of history is to determine, by action, how far those limits may go. Conservative critics like to say that "man's fallen nature" makes unrealistic the liberal-radical vision of the good society—apparently, when Eve bit the apple she predetermined, with one fatal crunch, that her progeny could work its way up to capitalism, and not a step further. But the liberal-radical vision of the good society does not depend upon a belief in the "unqualified goodness of man"; nor does it locate salvation in society: anyone in need of being saved had better engage in a private scrutiny. The liberal-radical claim is merely that the development of technology has now made possible—possible, not inevitable—a solution of those material problems that have burdened mankind for centuries. These problems solved, man is then on his own, to make of his self and his world what he can.

The literary prestige of Original Sin cannot be understood without reference to the current cultural situation; it cannot be understood except as a historical phenomenon reflecting, like the whole turn to religion and religiosity, the weariness of intellectuals in an age of defeat and their yearning to remove themselves from the bloodied arena of historical action and choice, which necessarily means, of secular action and choice. Much sarcasm and anger has been expended on the "failure of nerve" theory, usually by people who take it as a personal affront to be told that there is a connection between what happens in their minds and what happens in the world; but if one looks at the large-scale shifts among intellectuals during the past 25 years, it becomes impossible to put *all* of them down to a simultaneous, and thereby miraculous, discovery of Truth, some at least must be seen as a consequence of those historical pressures which make this an age of conformism. Like other efforts to explain major changes in belief, the "failure of nerve" theory does not tell us why certain people believed in the '30's what was only to become popular in the '50's and why others still believe in the '50's what was popular in the '30's; but it does tell us something more important: why a complex of beliefs is dominant at one time and subordinate at another.

V

I have tried to trace a rough pattern from social history through politics and finally into literary ideology, as a means of explaining the power of the conformist impulse in our time. But it is obvious that in each intellectual "world" there are impulses of this kind that cannot easily be shown to have their sources in social or historical pressures. Each intellectual world gives rise to its own patterns of obligation and preference. The literary world, being relatively free from the coarser kinds of social pressure, enjoys a considerable degree of detachment and autonomy. (Not as much as it likes to suppose, but a considerable degree.) That the general intellectual tendency is to acquiesce in what one no longer feels able to change or modify, strongly encourages the internal patterns of conformism in the literary world and intensifies the yearning, common to all groups but especially to small and insecure groups, to draw together in a phalanx of solidarity. Then too, those groups that live by hostility to the dominant values of society—in this case, cultural values—find it extremely difficult to avoid an inner conservatism as a way of balancing their public role of opposition; anyone familiar with radical politics knows this phenomenon only too well. Finally, the literary world, while quite powerless in relation to, say, the worlds of business and politics, disposes of a measurable amount of power and patronage within its own domain; which makes, again, for predictable kinds of influence.

Whoever would examine the inner life of the literary world should turn first not to the magazines or the dignitaries or famous writers but to the graduate students, for like it or not the graduate school has become the main recruiting grounds for critics and sometimes even for writers. Here, in conversation with the depressed classes of the academy, one sees how the Ph.D. system—more powerful today than it has been for decades, since so few other choices are open to young literary men—grinds and batters personality into a mold of cautious routine. And what one finds among these young people, for all their intelligence and devotion and eagerness, is often appalling: a remarkable desire to be "critics," not as an accompaniment to the writing of poetry or the changing of the world or the study of man and God, but just critics—as if criticism were a *subject,* as if one could be a critic without having at least four non-literary opinions, or as if criticism "in itself" could adequately engage an adult mind for more than a small part of its waking time. An equally astonishing indifference to the ideas that occupy the serious modern mind—Freud, Marx, Nietzsche, Frazer, Dewey are not great thinkers in their right, but reservoirs from which one dredges up "approaches to criticism"—together with a fabulous knowledge of what Ransom said about Winters with regard to what Winters had said about Eliot. And a curiously humble discipleship—but also arrogant to those beyond the circle—so that one meets not fresh minds in growth but apostles of Burke or Trilling or Winters or Leavis or Brooks or neo-Aristotle.

Very little of this is the fault of the graduate students themselves, for they, like the distinguished figures I have just listed, are the victims of an unhappy cultural moment. What we have today in the literary world is a gradual bureaucratization of opinion and taste; not a dictatorship, not a conspiracy, not a coup, not a Machiavellian plot to impose a mandatory "syllabus"; but the inevitable result of outer success and inner hardening. Fourth-rate exercises in exegesis are puffed in the magazines while so remarkable and provocative a work as Arnold Hauser's *Social History of Art* is hardly reviewed, its very title indicating the reason. Learned young critics who have never troubled to open a novel by Turgenev can rattle off reams of Kenneth Burke, which gives them, understandably, a sensation of having enlarged upon literature. Literature itself becomes a raw material which critics work up into schemes of structure and symbol; to suppose that it is concerned with anything so *gauche* as human experience or obsolete as human beings—"You mean," a student said to me, "that you're interested in the *characters* of novels!"—is to commit Mr. Elton alone knows how many heresies. (Cf. The *Glossary,* now in its fifth edition, which proves that bad reviews can't kill ponies.) Symbols clutter the literary landscape like the pots and pans a two-year-old strews over the kitchen floor; and what is wrong here is not merely the transparent absence of literary tact—the gift for saying when a pan is a pan and when a pan is a symbol—but far more important, a transparent lack of interest in represented experience. For Mr. Stallman the fact that Stephen Crane looking at the sun felt moved to compare it to a wafer is not enough, the existence of suns and wafers and their possible conjunction is not sufficiently marvelous: both objects must be absorbed into Christian symbolism (an ancient theory of literature developed by the church fathers to prove that suns, moons, vulva, chairs, money, hair, pots, pans and words are really crucifixes). Techniques for reading a novel that have at best a limited relevance are frozen into dogmas: one might suppose from glancing at the more imposing literary manuals that "point of view" is the crucial means of judging a novel. (Willa Cather, according to Miss Caroline Gordon, was "astonishingly ignorant of her craft," for she refrained from "using a single consciousness as a prism of moral reflection." The very mistake Tolstoy made, too!) Criticism itself, far from being the reflection of a solitary mind upon a work of art and therefore, like the solitary mind, incomplete and subjective, comes increasingly to be regarded as a problem in mechanics, the tools, methods and trade secrets of which can be picked up, usually during the summer, from the more experienced operatives. In the mind of Mr. Stanley Hyman, who serves the indispensable function of reducing fashionable literary notions, criticism seems to resemble Macy's on bargain day: *First floor, symbols; Second floor, myths (rituals to the rear on your right); Third floor, ambiguities and paradoxes; Fourth floor, word counting; Fifth floor, Miss Harrison's antiquities; Attic, Marxist remnants; Basement, Freud; Sub-basement, Jung. Watch your step, please.*

What is most disturbing, however, is that writing about literature and writers has become an industry. The preposterous academic requirement that professors write books they don't want to write and no one wants to read, together with the obtuse assumption that piling up more and more irrelevant information about an author's life helps us understand his work—this makes for a vast flood of books that have little to do with literature, criticism or even scholarship. Would you care to know the contents of the cargo (including one elephant) carried by the vessel of which Hawthorne's father was captain in 1795? Mr. Cantwell has an itemized list, no doubt as an aid to reading *The Scarlet Letter*. Mr. Leyda knows what happened to Melville day by day and it is hardly his fault that most days nothing very much happened. Mr. Johnson does as much for Dickens and adds plot summaries too, no doubt because he is dealing with a little-read author. Another American scholar has published a full book on *Mardi*, which is astonishing not because he wrote the book but because he managed to finish reading *Mardi* at all.

I have obviously chosen extreme examples and it would be silly to contend that they adequately describe the American literary scene; but like the distorting mirrors in Coney Island they help bring into sharper contour the major features. Or as Mr. Donald Davie writes in *Twentieth Century:*

> The professional poet has already disappeared from the literary scene, and the professional man of letters is following him into the grave. . . . It becomes more and more difficult, and will soon be impossible, for a man to make his living as a literary dilettante. . . . And instead of the professional man of letters we have the professional critic, the young don writing in the first place for other dons, and only incidentally for that supremely necessary fiction, the common reader. In other words, an even greater proportion of what is written about literature, and even of what literature is written, is "academic". . . . Literary standards are now in academic hands; for the freelance man of letters, who once supplemented and corrected the don, is fast disappearing from the literary scene. . . .
>
> The pedant is as common as he ever was. And now that willy-nilly so much writing about literature is in academic hands, his activities are more dangerous than ever. But he has changed his habits. Twenty years ago he was to be heard asserting that his business was with hard facts, that questions of value and technique were not his affair, and that criticism could therefore be left to the impressionistic journalist. Now the pedant is proud to call himself a critic; he prides himself on evaluation and analysis; he aims to be penetrating, not informative. . . .
>
> The pedant is a very adaptable creature, and can be as comfortable with Mr. Eliot's "objective correlative," Mr. Empson's "ambiguities" and Dr. Leavis's "complexities" as in the older suit of critical clothes that he has now, for the most part, abandoned.

Mr. Davie has in mind the literary situation in England, but all one needs for applying his remarks to America is an ability to multiply.

VI

All of the tendencies toward cultural conformism come to a head in the assumption that the *avant garde,* as both concept and intellectual grouping, has become obsolete or irrelevant. Yet the future quality of American culture, I would maintain, largely depends on the survival, and the terms of survival, of precisely the kind of dedicated group that the *avant garde* has been.

The *avant garde* first appeared on the American scene some 25 or 30 years ago, as a response to the need for absorbing the meanings of the cultural revolution that had taken place in Europe during the first two decades of the century. The achievements of Joyce, Proust, Schoenberg, Bartók, Picasso, Matisse, to mention only the obvious figures, signified one of the major turnings in the cultural history of the West, a turning made all the more crucial by the fact that it came not during the vigor of a society but during its crisis. To counter the hostility which the work of such artists met among all the official spokesmen of culture, to discover formal terms and modes through which to secure these achievements, to insist upon the continuity between their work and the accepted, because dead, artists of the past—this became the task of the *avant garde.* Somewhat later a section of the *avant garde* also became politically active, and not by accident; for precisely those aroused sensibilities that had responded to the innovations of the modern masters now responded to the crisis of modern society. Thus, in the early years of a magazine like *Partisan Review*—roughly between 1936 and 1941—these two radical impulses came together in an uneasy but fruitful union; and it was in those years that the magazine seemed most exciting and vital as a link between art and experience, between the critical consciousness and the political conscience, between the *avant garde* of letters and the independent left of politics.

That union has since been dissolved, and there is no likelihood that it will soon be re-established. American radicalism exists only as an idea, and that barely; the literary *avant garde* — it has become a stock comment for reviewers to make — is rapidly disintegrating, without function or spirit, and held together only by an inert nostalgia.

Had the purpose of the *avant garde* been to establish the currency of certain names, to make the reading of *The Waste Land* and *Ulysses* respectable in the universities, there would be no further need for its continuance. But clearly this was not the central purpose of the *avant garde*, it was only an unavoidable fringe of snobbery and fashion. The struggle for Joyce mattered only as it was a struggle for literary standards; the defense of Joyce was a defense not merely of modern innovation but of that traditional culture which was the source of modern innovation. And at its best it was a defense against those spokesmen for the genteel, the respectable and the academic who had established a stranglehold over traditional culture. At the most serious level, the *avant garde* was trying to face the problem of the quality of our culture, and when all is said and done, it faced that problem with a courage and honesty that no other group in society could match.

If the history of the *avant garde* is seen in this way, there is every reason for believing that its survival is as necessary today as it was 25 years ago. To be sure, our immediate prospect is not nearly so exciting as it must then have seemed: we face no battle on behalf of great and difficult artists who are scorned by the official voices of culture. Today, in a sense, the danger is that the serious artists are not scorned enough. Philistinism has become very shrewd: it does not attack its enemies as much as it disarms them through reasonable cautions and moderate amendments. But this hardly makes the defense of those standards that animated the *avant garde* during its best days any the less a critical obligation.

It has been urged in some circles that only the pressure of habit keeps serious writers from making "raids" upon the middlebrow world, that it is now possible to win substantial outposts in that world if we are ready to take risks. Perhaps. But surely no one desires a policy of highbrow isolation, and no one could oppose raids, provided that is what they really are. The pre-condition for successful raids, however, is that the serious writers themselves have a sense—not of belonging to an exclusive club—but of representing those cultural values which alone can sustain them while making their raids. Thus far the incursions of serious writers into the middlebrow world have not been remarkably successful: for every short-story writer who has survived the *New Yorker* one could point to a dozen whose work became trivial and frozen after they had begun to write for it. Nor do I advocate, in saying this, a policy of evading temptations. I advocate overcoming them. Writers today have no choice, often enough, but to write for magazines like the *New Yorker*—and worse, far worse. But what matters is the terms upon which the writer enters into such relationships, his willingness to understand with whom he is dealing, his readiness not to deceive himself that an unpleasant necessity is a desirable virtue.

It seems to me beyond dispute that, thus far at least, in the encounter between high and middle culture, the latter has come off by far the better. Every current of the *Zeitgeist*, every imprint of social power, every assumption of contemporary American life favors the safe and comforting patterns of middlebrow feeling. And then too the gloomier Christian writers may have a point when they tell us that it is easier for a soul to fall than to rise.[6]

[6] Thus Professor Gilbert Highet, the distinguished classicist, writing in *Harper's* finds André Gide "an abominably wicked man. His work seems to me to be either shallowly based symbolism, or else cheap cynicism made by inverting commonplaces or by grinning through them. . . . Gide had the curse of perpetual immaturity. But then I am always aware of the central fact about Gide—that he was a sexual pervert who kept proclaiming and justifying his perversion; and perhaps this blinds me to his merits . . . the garrulous, Pangloss-like, pimple-scratching, self-exposure of Gide."

I don't mean to suggest that many fall so low, but then not many philistines are so well educated as Mr. Highet.

Precisely at the time that the highbrows seem inclined to abandon what is sometimes called their "proud isolation," the middlebrows have become more intransigent in their opposition to everything that is serious and creative in our culture (which does not, of course, prevent them from exploiting and contaminating, for purposes of mass gossip, everything that is serious and creative in our culture). What else is the meaning of the coarse attack launched by the *Saturday Review* against the highbrows, under the guise of discussing the Pound case? What, for that matter, is the meaning of the hostility with which the *Partisan Review* symposium on "Our Country and Our Culture" was received? It would take no straining of texts to see this symposium as a disconcerting sign of how far intellectuals have drifted in the direction of cultural adaptation, yet the middlebrows wrote of it with blunt enmity. And perhaps because they too sensed this drift in the symposium, the middlebrows, highly confident at the moment, became more aggressive, for they do not desire compromise, they know that none is possible. So genial a middlebrow as Elmer Davis, in a long review of the symposium, entitled with a characteristic smirk "The Care and Feeding of Intellectuals," ends up on a revealing note: "The highbrows seem to be getting around to recognizing what the middlebrows have known for the past thirty years. This is progress." It is also the best possible argument for the maintenance of the *avant garde,* even if only as a kind of limited defense.

Much has been written about the improvement of cultural standards in America, though a major piece of evidence—the wide circulation of paperbound books—is still an unweighed and unanalyzed quantity. The basic relations of cultural power remain unchanged, however: the middlebrows continue to dominate. The most distinguished newspaper in this country retains as its music critic a man named Olin Downes; the literary critic for that newspaper is a man named Orville Prescott; the most widely read book reviewer in this country is a buffoon named Sterling North; the most powerful literary journal, read with admiration by many librarians and professors, remains the *Saturday Review;* and in the leading American book supplement it is possible for the head of the largest American museum to refer, with egregious ignorance, to "the Spenglerian sterility which has possessed Europe for the past half century and [has] produced Proust, Gide and Picasso. . . ." Nothing here gives us cause for reassurance or relaxation; nothing gives us reason to dissolve that compact in behalf of critical intransigence known as the *avant garde.*

No formal ideology or program is entirely adequate for coping with the problems that intellectuals face in the twentieth century. No easy certainties and no easy acceptance of uncertainty. All the forms of authority, the states and institutions and monster bureaucracies, that press in upon modern life—what have these shown us to warrant the surrender of independence?

The most glorious vision of the intellectual life is still that which is loosely called humanist: the idea of a mind committed yet dispassionate, ready to stand alone, curious, eager, skeptical. The banner of critical independence, ragged and torn though it may be, is still the best we have.

A MIND'S TURNINGS

There are grey moments when I charge myself with some small responsibility for the endless chatter about "conformity" that has swept the country. Six years ago, when McCarthyism was at its worst and the response of many intellectuals somewhat less than heroic, I wrote a sharp polemic for *Partisan Review* called "This Age of Conformity." Much of what appeared there still seems to me true, but I could not then know that, unintentionally, I was helping to make the outcry against conformity into a catch-word of our conformist culture.

Despite a small circulation, *Partisan Review* is an influential magazine. Editors and "opinion-makers" read it to keep up with the latest thoughts and moods of the intellectuals; it serves, also, as one of the sources from which middlebrow culture appropriates serious ideas. No one is surprised these days to find a notion or phrase migrating directly from the quarterlies to a cigarette ad, since the man writing the ad may well be an intellectual *manqué* who sneers at *Partisan Review* yet dreams of having it accept his story about the spiritual ordeals of Madison Avenue. As with cigarette ads, so with denunciations of conformity.

Intellectuals used to complain that society ignored or re-

This essay was written in 1960.

jected their ideas; they could hardly have imagined what might happen when, for ends of its own, society learned to "adapt" those ideas. During the past few decades the most remarkable trait of American culture has been neither conformity nor conservatism, not even its truly astonishing dullness; it has been an unprecedented capacity for assimilating—and thereby depreciating—everything on its own terms, both lavish praise and severe attacks.*

Assaults upon mass culture become an indispensable element of culture: the spice for the stew. *One idea seems as good as another, since none seems to matter very much*—this amiably nihilistic version of *chacun à son goût* is the most authentic sentiment of the age. And there seems no way of escaping it.

Perhaps so. But that does not mean that one should seek it and rush to embrace it. Adulteration may await whatever you say, yet that does not relieve you of the obligation to speak.

One mode of resistance, almost never considered by radicals, is silence. No one has yet found a way of popularizing silence, and for many people it must have a genuine value, which we should not scorn. But for the intellectual it will not do. The intellectual, alas, is a *noise-maker;* he is the man who keeps talking even after the room has been emptied and the shades drawn.

Another possibility for resistance is the scholar's kind of specialization. The mass media are quick to grasp phrases about "conformity," and recently have begun to make raids upon literary criticism and discussions of "action painting"; but they leave genuine scholarship untouched, except in those rare circumstances when it promises to yield a tremor of novelty. Still, no matter how much the intellectual may admire and envy the scholarly specialist, he cannot emulate him. In

---

* "To make enemies is perfectly easy; the difficult thing is to keep them."
—William Dean Howells

the nature of things, the intellectual deals with precisely the kinds of topics that the mass media will want to aggrandize. By impulse, if not definition, the intellectual is a man who writes about subjects outside his field. He has no field.

Will a magnified reiteration of radicalism protect him from the raids of mass culture? Probably not. At some moments, it may even help make him more popular, since it can lend him a certain individuality, a flavoring, that sets him apart from the bleached liberalism of the American scene. Recognizing all this, the intellectual can only maintain his moral guard, nourish his sense of humor, try to avoid needless self-pity, self-righteousness and snobbism—and keep doing his work.

In some limited circles, now that Cold War chauvinism is dying out, radicalism seems again to be taking on a sickly sort of popularity. No one, to be sure, wants it for himself, but everyone is ready to admit that it might be good to have a "constructive radical voice" in America. Some people even suggest they know what such a voice should say, though they tend to be chary of providing examples. But if you so much as mention socialism, then you are likely to be considered dangerous (by the readers of *Life*, whose minds seldom change) or absurdly old-fashioned (by the readers of *Partisan Review*, whose minds have been nourished on a diet of novelties). And that may be a good reason—surely not the only or main reason—why those of us whose Marxism is vestigial and whose socialism is primarily a commitment to a value and a problem, should continue to regard ourselves not merely as radicals but also as socialists. If nothing else, it helps suggest that we do not wish to be accepted as members of the Establishment, not even as members who by their frolicsome naysaying make it easier for the rest to stay comfortable and cool.

II

An intellectual, Harold Rosenberg once said to me in an amusing improvisation, is someone who turns answers into questions. This vivid sentence suggests all the invited discomfort, the principled worrying at one's own assumptions, that ought to be characteristic of intellectual life. But there is something else, so utterly commonplace that by now it needs to be cried from rooftops: an intellectual is a man who, by the very fact of his existence, is pledged to freedom.

To many other things as well: but to freedom above all, to freedom as it manifests itself in a series of definite and particular rights, and, equally important, as it is a commanding and moving idea.*

That I am here talking about intellectuals in a special way —by normative fiat more than historical observation—is clear. Yet there is also some historical ground for doing this, if only because over the past two centuries a whole series of norms and ideals have accumulated around the term "intellectual." The ideal construct, so obviously unrealized in many situations, which I here give to the term "intellectual" has itself become part of our history.

Intellectuals have often enough allowed themselves to become mere sycophants of ruling power, even a ruling power that was repressive and inhumane. At other times they have performed, reasonably and constructively, a variety of technical or political tasks. In such instances the judgment of their relationship to the dominant power cannot be made on *a priori* grounds, but depends on a series of specific historical estimates. At the same time, there is always a side to the intellectual—the side that makes him preeminently and uniquely an intellectual—which stands apart, as critic and observer, as the man who in the name of freedom casts a cold

---

* When the Polish intellectuals in 1956 started their opposition to Stalinism, they demanded a series of definite and particular rights, which were valuable not only to them but to other sections of the population; but in a remarkably short time they began to see that their struggle derived from, and could not be sustained without, a general idea of freedom. They began by struggling for the right to existence, but inevitably this led them to a struggle for the right kind of existence.

eye upon considerations of expediency. (In the modern totalitarian state, or in relation to it, intellectuals who become involved with History, Progress and Plans cease, in the sense that I have here used the term, to be intellectuals. They take on other roles: scribe, publicity man, political adjutant.)

For an intellectual to defend freedom is no particular cause for self-congratulation: it ought to be as instinctive with him as for a child to reach for food. That is why the flabbiness of spirit which characterized a good many American intellectuals during the McCarthy period is a deep and lasting blotch. And that is why it is so disquieting to hear intellectuals who but yesterday were professional anti-Stalinists now expressing the kind of rationalizations for Communist power that one has become accustomed to hearing from Paul Sweezy, Paul Baran and Isaac Deutscher.

To keep saying such things is not artificially to preserve a grudge; it is to assume that even in a country like ours, where memory is notoriously short, experience does matter.

III

Unexpectedly my mind keeps turning to Dostoevsky—not, as in the past, the novelist of extreme psychic states but the thinker whom radicals used uneasily to belittle. I mean the Dostoevsky who foresaw a situation in which the movement of history would drive men into a fearful choice between the risks of freedom and the security of a false collective. In the past this has seemed an excessively abstract and apocalyptic view, since the actual choices were seldom as total as Dostoevsky assumed. But now, for the first time, it becomes possible to foresee, in the future just beyond the immediate horizon, a Dostoevskian choice.

The Grand Inquisitor, anticipating his reign on earth, tells Christ:

> We shall give them the quiet humble happiness of weak creatures such as they are by nature. Oh, we shall persuade them

at least not to be proud, for Thou didst lift them up and thereby taught them to be proud. We shall show that they are weak, that they are only pitiful children, but that child-like happiness is the sweetest of all . . . They will marvel at us and will be awe-stricken before us, and will be proud at our being so powerful and clever . . . Yes, we shall set them to work, but in their leisure hours we shall make their life like a child's game . . . Oh, we shall allow them even to sin, they are weak and helpless . . .

And they will be glad to believe our answer, for it will save them from the great anxiety and terrible agony they endure at present in making a decision for themselves. And all will be happy, all the millions . . .

How much "translation" is required to see that this vision, though expressed in the terms of Dostoevsky's anarchist Christianity, anticipates the dominant trend of bureaucratic society, the Communist version primarily but surely not alone? A few elements are missing: the role of technology, the growth of functional rationality—Dostoevsky had not read Max Weber. But the anticipation is there.

When one is engaged in concrete political analysis which involves firm and immediate political choices, it seems to me both intellectually facile and morally catastrophic to affirm an identity between the societies of East and West. Though there is a tendency for the two to move closer to each other, the differences remain enormous and crucial. But if one turns from the immediate political struggle to a kind of socio-cultural speculation by means of which certain trends are projected into an indefinite future, there may be some reason for anticipating a society ruled by benevolent Grand Inquisitors, a society of non-terroristic and bureaucratic authoritarianism, on top of which will flourish an efficient political-technical elite—a society, in short, that makes Huxley's prophecy seem more accurate than Orwell's, except insofar, perhaps, as Orwell's passion and eloquence helped invalidate his own prophecy.

If there will not be a war within the next decade, and if ways are found for controlling the birth rate, it becomes possible to envisage a world in which material wants will be moderately satisfied. This possibility arises not, as radicals once thought, because there is an immediate likelihood that the human race will create for itself a free and humane order, but largely because of the sheer cascading growth of technology. The struggle between East and West has brought obvious catastrophic consequences for modern life; but one ironic consequence has been that the inner tendencies toward social crisis within both capitalist and Communist society are held in check by the need each has to combat the other. And more: the struggle between East and West accelerates the technological growth that makes it possible to foresee a life without severe material want.

To advance this speculation at a time when the majority of human beings on our planet still suffer from terrible poverty, may seem irrelevant and even heartless. It is a speculation which rests upon grossly simplified ideas, partly on the kind of technological determinism which I have repeatedly attacked. But I offer it *not* as a prediction, only as a conceptual possibility. That this possibility will not be realized in the next several decades, for a variety of reasons having to do with our political and social arrangements, seems almost certain. But the possibility remains worth considering in its own right.

Suppose, then, that the goal of moderate material satisfaction is reached after the next several decades in large areas of the world and by societies that are not socialist and often not democratic. What would the intellectuals say? We may assume that large numbers of ordinary people, fed regularly and diverted by the mass media, would be satisfied—as, by comparison with their previous condition, they might have good reason to be. But the intellectuals? Snug in their posts and aglow with honors, would they still remember or care about the vision of human freedom? Would they still feel the force of Dostoevsky's legend with its either-or of freedom and happiness? Or would they comfort themselves by regarding it as a mere dusty remnant of the nineteenth century?

For in our time the Grand Inquisitor is no longer a withered Churchman: stern, ascetic, undeluded. He is now a skilled executive who knows how to manage large-scale enterprises and sustain the morale of his employees. In the West he is a corporation official, in the East he belongs to the Central Committee. He is friendly. And he feeds the hungry.

At the end of Dostoevsky's legend, Christ says not a word but meekly kisses the Grand Inquisitor. Berdyaev and other Christian commentators see this as a triumph of love over power, Christ's readiness to embrace even his greatest enemy, His wisdom in rising above mere argument. No doubt. But perhaps Dostoevsky also meant something else. Perhaps Christ's kiss, as D. H. Lawrence thought, is a sign of loving helplessness: He has nothing to say to the Grand Inquisitor, He cannot struggle with him for possession of the world. The kiss is a kiss of despair, and He retreats, forever, in silence.

GOD, MAN AND STALIN

That Whitaker Chambers told the truth and Alger Hiss did not, seems to me highly probable. Personal tragedy though their confrontation was, it had another, almost abstract quality: the political course of the thirties made it inevitable that, quite apart from this well-groomed man and that unkempt one, there be a clash between two men, one a "liberal" recruited from the idealistic wing of public service, the other a former Communist who repudiated his past and then, as *Witness* testifies, swung to the politics of the far right. If not these two, then two others; if not their shapes and accents, other shapes and accents. And that is why most of the journalistic speculation on their personalities proved so ephemeral: for what did it finally matter whether Hiss was a likable man or Chambers an overwrought one? what did it matter when at stake was the commitment of those popular-front liberals who had persisted in treating Stalinism as an accepted part of "the Left"? and why should serious people have puzzled for long over the private motives of Chambers or Hiss when Stalinism itself remained to be studied and analyzed?

Chambers has told his story and put down his ideas. *Witness* is a fascinating grab-bag: autobiography, account of un-

---

This essay was written in 1952.

derground work, religious tract, attempt at an explanation of Stalinism. As confession, it has an almost classical stature: whatever opinions Chambers may now superimpose on his memory, the narrative itself demands the attention of anyone interested in modern politics. As autobiography, the book is embarrassing: Chambers' memoir of his family seems a needless act of masochism while the portrait of his adult self suggests a man whose total sincerity is uncomplicated by humor, irony, or persuasive humility.

The most remarkable fact about *Witness* is that as a work of ideas it should be so ragged and patchy. In all its 800 pages there is hardly a sustained passage of, say, five thousand words devoted to a serious development of thought; everything breaks down into sermon, reminiscence, self-mortification, and self-justification. Service in the G. P. U. is not, to be sure, the best training for the life of the mind; but there is something in Chambers' flair for intellectual melodrama that seems particular to our time and to the kind of personality always hungry for absolutes of faith. Writes Chambers: "I was not seeking ethics; I was seeking God. My need was to be a practising Christian in the same sense that I had been a practising Communist." A little time spent in "seeking ethics" or even a breather from "seeking" anything, might seem to have been in order.

The world, as Chambers sees it, is split between those who acknowledge the primacy of God and those who assert the primacy of man; from this fundamental division follows a struggle between morality and murder, with Communism merely the final version of the rationalist heresy; and the one hope for the world is a return to Christian virtue, the ethic of mercy. These views Chambers announces with an air of abject righteousness. Indifferent to the caution that the sin of pride takes no more extreme form than a belief in God as one's personal *deus ex machina*, he several times acknowleges a Mover at his elbow and declares the appointment of Thomas

Murphy as government prosecutor in the Hiss case to be evidence that "It pleased God to have in readiness a man." From *Witness* an unsympathetic reader might, in fact, conclude that God spent the past several years as a special aid to the House Committee on Un-American Activities.

In reading this book one is nonplussed by the way its polemics violate its declared values. A few illustrations may suggest the quality of Chambers' thought:

Again and again he declares himself interested in presenting the facts. Without questioning his personal story, I must doubt his capacity as historian and social observer. It is not true that Trotsky "led in person" the Bolshevik troops that suppressed the Kronstadt rebellion. It is not true that "Lenin gave up listening to music because of the emotional havoc it played with him"; the man merely said, if Gorky's report of a casual remark be credited, that music made him want to stroke heads at a time when he felt it necessary to make revolutions. It is not true that "Communists are *invariably* as prurient as gutter urchins." It is an exaggeration to say that in the 1927 faction fight in the United States Communist Party, dirty as it was, each side "prompted scandalous whispering campaigns, in which embezzlement of party money, homosexuality, and stool pigeon were the preferred whispers." And it is a wild exaggeration to assert that the Communist agents in Washington, dangerous as they were, "if only in prompting the triumph of Communism in China, have *decisively* changed the history of Asia, of the United States, and therefore, of *the entire world*" (italics mine—I.H.). Mao, alas, recruited his armies in the valley of Yenan, not the bars of Washington.

Chambers' extreme political turn has dizzied his historical sense. By noting that Alger Hiss was counsel for the Nye committee during the thirties, he tries to discredit its exposure of the munitions industry. "The penetration of the United States government by the Communist Party," adds Chambers, "coincided with a mood in the nation which lightheartedly baited the men who manufactured the armaments indispensable to its defense as 'Merchants of Death.'" But surely more was involved: the Nye committee revealed that some arms manufacturers had not hesitated to sell in bulk to Hitler, that their profits had been unconscionably high, that some had pressured both sides in the Chaco to buy their products and thus to prolong the war. The truth of these disclosures does not depend on whether Hiss was counsel for the committee that made them.

Chambers complains bitterly, and with justice, about the smears he has suffered from many Hiss supporters. Unfortunately, he is not himself above the use of similar methods. One of Hiss's attorneys was Harold Rosenwald, about whose face Chambers darkly pronounces: "I had seen dozens much like it in my time." The notion that people can be "placed" politically by the shape of their faces, is both preposterous and, at least in this century, sinister. It may be that Rosenwald does hold the political views Chambers hints at, but this attribution must seem completely shabby when it rests on nothing more than the fact that Rosenwald worked for O. John Rogge in the Attorney General's office and that Rogge "is now the legal representative of the Tito government."

In the course of breaking away from Stalinism, Chambers came to feel that "it is just as evil to kill the Czar and his family . . . as it is to starve two million peasants or slave laborers to death." What, if anything, does this highly charged statement mean? Coming from a pacifist, it would be perfectly clear, for it would suggest that killing is forbidden under any circumstances. We might then hope to hear as a sequel that "It is just as evil to kill 60,000 civilians in Hiroshima as it was to kill the Czar and his family." But Chambers is not a pacifist, he is willing to "struggle against [Communism] by all means, including arms." So the evil of killing the Czar cannot for him be simply that it was a killing, but must be that it was an unjustified killing—which leaves him with the moral enormity: "Several unjustified killings are just as evil as two million unjustified killings."

Throughout the book Chambers praises the Christian virtues of humility and meekness. Unfortunately, this credo does not prevent him from declaring "the left-wing intellectuals of almost every feather" to have been Hiss supporters and then from calling them "puffins, skimmers, skuas, and boobies." These delicate designations prompt one to remind Chambers that a good many "left-wing intellectuals" of one or another feather—those who truly deserved to be called "left" and "intellectual"—fought a minority battle against Stalinism at a time when *both* he and Hiss were at the service of Messrs. Yagoda and Yezhov.

What is Stalinism? It is evil, declares Chambers; a proposition neither disputable nor enlightening. Nowhere in his 800 pages does he attempt sustained definition or description, nowhere does he bound the shape of the evil. He seems unconcerned to examine the workings of Russian society, the social role of the Western Stalinist parties, the relation of the Asian parties to native nationalism. And with good reason. If you believe that the two great camps of the world prepare for battle under the banners, Faith in Man and Faith in God, what is the point of close study and fine distinctions? You need only sound the trumpets.

Almost unwittingly, Chambers moves toward the view that the source of our troubles is the Enlightenment: "The crisis of the Western world exists to the degree in which it is indifferent to God." The French Revolution becomes the villain of history, its progeny every godless society of our time. Chambers accepts, of course, the common, crude identification of Stalin's totalitarianism with Lenin's revolutionary state; both seem to him forms of fascism; the New Deal was a social revolution which crippled "the power of business"; and the motto of "the welfare state" is best expressed by his former associate, Colonel Bykov: "Who pays is boss, and who takes money must also give something." Everyone might thus be lumped together: Voltaire, Jefferson, Lenin, Roosevelt, Hitler, Stalin; not all equally evil, but all, apparently, "indifferent to God." A man who thinks in such patterns can hardly be expected to notice—or have much reason to care—that Stalinism and fascism, while symmetrical in their political devices, have different historical origins, class structures, political ideologies, and social rationales. Or that the Keynesian measures of the New Deal, far from constituting a revolution, proved a crutch for a stumbling capitalism.

Chambers' approach to history rests, finally, on no social theory at all; it is a return to Manichean demonology. Since for him everything depends on whether one takes God or man to be primary, he can write that "as Communists, Stalin and the Stalinists were absolutely justified in making the Purge. From a Communist point of view, Stalin could have taken no other course.... In that fact lay the evidence that Communism is absolutely evil. The human horror was not evil, it was the sad consequence of evil." The first two of these sentences are historically false; various Communists opposed the purge and proposed other courses of action, among them the removal of Stalin from power. The last sentence is shocking in its moral callousness. In effect, Chambers is saying that those of us who attack Stalinism for its inhumanity are sentimental, lacking in his austere disdain for what he calls "formless good will." Is it, however, more important to attack Stalin for disbelieving in the primacy of God than for killing millions of men? If the killing is to be regarded as a mere "consequence" of first principles, specific moral criticism of it can only seem superficial. But, in fact, the purges were the result of a decision by men in power, a decision for which they must be held responsible. A society is to be judged less by its philosophical premise about God and man, if it has any, than by its actual treatment of men; "the human horror of the purge" was evil, not merely "sad." What matters is not the devil's metaphysics, but his morals.

Chambers' major insight into the problem of Stalinism is his insistence that in this era of permanent crisis it provides a faith, a challenge, even an ideal. Feeding on crisis, Stalinism offers a vision. "The vision inspires. The crisis impels. The workingman is chiefly moved by the crisis. The educated man is chiefly moved by the vision." This is an important observation and a necessary corrective to vulgar theories which make of Stalinism mainly an atavistic drive for power. But Chambers, ignoring the fact that the vision of Stalinism is corrupt, treats it as if it were a legitimate form of socialism, and pays slight attention to the counterrevolution that occurred in Russia during the very years he was its underground agent.

Is this an academic matter? Not at all; for the essence of Stalinism, in its Russian form, is that it rests on a new kind of bureaucratic ruling class which engaged in "primitive accumulation" by destroying the revolutionary generation and appropriating to itself total economic and political power. Outside of Russia, Stalinism utilizes the socialist tradition of Europe and the nationalist sentiment of Asia for its domestic class needs and international power maneuvers. Drawing on a unique blend of reactionary and pseudo-revolutionary appeals, Stalinism attracts, in this age of crisis and decay, all those who feel the world must be changed but lack the understanding or energy to change it in a libertarian direction. Dynamic but not progressive, anti-capitalist but not socialist, Stalinism causes, in the words of Marx, all the old crap to rise to the top; under its domination, the best impulses of modern man are directed toward the worst consequences. And the problem for the historian is to determine precisely the blend of seemingly contradictory elements that Stalinism comprises.

Chambers himself provides an anecdote which dramatically confirms these remarks. His boss in the underground, Colonel Bykov, was a perfect specimen of the new Stalinist man, the Gletkin type: coarse, obedient, unintellectual, brutal. To Bykov "the generation that had made the Revolution . . . seemed as alien and preposterous . . . as foreigners. They belonged to another species and he talked about them the way people talk about the beastly or amusing habits of cows or pigs." So disgusting was Bykov that Chambers felt, before introducing him to Hiss, that he would have to apologize for the Russian. Yet, after a brief conversation, Hiss found Bykov "impressive." Why? I would guess that it was the attraction of an extreme bureaucratic personality for a mild bureaucratic personality, of one man who instinctively scorned the masses of people for another who had been trained to think of them as objects for benevolent manipulation. If Hiss had possessed a trace of revolutionary or liberal spirit, he would have been contemptuous of Bykov, he would have seen on Bykov's hands the blood of Bukharin and Tomsky and thousands upon thousands of others.

Where will Chambers go? His strength lies in a recognition that we live in an extreme situation; he agrees that "it is necessary to change the world." No longer a radical, scornful of liberals, convinced that "in the struggle against Communism the conservative is all but helpless," he accepts, formally, the position of those reactionaries *manqués* who edit the *National Review*. But only formally; for unlike them, he is drenched with the consciousness of crisis, he has none of their complacence, he continues a disturbed and dissatisfied man, given to extreme gestures and ultimate statements. What remains? Only the fact that estranged personality and reactionary opinion form an explosive mixture.

In his final sentence Chambers hints that he believes a third world war both inevitable and necessary. Yet he yearns for some spiritual reformation, a turn to God. What likelihood there is that spiritual or any other desired values would survive in a world-wide atomic war, he does not discuss. Would there, in any case, be much point in reminding him that religious faith has rarely prevented despots from being despotic? that many of our most precious concepts of liberty are the work of skeptics? that Stalinism thrives in pious Rome as in worldly Paris? that it wins supporters in an Orient which has not known a loss of religious faith comparable to that of the West? that if Stalin is an atheist, Franco is a believer? that the priests in Russia pray for Stalin as in Germany they prayed for Hitler?

Very little point, I fear; little more than to have told him during the 'thirties that Stalinism was betraying the German workers to Hitler or by its trials and purges murdering thousands of innocent people. Those who abandon a father below are all too ready for a father above. But this shift of faith does not remove the gnawing problems which, if left unsolved, will drive still more people to Stalinism; it gives the opponents of the totalitarian state no strategy, no program with which to remake the world; it makes our situation appear even more desperate than it already is. For if Chambers is right in believing the major bulwark against Stalin to be faith in God, then it is time for men of conviction and courage to take to the hills.

EDMUND WILSON AND THE SEA SLUGS

Edmund Wilson is not only a superb literary critic; he is also an extremely gifted writer; and there are ways in which his book about the American Civil War, *Patriotic Gore*, is a masterpiece. As an evocation of the literary and intellectual figures whose experience was shaped by the Civil War, the book is Plutarchian in its vividness. It displays to full advantage Wilson's gifts for historical narrative and critical description; it moves from writer to writer, topic to topic, with an ease that is astonishing; it vibrates with the passions of a supreme national crisis. But since all this has already been said elsewhere, let me simply join in the praise and proceed to glance at certain problematic assumptions behind Wilson's book. What follows, then, is not a discussion of *Patriotic Gore* as such but a word about its introduction.

Edmund Wilson is not at home in the modern world. He dislikes its cheap-jack commercialism, its frantic vulgarity, its ingrained deceit. He detests American chauvinism, and looks with a cold eye upon our claims to moral superiority in the Cold War. He fears the centralization of the bureaucratic state, and takes toward it an attitude of hostility such as, he implies, might have won the approval of nineteenth-century

---

This essay was written in 1963.

American intellectuals like Oliver Wendell Holmes in the North and Alexander Stephens in the South, men who were their own masters and lived by standards of public service and stoic virtue. Whether the attitudes expressed by Wilson can be called radical is less important than that they convey a criticism of modern society with which many radicals sympathize.

Now, it is from this perspective of disenchantment that Wilson approaches the Civil War. He is concerned not merely with the political meaning and cultural reverberations of the war, but also with the chain of causation which has transformed America from a country where republican virtues were once cherished by an austere minority to a country where

> We Americans whose public officials kept telling us we were living in "the Free World," discovered that we were expected to pay staggering taxes of which it has been estimated that 70 per cent has been going not only for nuclear weapons capable of depopulating whole countries but also for bacteriological and biological ones which made it possible for us to poison the enemy . . . We are, like the Russians, being spied upon by an extensive secret police, whose salaries we are required to pay, as we are required to pay, also, the salaries of another corps of secret agents who are infiltrating foreign countries. And while all this expenditure is going for the purpose of sustaining the United States as a more and more unpopular world power, as few funds as possible are being supplied to educate and civilize the Americans themselves . . .

Borrowing perhaps from the Marxism to which he was once drawn and of which there remains a sediment in his writing—though a Marxism that in regard to historical (as distinct from literary) problems never achieved a sufficient flexibility in his hands—Wilson sees this monster state of our time, this "Demon of Centralization," as rooted in the triumph of the industrial North. Memories of Charles Beard come to mind: the Beard who educated a generation into regarding the Civil War not merely or primarily as a holy crusade to abolish slavery and preserve the union but also as "the Second American Revolution" confirming the power of capitalist economy. But despite this deflation of Northern war aims, Beard never showed any doubts as to the relative merits of North and South. He was trying to describe an historical event in its full complexity, so that our awareness of the social transformation signalled by the Civil War would lead us to qualify *but not eliminate* both Northern and Southern claims to moral and ideological purposes. Wilson, however, in his distaste for what he regards as the consequences of Northern victory, will not consider seriously the professed Northern aims; his inclination is to dismiss both Northern and Southern statements as mere propaganda and self-delusion; he comes close to accepting the view that ideology, as Henry Ford once remarked about history, is "the bunk." He speaks of "the myth that [the North] was fighting to free the slaves," a myth that "supplied the militant Union North with the rabble-rousing moral issue which is necessary in every modern war to make the conflict appear as a melodrama." He compares the Civil War to other American wars, such as the one against Mexico, that were openly imperialist in character. He accepts all too readily a good part of the Southern view of the Reconstruction period, even permitting himself a reference to "the premature enfranchisement of the Negroes." And despite his contempt for Southern apologetics, he finds himself expressing admiration for Alexander Stephens, the Confederate Vice President who saw the Southern cause as a crusade against federalist centralization and in behalf of that crusade repeatedly embarrassed Jefferson Davis.

There is more to Wilson's discounting of ideology. He puts forth a view of history that might be described as a reductive biological determinism:

> In a recent Walt Disney film showing life at the bottom of the sea, a primitive organism called a sea slug is seen gobbling up smaller organisms through a large orifice at one end of its body;

confronted with another sea slug of an only slightly larger size, it ingurgitates that too. Now, the wars fought by human beings are stimulated as a rule primarily by the same instincts as the voracity of the sea slug.

If this be true, even "as a rule," then political ideas and moral sentiments can play only a trivial role in history; the past is a mere horror of ingurgitating voracity; and the future doomed to a nightmare-repetition of the past.

The complexity of human events, either in the American past or elsewhere, can hardly be grasped by anyone seriously adhering to such notions; and one reason *Patriotic Gore* is so fine a book is that Wilson's critical practice is superior to his theory. Plunging into his rich materials, he ignores most of what he has said in his introduction. But my interest here is with more than his critical or historical method: for the kind of disgust that motivates Wilson's reflections upon American history is often shared by people who find themselves disenchanted with the Cold War and who turn therefore to a kind of absolutist emotional radicalism, a radicalism without or even against politics, a radicalism of nausea.

It is a nausea we all know. Human history can be regarded, easily enough, as a nightmare; Wilson's analogy with the sea slugs has great emotional force, releasing as it does a wish to be done with the whole bloody mess; and who can deny that much of the past, as also the present creeping into the future, can be fitted into the scheme of ingurgitation? If men behave like sea slugs, the power of the comparison rests in the idea that they, like the sea slugs, cannot help doing what they do, for as Wilson remarks, they do it "by the same instinct." And that leaves little to say, since the problem of history has then been not solved but dissolved.

But the comparison with the sea slug is too grandiose, too monolithic, too apocalyptic. Claiming to encircle the whole of behavior, it fails to discriminate among the many kinds. Isolating the beast-like element in history, it distracts attention from those forces which even as they cause men to act like beasts are nevertheless peculiar to men. One need not cling to theories of inevitable progress in history to find purpose and direction, morals and sentiments, ideas and ideals, all contributing to the outcome of events and all a good deal more than mere disguises for the urge to power. Whoever doubts this need only read *Patriotic Gore* and follow Wilson's sensitive account of the way thinking men on both sides tried to cope with their experience during the Civil War.

Wilson's sea slug theory of history implies an answer to the problem of evil and violence, an answer that lies forever ready as a biological constant, an answer that precedes the problem. Meanwhile, it is an approach to human affairs which creates a special illusion of "realism": for what could seem more tough-minded than treating men as insatiable beasts whose thinking is little more than a cover for appetite? And in that "realism" there lies, also, a justification for impatience with political nuance and analytic shading: for if men are indeed like sea slugs, then there is no need to discriminate and choose among contending forces, either in 1865 or 1963, and all can be dismissed as ingurgitating organisms, while we unhappy few fall back upon a trench of rectitude, the Holmes's and Stephens' of the twentieth century.

Once into the heart of his book, Wilson quite forgets the sea slugs and becomes embroiled with the ideological disputes of his protagonists. Though contemptuous of the conventional Southern apologists and by temperament and belief himself a man of the North, Wilson bears down hardest on the claims for Northern idealism. Yet are his discoveries here quite so novel as he seems to suppose? That the North was driven by the pressures of an expanding capitalism and the South by the needs of a besieged slave economy; that a fundamental clash between two orders of society was often masked by the vocabulary of righteousness; that many Northern leaders were hostile to the Negroes and some indifferent to the horrors of slavery; that important Southern figures were humane gentlemen fastidious about trading in black flesh; that the Northern armies were often brutal; that it is much too simple to see the Civil War as an unambiguous conflict between good and evil —all this was pressed upon the consciousness of anyone who grew up and read books twenty-five years ago. Yet it does not follow, as Wilson so strongly implies, that the war was an utter disaster without moral value which set loose the sequence of events leading to bureaucratic centralization. Nor does it follow that the issue of slavery was a mere propagandistic mirage.

There is a sense, of course, in which the Civil War *was* a disaster: the sense that all wars are. Whether the Civil War was inevitable is a problem to be avoided here, since it is so hard to formulate, let alone solve. I would say that the clash between the two systems in the Civil War could not have been mediated: one or the other side had to win, and rarely in history has this kind of clash been resolved peacefully. The truth here is a double truth. The Civil War did mark the victory of modern capitalism and let loose those tendencies toward a centralized state which Wilson deplores; but also, the Civil War brought to an end the system by which one man could own another and therefore, despite all the necessary discounts, it represents a major turning in the moral development of the United States.

The point needs to be added that while the victory of the North helped to speed the growth of the bureaucratic state, it was surely not the *source* of that growth. More usefully, the Civil War can be regarded as a crucial moment in a historical development which is extremely complex and ambiguous, containing elements that promote freedom and others that stifle it. If Wilson were to push his reasoning a little further, he would have to go back in time and reject a good deal more of Western history—or, with whatever grimace, he would have to accept the two-sidedness of Western history, with the hope that through intelligence and will men may yet succeed in choosing freedom.

When discussing so complex an event as the Civil War—for that matter, the present-day Cold War as well—one must distinguish between a proper skepticism concerning announced political aims and an estimate of the probable consequences. The sincerity or duplicity of Northern claims was not a decisive factor in regard to at least one major outcome of the Civil War: Northern politicians may have been hypocritical and Northern publicists self-righteous, but the slaves were freed. Had the South won, they would not have been. There can be no evading this central fact. I am not saying that the falseness of much Northern writing had no consequence: it had a great deal to do with allowing the former slaves to sink back into semi-serfdom. Yet the fact remains that between North and South there were fundamental differences in social system which vitally affected the destinies of enslaved human beings; and as a result, the war must be regarded as more than a mere struggle for power veiled by moral phrases.

Wilson, in his revulsion from Northern cant and his disgust with the evolution of Nothern society, leans over backward in writing about the South. He is not of course pro-Southern; he has too richly developed a sense of justice and too keen a sense of the ridiculous to fall into that trap; and besides, he finds most Southern apologetics simply boring. Yet he can write, astonishingly, that "there are moments when one may wonder today—as one's living becomes more and more hampered by the exactions of centralized bureaucracies—whether it may not be true, as Alexander Stephens said, that "the cause of the South is the cause of us all." Each to his own wonderings; though I must confess that while recent years have led me to wonder about many things, identifying with the Confederacy has not been one of them. Alexander Stephens was obviously a man of probity and intellectual attainments; the idea of states rights which other politicians used as a handy slogan he took seriously; but he was caught up, as he had to be, in the moral shame of the South. He wrote with cogency about "the Demon of Centralization," but he also could write that the Confederacy rested "upon the great truth that the Negro is not equal to the white man, that slavery . . . is his natural and normal condition . . ."

Most of us share Wilson's desire to find intellectual ancestors in order to confront American life in the mid-twentieth century; it is a desire both understandable and necessary in a time of chaos. But if we cannot do better than Alexander Stephens, then perhaps we ought to try making it on our own. After all, hasn't that repeatedly been the lesson of Edmund Wilson's own career?

ACKNOWLEDGMENTS

Acknowledgments are made to the magazines in which the essays in this book have appeared, some in an earlier form: *The Hudson Review, The Nation, Partisan Review, The New Republic Dissent,* and Prentice-Hall, Inc. for the Introduction to *The Achievement of Edith Wharton* and to Houghton Mifflin Company for *In Quest of Moral Style* and for *George Gissing: Poet of Fatigue.*

```
PN
771        Howe, Irving
.H6
1970       A world more at-
              tractive
```

DATE DUE: JUN 16 1980

ERIE COMMUNITY COLLEGE/NORTH
RICHARD R. DRY MEMORIAL LIBRARY
MAIN ST. AND YOUNGS RD.
WILLIAMSVILLE, NEW YORK 14221